THE
POLITICAL
PERFORMERS

THE
POLITICAL
PERFORMERS

CBS Broadcasts in the Public Interest

MICHAEL D. MURRAY

Westport, Connecticut
London

Library of Congress Cataloging-in-Publication Data

Murray, Michael D.
   The political performers : CBS broadcasts in the public interest /
Michael D. Murray.
     p.   cm.
   Includes bibliographical references and index.
   ISBN 0-275-94490-5
   1. CBS News. 2. Press—United States—Influence. 3. Press and
politics—United States. 4. Television broadcasting of news—United
States. 5. Radio journalism—United States. 6. Public opinion—
United States. I. CBS Inc. II. Title.
PN4888.I53M87 1994
384.55'4'06573—dc20   93-30985

British Library Cataloguing in Publication Data is available.

Library of Congress Catalog Card Number: 93-30985
ISBN: 0-275-94490-5

First published in 1994

Praeger Publishers, 88 Post Road West, Westport, CT 06881
An imprint of Greenwood Publishing Group, Inc.

Printed in the United States of America

(∞)™

The paper used in this book complies with the
Permanent Paper Standard issued by the National
Information Standards Organization (Z39.48–1984).

10 9 8 7 6 5 4 3 2 1

To my father
and the memory of my mother

CONTENTS

PREFACE

The Political Performers explores some key news and public affairs broadcasts and the people behind them. It is offered in the hope of providing much-needed perspective on the early era of broadcasting, thus enriching our understanding of how and why CBS News became recognized for excellence in public affairs programming. No claim is made that examination of these broadcasts will exhaust the need for further study. The aim is to describe briefly the contents of some key broadcasts, evaluating why they made a difference with the public, exploring especially how they altered attitudes, perception, and decision-making in their day and sometimes over a more extended period of time.

Some of my students have suggested that a better title for the book would be *The Big CBS Broadcasts* or, taking a hint from Irving Fang's early work on individual broadcasters, perhaps *Those Great CBS Broadcast Documentarians!* But it is unlikely that we could agree on the "bigness" or even "greatness" of some of the programs or people selected for examination here. They do not all fit neatly into one category or classification. And even a cursory glance at the table of contents of this book will show that the author has not planned or delivered a comprehensive catalogue of important CBS programs, and no suggestion is made that they are our only available resources for examples of import or impact by CBS News.

The working premise is essentially the search for some concrete models of excellence in the field of broadcast news and public affairs, acknowledging and, it is hoped, encouraging depth and range of understanding in a most ephemeral medium. The analysis of broadcast programming in the context of the times is also intended as an additional framework of this book. Contained in it are what I believe to be striking illustrations of historic and, in some instances, heroic efforts. I expect and hope that these may propel others to better understand and pursue superior performance in the field of broadcasting. In many cases, the influence of some of the programs is widely acknowledged as having already taken place. Indeed, some of the broadcasts and their creators have acquired a symbolic stature, while others are all but forgotten.

It is my hope that the documents addressed here will provide the reader with a better understanding of their importance and vitality, big and small, and additionally institute an appropriate context in which to move on to examine and, in alternate cases, to create other historic programs. The reader should approach chapters, then, not as describing the ultimate or definitive broadcasts of an era or subject area, but rather as representing one approach, using one set of data and standards, raising particular questions about a problem or set of problems relative to the content. As an additional feature, I have tried to offer the reader some perspective on the manner in which some of the broadcasts were received in home communities, on those occasions when CBS went into the field for analysis.

Selecting documents for this book from an exceptionally rich collection from the CBS Archives was a challenge. Those selected are not intended to represent the "Top Ten" list (or top twenty) of documentary and other programs of distinction nor should those excluded be considered of lesser value or quality. Arguing that the "CBS Reports" program "Black History: Lost, Stolen or Strayed" is a program of greater merit or worth than others because of the quality of writing in the telecast, for example, would be futile. Writing quality was a major criterion for choice in many instances, but not the sole one: Selection was also influenced by a desire to represent diversity of content and approach. As an analysis of collected works, the scope of this study forms only a fragment of a richer historical fabric; as a result, the commentary can only offer a fragmentary sense of CBS performance in the public interest, set in time. In spite of these limitations, an attempt is made to go beyond discussion of individual programs and show the relationship of projects to the bigger picture, otherwise erased by the passage of time.

Someone else might choose to apply a different set of standards and pursue different questions regarding an entirely different slate of programs, with a different cast of characters under the microscope. I cannot prove, for example, that programs produced during the war years are superior to those looking at more contemporary problems of urban American life or that Edward R. Murrow's work is superior to that of those who came later, even though he is still recognized as the standard-bearer for others in the field. Such decisions are matters of personal taste, of course, and the imposition of individual preference is not the objective here.

The reader can critically consider the evidence offered in these pages and decide which CBS broadcasters and broadcasts have done the most to advance the cause of excellence in the field through selections of their work. Murrow and "See It Now" are obviously overrepresented, as are "CBS Reports" documentaries, but others are included. These broadcasts and the creative forces behind them should be viewed as suggestive examples of what some informed observers regard as noteworthy, an inductive guide to just a few of the more useful and critically successful broadcasts on important issues.

The enterprising reader should also, of course, supplement what is presented here with additional study. This can serve as an assurance that prominent examples of broadcast public affairs and news reporting will be used to contribute significantly to our lives in attempting to address and answer the critical questions of the present day.

IN GRATITUDE

As far as levels of support in this endeavor, my wife, Carol, and daughters, Katherine and Ellen, were, of course, always encouraging and usually kind, when they were not using the computer. On that score, I should also thank my sister Maryellen and her husband, Don Bowman, who encouraged me to invest in a new personal computer to expedite progress on this manuscript. Financial and moral support for this project has come from my dean, E. Terrence Jones, and chair, Thomas McPhail, at the University of Missouri–St. Louis, who successfully nominated me for more grants and enhancement opportunities than I deserved during the period when the book was being written. My friends and colleagues Sid Savan and Ellen Wallach also kept me on track and in good humor during this venture. Department secretaries Diana Davis and Linda Thompson, as well as student assistants Lori Morgan, Maria Whitter, Carla Gray, and Maurine Burns, did the bulk of the typing; they earned my sincerest thanks. Those who assisted me when I first got interested in documentary television over twenty years ago, namely, John Kline, Keith Sanders, James W. Gibson, Paul Nelson, Loren Reid, and G. Joseph Wolfe, are gratefully acknowledged, as well as the late Edward C. Lambert and William Stephenson, also of the University of Missouri–Columbia campus.

Members of my extended professional family from the American Journalism Historians Association (AJHA) have been a constant source of inspiration, information, and support, particularly Maurine Beasley, William David Sloan, and James Startt as well as Tom Reilly and John Pauly, former editors of *Journalism History* and *American Journalism*, respectively, who permitted me to reprint interviews I had conducted with two key sources. Former CBS News presidents Fred Friendly and Bill Leonard were also both very generous with their time and encouragement. AJHA conferences allowed me to try out ideas on some of the broadcasts in earlier form, and my good friend Barbara Cloud was kind enough to present one chapter on my behalf at a meeting of the Western Journalism Historians at Berkeley and to provide feedback on its contents.

Former CBS "See It Now" staffers Don Hewitt, Joe Wershba, Palmer Williams, Gene DePoris, and William McClure, as well as network information specialists Marcia Stein, May Dowell, Beverly Morgan in Don Hewitt's office, and Suzanne Bell Grainger and Marlene Adler of the Cronkite unit at CBS, all provided information and assistance, as well as Jeneane Fountaine Murray of CBS law, Murrow biographer Ann Sperber, and James Seward, co-trustee of the estate of Edward R. Murrow. Former CBS senior executives Frank Stanton, William Small, and Robert Chandler all graciously responded to inquiries and requests for information, as did premier anchorman Walter Cronkite.

My interest in seeing historic broadcasts examined in book form was also encouraged by Michael Schudson of the University of California–San Diego, who supported my efforts to examine public affairs programming and documentary television as part of his National Endowment for the Humanities Seminar, "American Journalism in Historical Perspective." Arthur Schlesinger, Jr., Albert Schweitzer Professor at the City University of New York, also provided assistance and important information.

Recently, a research award from the Shorenstein Barone Center at Harvard University enabled me to visit the Murrow Center at Tufts University on one day and to talk to Janet Murrow back in Boston the next. The inauguration of the Goldsmith Awards brought "60 Minutes" executive producer Don Hewitt and Bob Woodward of the *Washington Post* to the Harvard campus at that same time, and Mr. Hewitt also assisted me with material for this project, as earlier acknowledged. The opportunity to take part in the Shorenstein Barone Center event was a very enlightening and, frankly, moving experience for me personally, as we screened the historic McCarthy broadcast with Mrs. Murrow. For this honor, I am deeply indebted to Marvin Kalb, Marina McCarthy, and Edith Holway of the Kennedy School of Government at Harvard, as well as Murrow Fellows Leonard Baldyga and Brian Regli of the Fletcher School of Law and Public Diplomacy at Tufts.

A few months earlier, I was fortunate to share the Stephen Coltrin Award from the International Radio and Television Society (IRTS) in New York, which provided an opportunity to talk to Dr. Frank Stanton, who was kind enough to share information and follow-up by having transcripts of historic programs forwarded for study and review. Also, as part of the IRTS meeting, I was able to complete a field assignment at CBS News in New York, which gave me an additional chance to talk to some current network news leaders: David Corvo, Lane Venardos, Missie Rennie, and Andrew Hayward. This outing was organized by CBS News vice president James McKenna, who also provided follow-up support in the way of videotape dubs. Thanks to IRTS for this opportunity and especially to administrators Joyce Tudryn and Maria De Leon and to the meeting host, network president Ellen Shaw Agress, for her kindness and assistance.

Over the recent summer months, through a media management fellowship at Stanford University, I was able to study decision-making and also make some key contacts with West Coast figures willing to share ideas and recollections on early broadcasts. I thank Michael Donovan and Carol Ann Riordan of the American Press Institute of Reston, Virginia, and the faculty at Stanford for making my participation in that program possible. Additional early support during the period the book was under way came from Anne Schlosser of the American Film Institute in California and Sam Grogg of the Kennedy Center in Washington, D.C. I am also grateful to the Poynter Institute for Media Studies in Florida and for special assistance from Robert Steele and Valerie Hyman of the Program for Broadcast Journalists, and to C-SPAN, the cable network, for a generous grant to purchase videotape.

Ray Oakes and his student assistant at Franklin Pierce College, Eric Feibel, helped me locate some rather obscure source material. Needless to say, I owe a great measure of thanks to many librarians and libraries including Caroline Kent, Head of Research Services in the Widener Library at Harvard University; Eleanor Horan, former Curator of the Murrow Collection at Tufts University; Eva Moseley, Curator of Manuscripts in the Schlesinger Library at Radcliffe College; and Margaret Goostray, Assistant Director of Special Collections at Boston University.

Also of assistance were Pete Johnson of the Reference Department at the Cecil H. Green Library at Stanford University, Catherine Heinz at the Broadcast Pioneers Library, George H. Curor and Benedick K. Zobrist of the Harry S. Truman Library, and E. William Johnson of the John F. Kennedy Library. Of course, the University of Missouri library staff, both in the Journalism School in Columbia and at the Thomas Jefferson Library on my home campus, were a great source of assistance, especially Frances Piesberger of the Reference Department at UM—St. Louis.

Finally, sincerest appreciation to the staff at Praeger, especially Anne Davidson Kiefer, for unflagging support and encouragement in the start-up of this publication, and a number of careful editors, including Marcia Goldstein and Deborah Ross. All errors and omissions are mine, and the selection process for important broadcasts included was, of course, made solely by yours truly.

THE
POLITICAL
PERFORMERS

Chapter 1

THE CBS TRADITION

Over the years, CBS News developed a reputation for excellence in broadcast journalism based largely on the quality of its news and public affairs programming. The purpose of this book is to review some of the network's key programs, which, in spite of their importance as part of both our social development and broadcast history, are now often unavailable to the general public. Surprisingly, some are almost extinct after the passage of less than fifty years. It is the desire of contemporary historians that the message of these documents should survive and be sought after, for what they tell us about ourselves, the times, and the development of the field of broadcast journalism. It is also hoped that students of broadcasting will have an opportunity to review the content of the programs, considering their import and implications for the profession.

Researchers should, ideally, be able to consider the role broadcast documentaries played, for example, in introducing and exploring relevant public policy issues and key political players, both in front of and behind the camera. Fortunately, and in spite of their limited accessibility, these efforts and indices of their impact are available through other sources. A great deal has been written about CBS and the many important programs that often made history by challenging our way of looking at some critical issue of the day. These written words have a history of their own, and many are especially noteworthy because they contribute to our understanding not only of the public policy issues but of the nature of television public affairs programming itself. They are frequently contributed by insiders who went beyond mere descriptions to offer analysis of programs, people, and network decision-making.

Shortly after Edward R. Murrow's death in the mid-sixties, his close friend and partner Fred Friendly published a perceptive account of his personal experiences in network broadcasting up to that time, in his classic *Due to Circumstances Beyond Our Control* (1967). Two years later another former colleague, Alexander Kendrick, published *Prime Time: The Life of Edward R. Murrow*, the first popular and very detailed biography of broadcasting's legendary "father figure." Prior to that, two sets of broadcast transcripts were published. One edited collection of "See It Now" programs was offered by Murrow and Friendly in 1955, just as previously, in 1948–1949, they put together a series of "I Can Hear It Now" radio programs on long-playing Columbia phonograph records.

The premier edition of "I Can Hear It Now" began in 1933 with the first inauguration of Franklin D. Roosevelt and extended through the war years and into the so-called Atomic Age. The album was a tremendous popular success, and a follow-up, Volume II, was initiated. The material in the second volume was distilled from a variety of sources. Most of the broadcasts were first gathered as part of "pool" reports, serving the then four major radio networks. Both Murrow's colleagues and competitors were offered: H. V. Kaltenborn, Walter Winchell, Elmer Davis, and Robert Trout. Highlights such as Fiorello LaGuardia of New York reading comic strips over the radio during the newspaper delivery strike of July 1945 gave listeners a unique insight into political personalities.

Coverage of important stories such as the International War Crimes Trial at Nuremberg (1945–1946), Winston Churchill's "Iron Curtain" speech, and Secretary of State George C. Marshall's introduction of the Marshall Plan at Harvard University in 1947 were offered, as well as speeches from both the Republican and Democratic parties' national conventions of the following year. Murrow and Friendly ended their written introduction to that album with the wish that they would some day have an opportunity to translate the miles of sound tape, including the five hundred hours of old broadcasts, they had collected for the project in book form, devoted solely to major historical events. These would include, for example, the five days at Munich and the first ninety days of the New Deal. Unfortunately, broadcasting chores interfered with the objective of providing a written account of the broadcast material.

CBS newswriter Edward Bliss was able to edit a composite of Murrow broadcasts in his collection, *In Search of Light*, in 1967, which is regarded by many as a substitute for the book Murrow never found time to write for the ages. Much later, Bliss authored a comprehensive history of broadcast news for the Columbia University Press entitled *Now the News* (1991). Two film biographies of Murrow were produced as well, one by CBS and the other by the BBC; and by the start of the decade of the seventies, a scholarly and analytic overview of American broadcasting was published by Columbia University film professor Eric Barnouw. *The Image Empire*, the concluding segment of his highly regarded three-volume history of broadcasting, focused specifically on television and often on CBS programs. Barnouw is considered a leader among broadcast historians, with his work offering insight on major themes and forming the basis for much of what would follow. His three-part history is often credited for having provided the impetus for subsequent works in the field.

Five years after publication of the last volume, Barnouw condensed all of the television content of his previous works into *Tube of Plenty: The Evolution of American Television* (1975). The volume received a very favorable response, in large measure because of the special attention offered to the interrelationship between society, politics, and broadcasting. Television news, as early as the 1960s, was starting to be discussed as the principal source of information in the United States, surpassing the influence of newspapers. As a result, television was beginning to be taken seriously as a force in America's cultural and political life. One chapter of Barnouw's composite work, for example, focuses specifically on the political and commercial effects of programming for television's first two decades, with special attention to critical issues such as blacklisting and McCarthyism. Television's treatment of political party conventions, big televised events of the early era such as Nixon's "Checkers Speech," Khrushchev's "kitchen debate" with Nixon, and the Kennedy campaign and its "Great Debates" were included. Accounts of Kennedy's decision-making and reporting on the Bay of Pigs and the Cuban missile crisis are also covered in some depth, as well as both the president's assassination in Dallas and his televised funeral in the nation's capital.

The era of what Barnouw labeled "No Guts Journalism" is described in his book as a prelude to Vietnam coverage, the protest movement, an imperial presidency, and Watergate, which, according to the author, provided the atmosphere in which cloak-and-dagger intrigue helped to explain trends in popular programming. CBS was frequently, although not exclusively, at the center stage of study. Interestingly, Barnouw described how entertainment values began to influence news programming and how some major political events were constructed and often simplified by both participants and program producers, to insure that no mistake was made about the outcome, interpretation, or significance of an event. The original version of Barnouw's work earned for him the Frank Luther Mott Journalism Award, the George Polk Award, the

Bancroft Prize in American History, and the gratitude of nearly every broadcast historian in the United States.

Broadcasting had arrived as a serious subject for study and debate, and even the specialized area of television documentary received scholarly attention with the publication of A. William Bluem's *Documentary in American Television* (1965), which also included examination of CBS programs. A follow-up effort by Charles Montgomery Hammond, Jr., entitled *The Image Decade: Television Documentary, 1965–1975*, was published in the early 1980s. Fortunately, by the mid-seventies, a couple of over-the-air efforts were also offered to reintroduce CBS News documentaries in the form of summer retrospective broadcasts. Instigated by news chief Bill Leonard, run in concert with "60 Minutes," and hosted by network veteran John Hart, they included the controversial McCarthy broadcasts and also gave viewers a wide range of issue-oriented programs, some undoubtedly long since forgotten.

INSIDE STORIES

For years after the publication of Barnouw's respected work, a decade later in fact, CBS broadcasts and the networks in general received limited attention from the publishing world. Ironically, some attempts had already been made by broadcasters to evaluate press performance. WCBS Radio in New York featured Don Hollenbeck with "CBS Views the Press," beginning in 1947, and Charles Collingwood performed a similar role on WCBS-TV in New York much later.[1] By the time Gary Paul Gates wrote *Air Time: The Inside Story of CBS News*, ten years had passed since the publication of Barnouw's book; the bulk of published material on broadcasting's premier network could be categorized primarily as personal reminiscences by insiders such as Friendly, Kendrick, Dan Rather, Dan Schorr, and network founder William S. Paley. Gates, a former CBS newswriter and coauthor with Dan Rather of *The Palace Guard* (1974), began his company history by identifying the four grim days in November 1963 as the period when television came into its own as a news medium. He was able to provide a short account of CBS News up to that date, while pointing out that television would have been unable to cover effectively the Kennedy assassination and funeral live just five years earlier, because it lacked both the remote, on-the-scene technology and the editorial capacity to do so.

Gates attempted to dispel the myths related to Edward R. Murrow's legacy as well as many of the subsequent books, including the decline in his relations with management after the McCarthy broadcast and before his departure for government service in the United States Information Agency. That author presented Howard K. Smith as television's premier analyst of events during that period, but one whose aggressiveness sometimes matched Murrow's, proving almost as embarrassing to the network. He labels Eric Sevareid the most cerebral of "Murrow's boys," the one who most disliked visual gimmickry, while his somber on-air style of delivery also caused concern for the network.

Gates reserves most of the praise for Murrow's successor on "Person to Person," Charles Collingwood, the third of Murrow's distinguished radio recruits and highly thought of as the most polished, but in some ways as least successful because of his reputation of being too soft. Also included in Gates's account is a detailed review of the career of Douglas Edwards, key reporter for CBS Television's first decade, and Don Hewitt, the network's veteran producer and leading man-behind-the-scenes. Hewitt, known today as the developer and the guru of "60 Minutes," later published a book of important stories from that program entitled *Minute by Minute.*

The anchor chair got a thorough going-over in Gates's account, as one might expect. Needless to say, Walter Cronkite is the center of attention, starting at a time when television news was a low-cost operation and leading up to Dan Rather's million-dollar contract. In Gates's book, the argument is made, however, that CBS developed an outstanding reputation in news because of a cadre of professionals who became stars in their own right and because of strong specialty areas, plus excellent writing and reporting ability. These star-quality reporters included Marvin Kalb, Charles Kuralt, Roger Mudd, Harry Reasoner, Morley Safer, and Daniel Schorr.

For many years, Gates's book constituted, for the most part, the limited diet of specialized CBS material offered to readers. Exceptions include Robert Metz's popular history, *CBS: Reflections on a Bloodshot Eye*, with an emphasis on entertainment programming and the celebrity broadcasters who populated early prime-time favorites. Other books included an analysis of network decision-making, with all three broadcast news organizations under the microscope, in Edward Jay Epstein's *News from Nowhere* (1973); a brief account of network development under William S. Paley, as well as background on other news leaders, as part of *The Powers That Be* (1979) by the distinguished reporter David Halberstam; Mike Wallace's *Close Encounters* (1984), an autobiography written with Gary Gates, focusing heavily on the years with "60 Minutes"; and finally, a historical but highly critical look at that all-time popular CBS News program itself, *60 Minutes* (1984) by Axel Madsen.

In *60 Minutes*, Madsen praises the series but also discusses some of what he views as unacknowledged conventions of program editing. According to this author, these frequently led to conflict, with the appearance of an allegorical drama and a good-guy, bad-guy image, a clear-cut plot, dramatic buildup, and successful resolution. In this scenario, Mike Wallace frequently came across as the good guy uncovering wrongdoing and attacking a source of investigation caught unaware, although Madsen also accuses program chief Don Hewitt of focusing on entertainment values and selective editing in simplifying stories to successfully attract an audience of close to 40 million. Another, more scholarly analysis on the program was produced by Richard Campbell, *60 Minutes and the News: A Mythology from Inside America* (1991), which includes a breakdown of techniques with script samples.

Within the last decade, over a half-dozen books on CBS have been published, with much of the emphasis devoted to the figures who shaped news and public affairs programming. These books include more of the "inside story" account as well as two more biographies on Murrow himself. The Iowa State University Press published five interpretive essays prefacing abstracts of panel discussions held at Murrow's alma mater, Washington State University, on the occasion of what would have been his fifty-seventh birthday. The book, entitled *The Edward R. Murrow Heritage: Challenge for the Future* (1986), was written by Betty Houchin Winfield and Lois B. DeFleur. It featured a keynote address by Diane Sawyer and discussions by a number of key figures in the history of CBS News, speculating on Murrow's role and those worthy to carry on the Murrow tradition. Charles Kuralt and Bill Moyers are, for example, highly regarded as latter-day contributors to the master's legacy. Other important works include Ann Sperber's *Murrow: His Life and Times* and another carefully researched biography by Joe Persico entitled *Murrow: An American Original* (1988).

An additional book by Barbara Matusow, *The Evening Stars: The Making of the Network News Anchor* (1983), looks specifically at the anchor chair and its inhabitants, including the major historical CBS figures Murrow and Cronkite, with a review of the challenge facing upstart anchor Dan Rather. Four of the recent popular books, like their predecessors on CBS, provide not only an update but also detailed accounts from within the network, offering a distinctly personal approach, with the focus on individual contributors as opposed to key broadcasts. The books all pay their respects to the early myths associated with the network, which the staff sometimes regarded as the broadcast equivalent to the *New York Times*.

In many ways, ironically, many of the new books contribute to the mythmaking, but many more villains than heroes tend to be discussed in these mostly contemporary works. They include detailed descriptions of Van Gordon Sauter's performance as CBS News president; the influence of talent agents, especially Richard Leibner; efforts to boost the "CBS Morning News"; and attempts by key personnel to bolster their own positions in an atmosphere of high turnover and radical change—a striking contrast to the years of stability and security that preceded them.

CURRENT OFFERINGS

In most of the recent books about CBS, the heavies are almost universally agreed upon or at least as clearly defined as the heroes of the early years at the network, often enshrined in organizational folklore. Two of the most recently published books, *Who Killed CBS? The Undoing of America's Number One News Network* (1988) by Peter J. Boyer and Ed Joyce's *Prime Times, Bad Times: A Personal Drama of Network Television* (1988), identify a funeral gathering for Charles Collingwood as the event signaling the end of the great era of news for CBS. In many instances in Boyer's book, the author reflects on contemporary attempts to resurrect the memory or trappings of the CBS News historic figures, Murrow and his "boys," by younger staffers.

Asked how the CBS tradition of news quality affects performance today, one producer described it as a double-edged sword, working to your advantage but also against you, in some contexts: working in your favor in that the institution has a marvelous history, but against you in deviating from the established culture, sometimes perceived as undercutting the institution and its traditional way of doing things. Thus the network was viewed as an institution that sometimes looked at change in a threatening way, and one in which more recently the bottom line might be suspected as the cause. Again, references to broadcast content appear less important than personal intrigue, infighting, and personalities in most of these books; and, of course, it is important to note that they were written for a popular audience.

Most of the recent additions to the literature on CBS News address the relationship between quality production and marketplace considerations. This theme became more and more prominent in press accounts of the network's condition, with the outcome interpreted in a way that always showed that, in the end, entertainment values beat out news at what was always viewed as the preeminent, "Tiffany" network. In one book former CBS News chief Ed Joyce discussed how 20 percent of the people under contract in the news division at one point were earning half of the network talent payroll, leading to a wide disparity among staff salaries and the obvious accompanying disenchantment. Escalating talent fees, including negotiations when Dan Rather accepted the network anchor reins from Walter Cronkite, were widely reported, with comprehensive coverage of this particular deal by the man who made it, Bill Leonard, in his book, *In the Storm of the Eye: A Lifetime at CBS.*

Other network news squabbles made public involve decision-making over the "CBS Morning News," subject to constant restructuring efforts at the breakfast hour, in an attempt to compete with NBC and ABC. In *Bad News at Black Rock* (1987), Peter McCabe also spends a great deal of time decrying the encroachment of entertainment values and says he was accused by network colleagues of sounding like one of "Murrow's Ghosts," a title used to disparage anyone attempting to mediate battles between competing hosts of the morning program during the decade of the 1980s. Another author, Robert Slater, goes to great lengths to describe fully the circumstances leading to earlier dissension at the network, including Fred Friendly's famed resignation from the CBS News presidency. Slater's book *This . . . Is CBS: A Chronicle of 60 Years* is able to update information and offer various details on additional key documentary programs, for example, not covered fully in earlier works by participants, such as Friendly's own *Due to Circumstances Beyond Our Control.*

Slater's work addresses the critical events of the sixties, such as the Vietnam conflict and the 1968 Democratic Convention. William S. Paley's personal memoir, *As It Happened* (1979), and two biographies of the CBS founder published about the same time offer an overview of the network from both an entertainment and a news perspective with emphasis on personality and, often, internal conflict. Other recent additions to the literature on the company include that long-awaited general history of broadcast information gathering and reporting mentioned earlier, *Now the News* by Edward Bliss, and another personal memoir, *On and Off the Air* by David Schoenbrun, who died shortly after the completion of his work.

The Bliss history is noteworthy because of the author's key role in the creation of many CBS News projects and his editing of Edward R. Murrow's broadcasts before joining academia and founding the broadcast journalism program at American University. This history is replete with inside stories on key figures and, as one might expect, often focuses on quality writing at the network, the lynchpin of Bliss's career working for both Murrow and Walter Cronkite. The book by Schoenbrun is unique in that it tells the exciting but stormy tale of a leading newsman who enjoys great success but ultimately leaves the network when he experiences a loss of independence as a CBS News correspondent, in the face of new management and new policy regulations in network decision-making.

Although works on CBS are not in short supply, few of them focus on the broadcasts themselves or examine the key issues addressed by major programs or series, such as the CBS documentaries that in large measure helped to create the news reputation of the network itself.

Almost all of the works published to date emphasize the players instead of the game. Even some academic accounts fall short in this area. They tell who the major players were but seldom explain the details of what they did in any kind of context. In an attempt to cover the entire terrain, they overlook important details on the critical broadcasts that helped the network become established as a leader in the field. Even the most widely used broadcast textbooks are forced, by space requirements, to relegate the important work of broadcast leaders to limited accounts.

STAR SYSTEM

The most important contemporary figure in the field, Walter Cronkite, is often discussed as being the leading CBS News personality, as he is in the long-standing front-runner among journalism history texts, *The Press and America* (4th edition) by Edwin and Michael Emery. Right after a section on Edward R. Murrow, Cronkite's status as one of the most admired men in America is highlighted, outlining important "firsts," emphasizing that he came out of a press association tradition. Cronkite is credited with inaugurating the half-hour national network news program for CBS in which he interviewed President John F. Kennedy about Vietnam.

Of course, Cronkite's coverage of the Kennedy funeral is mentioned, along with the personal setback he suffered when he was replaced at the 1964 Democratic National Convention. Four years later he was back on track, and his condemnation of police actions at the Chicago convention is duly noted. His public stand on Vietnam policy and relations with LBJ are discussed, along with his identification with issues such as Watergate, space, and ecology and his service as moderator of radio talks with Jimmy Carter. These highlights cover about a page and a half of Cronkite's contributions.[2]

Almost every account of Cronkite's life credits his early experience as a wire service reporter for his success as a television newsman, sometimes ignoring other aspects of his career. The Emery and Emery coverage lists his involvement in documentary projects such as *Eyewitness to History* and *Twentieth Century* without mentioning his role as host of "You Are There" from 1953 to 1957, television's first attempt to re-create historical events based on authentic material. Topics in the series included the Revolutionary War, the Civil War, the Lincoln/Douglas debates, and the Gettysburg Address. Some broadcast historians, such as Robert Horowitz, writing in *American History/American Television* (1983), pointed out that Cronkite learned to project trust and authority at the same time on this show.[3]

In his general history of the network, Gary Gates explains how Cronkite fostered an image of professionalism as CBS anchorman by stressing his role as an active participant in the newsgathering process as he did by insisting on the title "managing editor," alluding to his responsibilities and work schedule. Unlike many of his contemporaries in television news, he was in the office early, actively involved in the creation of the news program and details of film or tape coverage of key stories. In this way, he could provide special attention to coverage of environmental problems, emphasizing the importance of good writing and letting producers handle the visual gimmicks of the newscast while he devoted a significant amount of attention to rewriting and editing, right up until air time.[4] These are all the positive images we tend to conjure up when we think of "Uncle Walter," based on historical accounts. With few very prominent exceptions, we tend not to associate him with issues-oriented broadcasts or important ideas.

Besides the lack of comprehensive treatment of major figures in favor of the personality profile approach, many important contributors have been overlooked. Those who produced and directed many of the very controversial works for "CBS Reports" are frequently absent from the literature on the television documentary, except in the specialized work of Alan Rosenthal and Roy Levin.[5] This oversight is especially unfortunate given the collaborative nature of the medium, a fact that has been emphasized time and again by broadcast bigwigs.

On a number of occasions, "60 Minutes" chief Don Hewitt has discussed the importance of good storytelling in network efforts to achieve important goals in television news and gain a popular following. In some instances, he has made a point of underselling the personality side of the story while stressing the value of his production staff, emphasizing their reporting responsibilities in story development, often prior to the involvement of the actual on-camera reporting staff. In short, according to Hewitt, there are times when the story can get lost in a cult of celebrity. Ironically, Richard Campbell recently pointed out that individualism takes precedence over institutions on most "60 Minutes" stories; and Hewitt has used the celebrity status of his reporters, especially Mike Wallace, as an integral part of his method of storytelling.[6]

It is the aim of this book, then, to examine important broadcasts and those who produced the reports that made a difference and helped CBS gain its reputation as an early model for news and public affairs programming. Interestingly, some of these broadcasts have achieved legendary status, almost as significant as the principals themselves. The "See It Now" "Report on Senator Joseph R. McCarthy" is perhaps the best example of such a broadcast. "The Selling of the Pentagon" on "CBS Reports" is, of course, of nearly comparable status. Because of their historic importance and the perspective offered, they will be reviewed here along with broadcasts of significant but often forgotten import. These include the follow-up report focusing specifically on the activity of the McCarthy committee, which both Murrow and Friendly regarded as a more effective, useful telecast.

Also discussed are early programs that helped establish the network, the documentaries from the "golden age" of the 1960s targeting the critical issues of that period: race, hunger, and the generation gap, all with political implications. Admittedly, a disproportionate number of these programs were hosted by network "stars" such as Murrow, Cronkite, Reasoner, Kuralt, Mudd, and Rather. In spite of the book's title, the intent here is to look as much at the message as the messenger, with special attention to story construction and overall content, the impact and the way the programs were received; evaluating, whenever possible, the motivation for the stories and their effects on public policy, public perception, and political action.

Fortunately, a number of scholars have recently examined network development and impact from the standpoint of their overall benefit for the image of the network and government relations. Some, such as James Baughman, have argued that the entire rationale for these public affairs programs emanated from a need on the part of the networks to change their public posture—that the image of television had become so badly tarnished by quiz show scandals that the development and support of documentary programming was a clear-cut effort to sacrifice financial interests for public relations aspirations and even cultural considerations. In his book *The Republic of Mass Culture* (1992), Baughman offers as evidence a statement by CBS News president Richard Salant, indicating that the CBS pretax profits at one point in the early sixties would have been 65 percent higher without the production of network public affairs programming.[7] Other researchers have also discussed the need to improve public perception of the medium as a means of avoiding government interference, although ironically some of the documents under study addressed government excess, abuse, or oversight, especially in the military, often getting a significant negative reaction.

In gauging effects, the work of individual broadcasters is also evaluated and, in looking at program influence, the writing of major American media critics is also examined. Frequently, as many of these national stories emanated from news developments in their respective home communities, the start-up and basic sources of the information are evaluated firsthand, frequently using the local press as a preliminary guide. It is hoped that in describing this series of broadcasts, which helped to establish CBS as the leading news network, the book will help the reader gain an appreciation for the myriad influences on American broadcasting, some of its important documents, and certainly those players, in key roles, who made them happen.

NOTES

1. See Marion Tuttle Marzolf, *Civilizing Voices: American Press Criticism, 1880–1950* (New York: Longman, 1991).

2. For another example, see the entry on Cronkite in Joseph McKerns's *Biographical Dictionary of American Journalism* (New York: Greenwood Press, 1989), pp. 126–128.

3. See Robert Horowitz, "History Comes to Life and You Are There," in John E. O'Connor, *American History, American Television* (New York: Frederick Ungar, 1983).

4. See popular accounts such as "Murrow: The Man, the Myth and the McCarthy Fighter," *Look*, August 24, 1954, pp. 27–34.

5. See, for example, Alan Rosenthal, *The New Documentary in Action* (Berkeley, CA: University of California Press, 1971).

6. See Richard Campbell, *60 Minutes and the News: A Mythology for Middle America* (Urbana, IL: University of Illinois Press, 1991), pp. 154–157.

7. Ironically, the prototype documentary series "See It Now" came into being because a major advertiser, the Aluminum Company of America (ALCOA), was making an attempt to improve its public image by sponsoring the Murrow/Friendly program. See Fred W. Friendly, *Due to Circumstances Beyond Our Control* (New York: Random House, 1967), p. xix.

Chapter 2

WAR OF WORDS

The CBS News tradition developed slowly at first. Two individuals are credited for the network's early competitive news orientation and high standards. Ed Klauber and Paul White joined CBS News just two years after William S. Paley took it over in 1928. Klauber was a stern and very demanding former city editor for the *New York Times*. Paul White earned his stripes while working for the United Press wire service. Both were knowledgeable and skilled newsmen with critical outlooks and high expectations. They both came to broadcasting from print journalism and were able to adopt strict newsgathering policies, with the support of William S. Paley, which would help to define what radio news could be. These established guidelines were meant to demonstrate objectivity and achieve credibility with the public while attempting to preserve, at least initially, an ability to interpret events and also to provide analysis.[1] The policy issues these guidelines raised would eventually cause headaches for all of the established networks during wartime and thereafter, questions that both Klauber and White were forced to address, such as the need to separate fact from opinion.

Their insistence on quality standards for news at CBS at the outset made it possible for the staff to adopt those criteria and expectations to a still-new medium. Their approach also helped to develop talent. H. V. Kaltenborn, Elmer Davis, John Daly, and Robert Trout all benefited from the White/Klauber partnership in that formative decade just before Murrow began to develop a corps of reporters for CBS overseas and in conjunction with international developments.

The position of early broadcast news was articulated by CBS News director Paul White, who often noted his network's efforts to cover key stories, such as the kidnapping of the Lindbergh baby in 1932, while competitors at first viewed that story as being too sensational.[2] White set up a radio news service anticipating the so-called Biltmore Agreement between newspaper and broadcast stations, and *Broadcasting* magazine interpreted this development as a concession that newsgathering was incidental to radio's primary mission, to entertain.[3] In spite of that view, about the same time, some print journalists were making the transition to radio broadcasting from newspaper posts. H. V. Kaltenborn left the *Brooklyn Eagle* in 1930, for example, to join CBS Radio. Harry Truman would eventually mimic Kaltenborn, publicly ridiculing both his clipped style of radio delivery and the broadcast prediction that Truman would be defeated for the presidency in 1948. However, during the decade of the 1930s, Kaltenborn was gaining innovations, broadcasting "live" from a haystack during the Spanish Civil War, then anchoring a series of reports lasting nearly three weeks in which he interpreted European negotiations involving Hitler and Chamberlain, a tremendous boost to radio news' credibility and a prelude to world war.[4]

Just prior to war, while the craft of broadcast journalism was still in its developing stages, an unusual challenge arose that would raise questions about the behavior of the network and the relation of fact and fiction on the airwaves. A single entertainment program at CBS created a national stir and riveted attention on the issue of the need for broadcast censorship to be applied during the war. Beyond that, the program also called into question the need for standards and practices as they relate to the presentation of fictional material.

What could Orson Welles's 1938 Halloween-night radio dramatization of "War of the Worlds" have to do with important network news and public affairs broadcasts? Is there a relationship between the most famous radio program of all time, announcing that fabricated invasion from Mars, and other programming of that era? Surprisingly, a number of areas relevant to both that legendary "Mercury Theatre on the Air" production of over fifty years ago and broadcast policy issues, including some relatively recent challenges, have come under scrutiny. Many of the major writers of the day addressed the issues; a major, now considered classic, study focusing specifically on effects of the program was conducted shortly after the broadcast.

Timing and context, of course, had a lot to do with the impact of the Welles program. When it aired in late October 1938, just before the outbreak of World War II, the nation was quite anxious over the uncertainty and anticipation of going to war. Hitler had carved up Czechoslovakia while France, England, and Italy stood idly by. It was in this milieu that America was introduced to alien creatures with firepower and all the panache of the brash young dramatist Orson Welles. Social scientists and psychologists were kept very busy in the aftermath, trying to draw parallels between the broadcast itself and the political environment of that day. These considerations included developments on the international scene.

The author of the most thorough analysis of the program, Hadley Cantril, made reference to both Hitler and his propaganda minister Joseph Goebbels, in his review of how the atmosphere for the broadcast was created.[5] The program painted a grim, bizarre picture, of course, one in which parts of the United States were said to be occupied by creatures from Mars, while military forces were defeated, munitions destroyed, communications disrupted, and the population fully demoralized in an unsuccessful effort to repel the attackers. The presentation of this mass destruction was accomplished in broadcast format over radio in less than the hour it took to present the program. Prepared by a relative novice, the program was written by Howard Koch, who was frequently asked to adapt a novel or short play for about a sixty-page broadcast treatment, assigned by Welles himself and John Houseman, the coproducer of the series.

The Welles/Houseman partnership began with a Federal Theatre project and extended to the formation of the Mercury Theatre, then advanced to radio. Koch said he had labored over a wide variety of broadcast copy on this series, which would then be edited by the production team, when H. G. Wells's novella *The War of the Worlds* was passed along with instructions by Houseman to rewrite and prepare it in the form of news bulletins. The revision consisted of a number of news items couched between live dance-music numbers from various locations in the East, a format considered neither novel nor unique for that era. What was challenging for the writer, Koch observed, was the change of location from the original work, since the H. G. Wells story was set in Great Britain, and the style of the first manuscript, which was at first straight narrative.

The key element of the story, a Martian invasion, was, according to Koch, the critical part of the treatment that could be retained, along with the look of the creatures and their exotic weaponry. The demands of the job and the fact that he was preparing what was, for all intents and purposes, an original treatment, plus being asked to do so in less than a week, concerned the fledgling broadcast writer a great deal. But he was told to proceed with the project posthaste because, among other things, it was Orson Welles's favorite idea and one which showed great promise. It provided a contemporary theme with lots of sound effects and dramatic action.

In an attempt to visit his family briefly before undertaking the monumental writing task, Koch left New York and made the journey up the Hudson River to his home, returning via a New Jersey expressway. It occurred to him that he needed to begin the project by identifying the spot where Martians might initiate their invasion. He stopped at a gas station to purchase a map and, according to his published account, took out a pencil and slapped it down inadvertently on a random location on the map. His eyes focused immediately on the small town of Grovers Mill, near Princeton, New Jersey.

He viewed as a plus the fact that the town was situated near a leading American university, which provided an opportunity to tie together an observatory and academic assistance, even a particular if mythical astronomy scholar, Professor Richard Pierson. Played by Orson Welles, Professor Pierson could be introduced in the program and presented as a major source of information in the field. This is one of the elements noted by many of those taken in by the broadcasts. Welles's character added the authenticity associated with a noted astronomer, a prestigious university, and a convincing performance, which included an admission by this credible source, in the early stages of the program, that such happenings were not feasible because Mars was so far away.

Besides Welles's Professor Pierson character, the names of three other academic specialists in the field were used, along with additional references to their institutions, as well as international scientific bodies in France, England, and Germany. Other credible but fictitious "expert" sources named in the broadcast included the commander of the state militia, the vice president of the Red Cross, an Army Signal Corps officer, and another character identified as the secretary of the interior, who, sources said later, sounded a lot like Franklin Roosevelt. In the aftermath of the broadcast, critics said that institutional prestige achieved through the use of titles had a dramatic effect on the influence the program had on laymen. The cumulative effect of having a wide range of sources plus a good number of details, including actual locations reported under attack, with names of specific towns and highways, gave credence to calls for action.

In his book *The Panic Broadcast*, Koch described the gargantuan feat of completing the work for the broadcast in one week. The format consisted of fantastic news flashes interjected into an equally fictitious program of dance music, a prevailing format of the day. First, "Ramon Raquello and his Orchestra" broadcast from the Meridian Room of the Park Plaza Hotel, and later, Bobby Millette and his orchestra were heard from the Hotel Martinet in Brooklyn. Before it was all over, the outrageous scenario included atmospheric disturbances on Mars, battle scenes between invading armies of Martians and U.S. troops, and the destruction of large areas all over the country, including New York City and the facilities of the Columbia Broadcasting System. At one point in the broadcast a roving CBS reporter who has provided reports on the emergence of creatures from a space vehicle on a farmer's field translates the scene as the most terrifying thing he has ever witnessed, describing an alien creature as being as big as a bear and glistening like wet leather, adding "But that face it . . . it's indescribable. I can hardly force myself to keep looking at it."[6] Before losing his ability to transmit, he reports direct movement of the Martian creatures and an attack on spectators on a local farm.

The on-the-spot reporter, a character named Carl Phillips, sounds to listeners as if he has been zapped by the Martian invaders just after he attempts to announce above the sound of screaming voices in the background. The actor playing the part of the reporter explained later that he was able to communicate a breathless panic by mimicking the voice of the real-life announcer at Lakehurst, New Jersey, the year before, who had been broadcasting at the time of the Hindenburg explosion. When another announcer breaks in, after a stall in transmission, to explain that the line to the network is being reestablished, listeners are calmly told of some technical difficulty that has interrupted the radio signal, before being returned to live dance music. In the course of the broadcast, it is explained that a national emergency has been declared, the aliens have wiped out all government military forces, and that New York City is being overrun by space creatures as tall as skyscrapers.

AFTERMATH

Over 6 million listeners tuned in. The CBS assistant vice president in charge of production, Davidson Taylor, reported inquiries into the network by the New York City police department.[7] By the end of the program, a single radio announcer, Ray Collins, is heard offering his view of how gas being sent from alien canisters is leveling the population of the entire United States. Radio stations, newspapers, and police departments across the country were besieged with telephone calls by concerned citizens. Many were obviously convinced, in spite of four warnings during the program and a concluding statement by Welles that it was meant as a Halloween put-on, that what they were listening to was fact, not fiction. Welles said it was the equivalent of dressing up in a sheet and saying "Boo." But many listeners missed or ignored these clues, obviously feeling that part of their world was coming to an end, brought about by the invading Martians.

Interestingly, the day after the broadcast, as postmortems were being conducted, Koch said he overheard references to invasion on the street and assumed that the anticipated world war had broken out or that perhaps Hitler had invaded some additional territory. His barber clarified the impact of the broadcast by showing him the front page of a newspaper, which showed Orson Welles, with outstretched arms, saying he had no idea that the program would have such a tremendous impact on listeners and the country as a whole. In the aftermath, Koch stated that those who had participated in the broadcast were uncertain of their fate as either heroes or villains. Most of the attention was directed at Welles, who became the source of numerous interviews, while both the network itself and the series were busy defending the program.

Fortunately, there were no fatalities associated with the aftermath of the broadcast, although it was reported that some people sustained minor injuries in an effort to avoid what they perceived to be their impending doom. All over the United States, people fled the destruction as best they could. Parents whose children were in theaters promptly removed them and sought shelter. They called police stations, weather bureaus, newspapers, and local universities for information. In a couple of instances, fleeing people stopped to interrupt religious services and to inform the congregation of the invasion. Koch noted that one person considered taking poison as a response to the program, but a thoughtful spouse was able to help avoid that disaster. Meanwhile, columnist Dorothy Thompson was one of the first to credit the program with helping to demonstrate the nation's vulnerability to panic, given any sort of prewar message; and this theme seemed to be picked up by various other elements of the press, with public opinion reportedly changing over a period of time.

Thompson referred to it as "the story of the century" and added that the work of Welles and his cohorts demonstrated more graphically than any other arguments the dangers existing at that time of mass illusion. In recognition of this valuable service, she recommended that Welles be given a Congressional Medal of Honor for his contributions to the social sciences and a better understanding of "Hitlerism, Mussolinism, Stalinism, anti-Semitism and all the other terrorisms of our times."[8] According to that columnist, the CBS creative team exceeded all of the journalists and commentators of that day in graphically communicating European developments and the bullying leading to the Munich Pact. She also pointed out how some demagogues were able to create fear and demoralize thousands in the same way that people had been frightened with political fanaticism abroad, but without any demonstrable show of force and no army or air force.

Thompson offered her assessment that to create an outside enemy and terrorize people into subservience in return for protection was the order of the day in some European quarters. This demonstrated a number of morals, not the least of which was that no political body should ever to allowed to monopolize radio broadcasting. She also lambasted the education establishment for not producing better critical thinking skills in the populace and even charged educators with the creation of superstition rather than skepticism and logic. She added that Welles had bettered the politicians of the day in showing the power of mass suggestion presented on an obscure entertainment program featuring theatrical demagoguery. That appeared, in the wake of the broadcast, to be a more powerful force than economic factors, with the outcome of the new warfare resting on who could frighten the other to death. This was demonstrated by the CBS program, the result of theatrical rather than political performers, and certainly not reflecting well on listeners' ability to discriminate between the two.

Some voices made it clear that the broadcast might be embraced by those seeking radio censorship. The network tried to dismiss some newspaper accounts with the knowledge that select print sources may have been motivated to some extent by radio's developing information status with the public. But CBS sources also noted the state of the world at the time, which gave credence to the wild rumors associated with the program. One military strategist and author on operational issues, Major George Fielding Elliot, discussed the military implications of the panic and cautioned against censorship, pointing out that in a democracy the full unvarnished truth is an excellent antidote to rumor transmission. He used as an example reports that German air power far exceeded their actual numbers, talk that unnecessarily frightened both English and French military authorities and the public at the time into overestimating their strength.

The entertainment trade publication *Daily Variety* ran a page-one banner headline on November 2, 1938, announcing "Radio Does U.S. a Favor." United Features Syndicate writer Hugh S. Johnson described the broadcast as absurd, "a teapot tempest." At the same time, he said that it was also highly significant because it revealed the state of the public mind regarding weaponry and could give the Federal Communications Commission a new excuse to introduce regulation and extend into areas of radio censorship and free speech.[9]

Noted journalist Heywood Broun commented on the need to establish a rule that nothing be put forward as news information on the radio unless it was legitimate news, a domain which, he said, should not be disturbed for comic effect. Broun also warned of efforts to exert censorship in the wake of this broadcast, saying the censors could be much more threatening, and their weapons more far-reaching and potentially devastating, than anything from the pseudoscientific fairy tale "War of the Worlds." As he put it, people had more to fear from "the silhouette of the censor than from the shadow of Orson Welles." Concerns about the broadcast's influence were reinforced when Hadley Cantril completed his study of the media event, the first analysis of its kind, which showed how and why many individuals had been affected in some way by the program.

ANALYSIS

Cantril's study, *The Invasion from Mars*, hypothesized that many Americans were irrationally caught up in the authenticity of the content of the broadcast, in spite of the opportunity to perform the simple check of switching to another channel, mostly because of the insecurity of the world at that time. He focused on one respondent's use of the term "troublesome world" to provide background and some of the reasons why listeners were taken in by the broadcast. The frequent mentions of the international political environment alluded to the idea that Hitler might have developed a weapon of mass destruction, which tied together nicely with accumulated fear for some listeners. The Cantril study also acknowledged that the world situation had created an unusually high listenership for radio news in the two-week period immediately preceding the broadcast. Interestingly, and as a foreshadowing of things to come, he pointed out that those in the lower educational levels had come to rely on radio as the primary source of news. Beyond that, with the then-recent history of poor economic conditions and prolonged insecurity, with the Depression of the early 1930s still in recent memory, additional causes of financial concern existed for many people.

A similar description was provided by researcher Herta Herzog, who was commissioned by CBS and reported to Dr. Frank Stanton.[10] In an effort to examine psychological reasons for the response to the event, she interviewed a number of New Jersey residents who were affected by the program. She mentioned the war scare in Europe as being of primary concern. Respondents suggested "permanent talk about war" and "strange developments in science" as being the most frequently listed factors in creating an atmosphere in which the program could be mistaken for a news broadcast. Some writers offered the view that because radio had been used most recently to relay critical information, it suddenly became the expected source of bad news.

Cantril reported that even before the end of the broadcast, some listeners were crying, praying, and trying to get as far away from death and destruction as they could. Telephone lines were jammed with people bidding adieu to their loved ones. College students lined up at pay telephones to say goodby to family members, and at one small college in Virginia, students stood in line for medical treatment, which seemed logical since the college dean himself had passed out as a result of the excitement. Researchers from Princeton gathered statements from individuals who described feelings of disbelief, while on the other hand reporting efforts to run to their roofs in an attempt to spot monsters wading across the Hudson on their way to Manhattan.

The American Telephone Company outlet in New Jersey reported an increase of telephone use of close to 40 percent over the usual volume during the hour the program was on the air, and CBS radio station managers said letters received by their stations in the aftermath exceeded normal volume by over 100 percent. The network's flagship station at the time, WABC, received close to 2,000 pieces of mail, and the "Mercury Theatre on the Air" almost matched that number of letters. Perhaps more important, the Federal Communications Commission (FCC) told of getting nearly 650 pieces of mail concerning the broadcast with over half of it, about 60 percent, unfavorable.

The FCC, which experienced challenges of its own during this period, was limited with respect to any overt efforts to curtail broadcasters' rights to air contact, but an informed gathering of network presidents, hosted by the Commission chair, resulted in an agreement that the terms "bulletin" and "flash" would be used sparingly in future dramatic programs.[11] Just one year prior to the broadcast, FCC chairman Frank McNinch had been appointed with the mandate from President Franklin Roosevelt to "clean up the mess" at the FCC. McNinch presided over the postmortem meetings just as he had earlier taken steps to reorganize the Commission as a result of public challenges to the vested interests and various broadcast business dealings that had hurt the Commission's credibility with the public and the press.[12]

When nearly 12,500 newspaper accounts related to the broadcast were analyzed, it was shown that the event created an unusually high level of interest, which was sustained for nearly a week after the program and with a wide variety of stories.[13] Because of the manner in which the various elements of the show were broken down for analysis, Hadley Cantril, on a couple of occasions, cautioned that the entire experience or context of the broadcast needed to be considered and explored to reach adequate conclusions on effects. He pointed out that the social context of the times, with social norms and corresponding personal habits in flux, should be of primary concern when reviewing the total event.

Another author, Joel Cooper, chairman of the psychology department at Princeton University, has more recently analyzed public reaction to the broadcast and also pointed to the anxiety of post-Depression

America as a factor in the response to the program: "On the surface, the broadcast was implausible and contradictory, but that didn't matter. In that one instance, people had an immediate explanation for all the unease and disquiet they had been feeling. And suddenly, they could do something. They could gather their families. They could run."[14] A few reports exist along these lines, one in a letter to Welles, in which an admission to that end is made. A writer told him that in response to the broadcast he had withdrawn all of his money from the bank in order to make a hasty exit from the area.

In addition to the psychological explanations, often requiring some considerable leap of logic, the study by Hadley Cantril also uncovered instances in which coincidence, such as power failure in some locales, fed concerns over the program. But the overview of the study demonstrated that a higher level of education created more skepticism and less of a likelihood of being taken in by the outrageous message. Some respondents recognized Welles as a broadcast performer and dismissed the program for that reason. A national survey conducted independently by CBS one week after the broadcast and an American Institute of Public Opinion questionnaire of more limited scope both indicated that those who tuned in late to the broadcast were much more likely to accept the program as a valid news report.

As for the orientation and preparation of the broadcast itself, Howard Koch speculated years later that, had the aliens been represented as friendly creatures out on a mission of good will and understanding, chances were much less that listeners would have been taken in by the program, even at that precarious time. William S. Paley's biographer, Lewis Paper, suggested that the "War of the Worlds" broadcast was consistent with the CBS chairman's plan to make sustaining programs, those without formal sponsorship, so dramatic that the listener could distinguish them from pure entertainment only with great difficulty.[15] In any case, the FCC made it clear that it did not consider the broadcast in the public interest and would not tolerate such abuses in the future. For its part, CBS, noting the use of "flash"-type news announcements common at that time, said that it was dropping simulated news broadcasts within drama programs and also the technique of production in which one story is contained within another. In an updated, 1966 foreword to his classic study of the broadcast, Hadley Cantril also speculated on whether a mediated threat could create as much havoc in contemporary America.

Cantril pointed to an electric power failure in the northeastern United States in the mid-1960s in which millions of people were thrust into darkness, many stranded in isolated places, as evidence that concerns existed from reported fantasies and speculation on the well-being of the country. At the same time, he commented on the deep sense of commitment and responsibility broadcasters now feel to avoid such incidents. This sense of responsibility, a legacy of the strong news commitment and philosophy of early CBS management, especially Ed Klauber and Paul White, was cultivated and reinforced by credible and sometimes heroic coverage by members of that network's news staff, beginning even before the "War of the Worlds" program was offered.

Although it may have competed poorly in the public mind with entertainment programming, the CBS News tradition was aided by a few individuals at the network who had already established name recognition and a news voice on radio. They included, for example, Hans Von Kaltenborn. In fact, H. V. Kaltenborn's wife insisted that listeners to the Welles hoax should have been aware that it was fiction; otherwise, Hans, she said, would have been on the scene, covering the event for radio listeners.[16] This is an element of the debate emanating from the broadcast that is still widely discussed: the extent of influence of that broadcast on the general public as compared to the news arm of the network and crisis reporting.

We know that the few nationally known voices in news were joined by Edward R. Murrow, from modest beginnings in building European outposts and staff for CBS. Often regarded as the father of broadcast journalism, Murrow is credited with setting the tone for newsgathering and with establishing CBS as the early network news leader. His voice and judgment on behalf of both his organization and his country during wartime would help to eliminate questions of credibility and establish norms and respect for broadcast news, because his voice became synonymous with a patriotic commitment and determination. As his work became associated with a number of critical issues and broadcasts, not the least of which were the survival of Great Britain during World War II and the "This Is London" series, he became known as an unofficial American ambassador and statesman. Orson Welles, of course, went on to Hollywood.

NOTES

1. Gary Paul Gates, *Airtime: The Inside Story of CBS News* (New York: Harper and Row, 1978), p. 99; Robert Slater, *This . . . Is CBS: A Chronicle of 60 Years* (Englewood Cliffs, NJ: Prentice-Hall, 1988), p. 101; Christopher H. Sterling and John M. Kitross, *Stay Tuned: A Concise History of Broadcasting* (Belmont, CA: Wadsworth, 1978), p. 167; and J. Fred MacDonald, *Don't Touch That Dial!* (Chicago: Nelson Hall, 1979), p. 71.

2. Paul W. White, *News on the Air* (New York: Harcourt, 1947), pp. 30–31.

3. See "Columbia News Service Has Troubled Start," *Newsweek*, October 7, 1933, pp. 27–28; and "New Plan to End Radio-Press War," *Broadcasting*, January 1, 1934, p. 10.

4. H. V. Kaltenborn, *Fifty Fabulous Years* (New York: Putnam, 1950).

5. Howard Koch, *The Panic Broadcast* (Boston: Little, Brown and Company, 1970). See also Charles Higham, *Orson Welles: The Rise and Fall of an American Genius* (New York: St. Martin's Press, 1985); and Frank Brady, *Citizen Welles* (New York: Charles Scribners Sons, 1989).

6. Hadley Cantril, *The Invasion from Mars* (Princeton, NJ: Princeton University Press, 1940).

7. See "Radio Listeners Alarmed by Fictional Broadcast of Attack by Men from Mars," *St. Louis Post-Dispatch*, October 31, 1938, p. 1, "Too-Realistic Radio Play Starts Wave of Hysteria over City, U.S. Told of Fictional 'Invasion from Mars,' " *Courier Journal*, October 31, 1938, p. 1; and "Radio Listeners in Panic, Taking War Drama as Fact," *New York Times*, October 31, 1938, p. 7.

8. Dorothy Thompson, "On the Record," *New York Tribune*, November 2, 1938, quoted in Howard Koch, *The Panic Broadcast* (Boston: Little, Brown and Company, 1970), pp. 92–93; and Raymond Moley, "Radio Dangers," *Newsweek*, November 14, 1938, p. 48.

9. "Radio Does U.S. a Favor," *Variety*, November 2, 1938, p. 1. See also Associated Press dispatch, "Radio Broadcast Causes Panic: Widespread Hysteria over War Drama," *St. Louis Globe-Democrat*, October 31, 1938, p. 1; "Dialed Hysteria," *Newsweek*, November 7, 1938, p. 13.

10. Herta Herzog, "Why Did People Believe in the 'Invasion from Mars'?" Memorandum to Dr. Frank N. Stanton, Columbia Broadcasting System, 1939, from Paul Lazarsfeld and Richard Rosenberg, *Language of Social Research* (New York: Free Press, 1955), reprinted in Lawrence W. Lichty and Malachi C. Topping, eds., *American Broadcasting: A Source Book on the History of Radio and Television* (New York: Hastings House, 1975), p. 494; Orrin E. Dunlap, "Radio Learns That Melodrama Dressed Up as a Current Event Is Dangerous," *New York Times*, November 6, 1938, pp. 1X, 12.

11. See "Communications Board Investigating Broadcast That Caused Hysteria," *St. Louis Post-Dispatch*, October 31, 1938, p. 1; "Proposes Congress Curb Radio "Abuses,' " *St. Louis Globe-Democrat*, October 31, 1938, p. 1; "Orson Welles on Problems of Making Drama More Intimate," *New York Times*, August 14, 1938, p. 10; and also, Hugh S. Johnson, " 'Mars Panic' Useful," and Heywood Broun, "It Seems to Me," both quoted in Howard Koch, *The Panic Broadcast* (Boston: Little, Brown and Company, 1970), pp. 90–91.

12. Federal Communications Commission, Washington, DC, Press Release #30432, November 7, 1938.

13. See "F.C.C. Shakeup," *Newsweek*, October 25, 1937, pp. 32–34; and "F.C.C.: History of a Flop," *Business Week*, February 4, 1939, p. 15.

14. Quoted in "The Night Martians Came to New Jersey," *People Weekly*, October 31, 1988, p. 45. Howard Koch went on to become a successful Hollywood film writer. He won an Oscar for *Casablanca* with Humphrey Bogart and sold the original "War of the Worlds" script at Sotheby's auction house for $143,000 in 1988. See " 'War of the Worlds' Fetches $143,000," *St. Louis Post-Dispatch*, December 16, 1988, p. 24E.

15. Lewis J. Paper, *Empire: William S. Paley and the Making of CBS* (New York: St. Martin's Press, 1987), p. 31.

16. Irving E. Fang, *Those Radio Commentators!* (Ames, IA: Iowa State University Press, 1977), p. 16; also see Eric Barnouw, *The Golden Web: A History of Broadcasting*, vol. 2: 1933–1953 (New York: Oxford University Press, 1968).

Chapter 3

MURROW: RADIO DAYS

For some observers, broadcast journalism began in the late 1930s when Edward R. Murrow covered the Austrian invasion, including a first-hand description of Adolf Hitler's entry into Vienna. Taking it a step further, Murrow offered American radio listeners shortwave reports from European capitals with expert CBS commentary by the likes of Robert Trout, William L. Shirer, and Eric Sevareid, experts he recruited, who affectionately became known as "Murrow's Boys." The goal of taking listeners on location to hear the sounds of internationally significant events with the eyewitness accounts and voices of newsmakers from the political arena was the result of careful planning by CBS News director Paul White and his boss, Ed Klauber, who had high expectations and set high journalistic standards. The CBS "World News Roundup" from Europe, which was established shortly after the Press-Radio Bureau ended in 1938, had Robert Trout and William L. Shirer playing pivotal roles. It also set the stage for international coverage in that the network gathered its own news and provided on-the-spot, factual coverage.[1]

Closely linked to this commitment to covering the "big picture" was Murrow's continuing effort to tell the story of little people caught up in challenging events. The decision to establish and support Murrow's "This Is London" radio series helped to create an atmosphere for broadcast news coverage that was unique and unprecedented. H. V. Kaltenborn, Graham McNamee, and some others were offering perspective via radio but the CBS News decision to establish European report-

Edward R. Murrow became well known as a broadcaster initially on his "This Is London" series for CBS News. He also recruited a number of talented newcomers to the field from his base of operations in Europe. Used with the permission of CBS Inc.

ing outposts based in London was on a par with the journalistic tradition of newsgathering associated with print reporting and leading newspaper organizations of the day. Of course, beyond this commitment to news was the obvious difference that listeners were getting information and descriptions of conditions firsthand, often directly from primary sources, filtered through American voices but from the perspective of listeners with their values and priorities at the forefront.

At times, the perspective offered on the airwaves created grave concerns. But Murrow and his colleagues offered an opportunity to associate with an international dilemma of epic proportions and add insight that would contribute to morale and rally the American public, often providing small slices of British life as informed, concerned observers and citizens of the world community. Murrow's early role in London enhanced his status as ex officio ambassador of good will in the United Kingdom. In short, American listeners identified with Murrow. He provided word pictures of key events and also communicated the mood of the country, the will to survive and overcome adversity. He frequently gave listeners a glimpse of life during wartime, addressing the concerns of those to whom he broadcast by sometimes bringing the oddities and awkwardness of the war home through his broadcasts.

LONDON SCENE

On Christmas Eve 1940, Murrow described, for example, a London scene somewhat at odds with the popular image of the staid British "business as usual" character, one in which church bells did not ring, except to announce invasion.[2] This was a London where rooftop observers were on the lookout with antiaircraft gunners standing at the ready, waiting for the sound of German air engines. Meanwhile, ambulance drivers and firefighters were equally prepared to battle whatever calamity might accompany the next attack. Murrow pointed out that this was not viewed as a "Merry Christmas," since well-wishers avoided making that time-honored wish of good cheer this time around because of its awkwardness at this dark hour.

Even though casualties were low, the future looked ominous indeed. Murrow, still growing in recognition among radio listeners, let Americans know of the need for Britons to celebrate as best they could under these circumstances, some from underground shelters. While feeling the challenge of offering Christmas cheer under such grim conditions, Murrow sought to offer the London phrase "So long and good luck," on that occasion, a variation of the familiar "Good night and good luck" sign-off he would adopt and use throughout his broadcasting career.

In an assessment of Prime Minister Winston Churchill's condemnation of Hitler, Murrow offered the prime minister's use of the label
"bloodthirsty guttersnipe" as evidence of his sense of impending misery
and desperation in requesting technological and economic assistance
from the Soviet Union, pledging that any state who fights the Nazis
should have the support of Great Britain. In the year following that
broadcast, Murrow frequently conveyed the sense of urgency in involvement and commitment or resolve on the part of the British people,
as shown by their efforts to volunteer for service.

He described individual acts of courage by British and Scottish sailors,
for example, and their desire to return to combat assignments even just
after undergoing hardship or injury. He continued to reflect favorably on
the Russian people as they faced up to the German war machine, while
speculating on America's role and the British appetite for good Anglo-
American relations, pointing out that there had never been a greater
desire on the part of the British to learn about America and its institutions.

By November 1942, Murrow was able to describe the feeling of
hearing church bells for the first time in twenty-nine months. He reported that this exercise was both exhilarating and odd, strange in that
the sound was now echoing through cavities in neighborhoods where
buildings once stood. The comfort that accompanied the sound of the
bells was testimony to those working on the North African campaign
that things were looking up on the home front but perhaps just as
dramatic a message for those who fought the battle at home with fire
hoses and buckets of sand.

By the next month, Murrow was reporting on war atrocities and the
cold-blooded massacre of Polish Jews, including those of the Warsaw
ghetto. Throughout Nazi-dominated territory, extermination camps
had been established. Murrow explained that it had reached the point
where the term "concentration camp" was no longer accurate. In light
of what would follow at Nuremberg, interestingly, Murrow reflected on
demands by British clergy and newspapers, insisting that postwar
punishment should be dealt out not only to those who gave orders, but
also to the underlings who carried them out.

In what is regarded as one of the most dramatic and hard-hitting
broadcasts ever made, Murrow reinforced the outrage of the world
when he broadcast from the just-opened camp at Buchenwald.[3] He
described how prisoners had been treated, housed and fed worse than
animals. As an unconventional effort to offer insight into the wretched
conditions of the camp he offered his reaction to the all-pervasive smell,
the ugly stench of those surroundings.

He personalized the message by identifying children who were incar-
cerated and tortured in the camp and added testimony by a former

mayor who had been humiliated by the Nazis and stamped for identification, something Murrow said the former prisoners including children would carry until the end of their lives. He made no effort to mask his personal anger at the result of atrocities he observed firsthand and vowed to make every effort to inform the public of the brutality, the murders, and inhumane treatment. That broadcast, when heard today, still conveys an emotion-charged, dramatic indictment of Nazi horrors that undoubtedly colored Murrow's perception of war from that point forward, including a well-known commitment to cover the Korean conflict more than a decade later.

Gradually, Murrow came to embody the news value of an infant medium[4]; like many prominent journalists, he occasionally took occasion to poke fun at himself and the parameters of his craft. On one occasion, for example, he broadcast the contents of a letter he had received from a radio listener who suggested the distinguished broadcaster change his early sign-off from "This is the news" to "This is some of the news." The writer went on to describe himself as very tolerant of the introductory verbiage but nonetheless concerned that some listeners might interpret these remarks as a reflection of egotism, pride, and self-assumed omniscience.

The concerned writer suggested that a slight change of pace might indicate an awareness to coverage of "all the cosmic facts of the universe." Murrow said he regarded it as sound advice and, as one might expect, signed off by acknowledging that he had indeed reported just "some of the news." This attempt to keep it somewhat lighthearted, not taking himself too seriously, served Murrow well, especially when he had to report on dire consequences of war.

KOREAN CONFLICT

In acknowledging the brutality and often futility of war, Murrow frequently described the rationale for conflicts in which American forces played a major role. He offered details on decision-making at home and speculated on how GIs would react if they were aware of the divisions of party politics or dissenting opinion, often reporting from the front or as a prelude to fighting that might lie ahead. With the Korean War at hand, he reviewed the various positions on the need for the conflict and characterized the views of leading political figures. At the site of the conflict in June 1950, Murrow described the military outlook, along with his own observations on the conduct of the war and a physical description of the sights and smell of the battlefield cast in everyday terminology—offering a comparison to home, the attitudes and actions of the everyday soldier seen from a reporter's vantage point. He described how one day's broadcast was written by candlelight on the school desk of a small child, just forty miles away from the fighting.

On other occasions, Murrow replicated previous commitments and conditions, going to the battlefield itself past burning villages, linking up with the 1st Cavalry, describing the action of a spotting plane in the course of correcting the fire of a six-gun battery firing maverick rounds while responding to air strike requests. Murrow, of course, frequently relied on military leaders to form the basis of his reports. On occasion, these sources gave conflicting information, sometimes critical of the conduct of the war effort itself. In one instance, on August 14, 1950, CBS elected not to use a Murrow broadcast recorded for playback on the evening news program, because it had the potential of putting the military in a bad light. It contained questions regarding command decisions based on personal conversations he had with commanders and troops relative to enemy troop strength and the American potential to mount an offensive with the military strength of that period. This editorial decision raised some eyebrows but was understood as a patriotic gesture, even in this era.

Korea had a special appeal to Murrow. He viewed the American military personnel of that conflict as young men, boys really, in contrast to his peers from the World War II experience. This was once reflected in broadcast references to his son Casey, seven years old at the time of Murrow's Christmas Eve broadcast of 1952. In offering a brief report specifically for his son, an occasion he said he hoped was not an abuse of privilege, Murrow talked about the American holiday rituals, the emphasis on family, gift-giving, and, of course, a Christmas tree.

Murrow discussed how the American soldiers displayed photos of their families and how, upon seeing a picture of Murrow's son, a soldier had suggested a talk aimed specifically at Casey and other little boys whose dads were on duty. Apologizing for the fact that he had been there such a short time and, unlike the soldiers, would have a chance to return home soon, Murrow proceeded with a description of life in Seoul.

He described the events which had taken place in Korea and the activity of the American forces. He provided a detailed description of the Headquarters Building, which included a huge Merry Christmas sign decorated with a cardboard reindeer and the colored lights one might expect to see this time of year in an American neighborhood. He went on to tell of the Korean children, how they looked and how they were handling the conditions of war. As far as the Korean soldiers were concerned, he praised their courage and strength, then advised an inspection of the famed Valley Forge painting, to gain some insight into their commitment to contemporary freedom.

In describing the work of American soldiers, he took time to tell of their living conditions, the lack of electricity and heat. He noted how some kids' dads were straining their eyes to insure that the enemy was not sneaking up the hill to threaten their position. When the dad gets relieved from his duty he will have a chance to get some coffee and look at those pictures of his loved ones at home, Murrow added, and maybe even get to write a letter home to express the sense of loneliness one experiences, especially on a holiday, in being far away from home. This was a loneliness under stark conditions, Murrow pointed out, that had to be lived to be fully understood. Similarly, in his stateside radio broadcasts and eventually on television, Murrow frequently identified challenges in an extended, long-form documentary format related to the security of home and country, often in a political context.

TRANSITION

As Murrow and his associate Fred W. Friendly made the successful transition from radio to television, at times the programs they produced attracted the attention of both media. For example, when Murrow interviewed former president Harry S. Truman for "See It Now" in February 1958, CBS elected to replay the program on radio when a labor union stepped forward with special advertising revenue to support the broadcast.[5] The hour-long conversation with Truman was filmed over a four-day period during the previous year in the Florida Keys. A total of ten hours of film was shot, with much of it reserved for release only after Truman's death.

The program, entitled "From Precinct to President," focused on Truman's experience in office, describing his background and his awe of the office of the presidency, his battles with Congress and conflicts with the press. He admitted that his criticism of a music critic who addressed the musical talents of his daughter Margaret was probably an error of judgment on his part. He also questioned how the song "Missouri Waltz" had somehow become attributed to him as a favorite. On more serious subjects, Truman clarified a report that said he had once backed General Eisenhower for president.[6] Truman had advised Eisenhower on the special difficulty of the job for military men who had held the office, but he said he never encouraged or supported the former war hero.

Truman also commented on the subject of hypocrisy among certain people who lay claim to religious orthodoxy. He offered his view that former presidents were compensated at a low level, forcing him to admit that if he had not inherited some property, he would have ended up on relief. He again called the decision to order troops into Korea his toughest decision, dismissing the dropping of the bomb on Japan as a necessity of war. Overall, Truman said he had no regrets about the conduct of his presidency. The documentary effort consisted of the former president in close-up for most of the program without any visual embellishment. In spite of that, Jack Gould of the *New York Times* called it an animated and absorbing interview, adding that it provided a rare three-dimensional portrait of a leader and the period in which he was in office.[7]

The former president admitted that his failure to pass health and education legislation was the greatest regret of his time in office, adding that the American Medical Association had sabotaged efforts to improve health care insurance. His position on improved education and urban security, he claimed, would have the effect of providing equality of opportunity for all Americans. These areas, which would get regular attention by Murrow, included one prominent occasion when he addressed the subject of urban violence and the young.

STREET STORY

Regarded by some as one of Murrow's best-constructed works and, in some ways, the most effective radio documentary ever, "Who Killed Michael Farmer?" examined violence in American society by putting urban youth gangs under a microscope.[8] Murrow offered an overview of the habits and peculiarities of gang members and their victims. He pieced together the details of a violent attack and murder in this program, with the participants describing the event and giving a first-hand account of their background motivations.[9] Parents were heard explaining what transpired before and after the assault, including the criminal trial of young gang members.

Police tell of being called to the crime scene and of their dealings with the offenders. Gang members say how and why, in their view, the attack took place. Psychologists and counselors try to offer an explanation for the attack, a portrait of individual gang members including their living conditions, and a rationale for their violent activity and criminal behavior. Both juvenile authorities and social workers comment on the conditions under which they are forced to work in trying to deal with the inner-city youth-gang problem. The broadcast explores in depth the motivation of gang members and their psychological makeup.

The documentary began with a remembrance of Michael Farmer by both his father and mother. They described an excellent student, good-looking and athletic, although he walked with a slight limp from an attack of polio. Next Murrow recounted the basic facts of the case. Farmer was stabbed and beaten to death on the evening of July 30, 1957, in a New York City park. In the aftermath, ten gang members under fifteen years of age were convicted of juvenile delinquency and committed to a state training school. Seven other members of the gang, ages fifteen to seventeen, stood trial for first-degree murder in a court proceeding that lasted ninety-three days.

Gang members were defended by twenty-seven court-appointed lawyers, and the verdict of the all-male jury was that two of the defendants were guilty of murder in the second degree, two were guilty of manslaughter in the second degree, and two were not guilty because they had been coerced into going along with the other gang members in the attack. One defendant was found not guilty due to mental illness. For all intents and purposes, the case appeared to be closed, and typical broadcast news treatment of that era might have ended at that point. But Murrow noted that the roots of this crime went very deep and it was his intent to explore the causes of youth violence, reiterating for instance that this broadcast was not a dramatization.

The murder of Michael Farmer first became news at 6:30 on what Murrow described as a steamy summer night on the upper west side of Manhattan in New York City. He began this segment of the broadcast by letting one of the leaders of the Egyptian Kings and Dragons gang, the group responsible for the murder, explain their efforts to gather members together from a twenty-block area that evening at a local candy store, their usual meeting place. The organizer of the meeting, a leading gang member, said he sent little children home in anticipation of a fight with the Jesters, the rival street gang from the adjoining neighborhood, Washington Heights, where Michael Farmer resided. The two gangs were feuding over the fact that boys from both groups had recently been beaten and stabbed. The goal was to find and fight any rival gang member they might encounter, and they prepared by bringing along weapons for this purpose.

Murrow let individuals from the group tell their story of how violent encounters were conducted by gangs. Remarks by some of the participants indicated some reluctance that evening because they anticipated trouble. On the other hand, they also feared being left out because of gang retribution regularly leveled at those who did not take part in fighting. The gang confrontation was planned to take place at the Hybridge Park swimming pool, identified as a frequent flash point for gang violence.

Meanwhile, Michael Farmer's mother explains in the broadcast how, in the hours preceding the attack, her son and his friend Roger McShane were listening to records at the Farmer household. When they finished with their music, Michael told his parents that he was going to walk Roger home. Mrs. Farmer said that both of the boys had been instructed to stay out of Hybridge Park at night after the pool was closed but that they decided to sneak a swim. At the same time the Egyptian Kings and

Dragons were waiting at the pool for scouts to return and report on the other gang's whereabouts. At this point in the narration, when the attack is about to begin, Murrow turned the story over to the surviving victim, Roger McShane.

At 10:30 P.M. the boys entered the park and observed members of the gang, he said. Within minutes, they were attacked with garrison belts and were hit and kicked, then Farmer was stabbed with a bread knife. McShane ran and gang members trailed after him, shouting that he was a member of the opposition gang. He was also knocked down and stabbed. The gang members retreated after he screamed for help. He was subsequently found and taken by ambulance to a hospital while his friend remained injured in the park. The gang members returned to their respective homes. Before undergoing surgery, McShane notified police that his friend was still in the park, and police were sent back to that location.

At this point in the broadcast, the parents of Michael Farmer explain what happened next. They were given a ride to the host hospital, where they were informed of their son's death. Murrow clarified that neither Farmer nor McShane had ever been gang members or, for that matter, in trouble with the police. Those who conducted the attack on the boys claimed that they had seen them accompanying the Jesters and assumed that they were members of that gang. The Jesters said neither had been a member and told the police who had been involved in the attack.

One gang member told of the police investigation and his denial of any involvement in the attack. Another gang member, the one who used a bread knife in the attack, was in juvenile court the next morning. He was pleading innocent to another crime, a recent robbery. In an interview with CBS, this boy also alleged police cruelty against him, claiming that while he was in custody, police officers wiped their shoes on his clothing while calling him a murderer and verbally threatening that he would receive a death sentence in this case. This boy commented that if he had a revolver, he would have shot all of the police at that point in the interview. Another gang member laughed about his reaction when the knife was taken from Michael Farmer's body because the victim said "thanks" for removing the weapon.

Police found hunting knives in the homes of gang members' girl friends. The boys were charged and made full confessions. Murrow mentioned the fact that this was the largest group of boys ever arrested for a New York City murder; seven were charged with homicide, two with attempted homicide, and ten more with juvenile delinquency. Murrow also offered some perspective on the juvenile crimes and the extent of the charges and pointed out that those charged were among fifty-eight youths arrested in New York City that year, 1957, for murder and nonnegligent manslaughter.

BACKGROUND

Murrow added that these were among the more than three thousand juvenile arrests in the nation during the preceding year for crimes of major violence and among an estimated 1 million youths arrested for all crimes nationally during that same period. Murrow reflected on the reaction of Michael Farmer's father when the preliminary hearing of gang members took place. He said Mr. Farmer categorized the killers as "savage animals" with no sense of civilization or remorse: "These boys didn't even hang their heads, most of them, when they came into court. They stood erect and looked around the courtroom at friends and relatives." He added that one of the killers exhibited a "small smirk" when he looked in the direction of the victim's parents.

As one might expect, Mr. Farmer expressed the view that these young criminals should be put away and kept away or, if the penalty is death, they should be executed, he said, because they had set themselves up as judge, jury, and execution squad in his son's case and it was done in a matter of minutes. Murrow offered the assessment of other courtroom observers, including two detectives, who also commented that the boys showed no remorse whatsoever in the hearing room. The boys themselves accused police officers of threatening and coercing them into confessing to the murder, charges the police denied under oath.

Early reports indicated that at least one of the attackers stabbed "for thrills," Murrow said, adding that the boy who used a bread knife in the attack reportedly told police, "He always wanted to know what it would feel like to stick a knife through human bone." The same boy told CBS News program producer Jay McMullen that he did not know what he was doing at the time because he was intoxicated. That boy also reiterated the point as well that he thought the victims were members of the opposing gang, the Jesters. He added that he acted in self-defense and that gang members frequently called him by the racial epithet "Spik," implying a defensive stance and saying that he had been beaten up himself on five different occasions.

He clarified his disposition toward the murder, saying that he also feared discipline by his own gang if he did not participate in the attack. Murrow again reviewed the situation that led to the event, summarizing the basic facts of the case, that gang members got drunk, sought revenge, then committed murder. He pointed out that one boy pleaded not guilty on grounds of insanity but was declared legally sane. A psychiatrist testified that the boy was epileptic and incapable of premeditating or deliberating a murder. No psychiatric examination was made of the other six boys on trial for their lives in this case.

CRIMINAL PROFILE

Murrow informed listeners that the jury convicting some of the boys heard very little about their mental or emotional makeup, but the program producer, Jay McMullen, questioned the director of psychiatric care at New York City's youth treatment center. Facility director Marian Cohen explained the purpose of her center, to hold individuals while they are remanded temporarily by the juvenile court. While they are held in this facility, their conditions are studied and a diagnosis is made, she said. In the case of those who attacked Michael Farmer, she added, the boys were not evaluated because the judge did not request it; the problems of the individual boys and their needs were not differentiated. No formal request had been made in the case, and there was a shortage of staff workers. Murrow described the staff as consisting of four caseworkers assigned to handle three hundred boys.

When asked if she could make generalizations about the gang members in this case, Ms. Cohen offered the view that these boys were intent on presenting a tough facade to outsiders because of internal feelings of weakness and inadequacy. Murrow then let one boy describe his condition at home, which was consistent with the evaluation of professional counselors. Murrow quoted one of the gang members as saying that he would have stabbed Roger McShane himself if he had a knife, because then the other members of the gang would have viewed him as a "cold killer," thus establishing his need to be regarded as a tough guy.

When the CBS reporter interviewed the mother of one of the attackers, she expressed shock and disbelief that her son would engage in such activity, but other parents of those involved in the attack showed much less concern. When Murrow interviewed the staff psychiatrist at juvenile court, Dr. Marjorie Rittwagon, she provided statistics on the emotional makeup of parents whose children commit serious crimes. Among other things, she pointed out that in close to 80 percent of cases in which children are brought to court, their parents are emotionally ill or have severe personality disorders. Ten percent of those are committably psychotic, she said, and most of the children come from homes in which there is no father, a theme that would be repeated in CBS documentaries.

Murrow added that of the seven members tried in the Farmer case, five had no father in the home. In a very emotional segment of the broadcast, one mother explained how her son grew up under the care of his grandfather because as a single parent she was overwhelmed by her own personal problems. Overall, Murrow explained, eleven of the seventeen boys arrested in the case came from broken homes. This recurring condition was reiterated by the psychiatrist, who said that at critical times in their lives the boys, unwilling to relate closely with their mothers, sought out superficial male role models through gang membership.

This environment, according to authorities interviewed for the program, promotes violent behavior and a tendency to "act out" rather than to discuss personal problems. Murrow investigated the daily routine of the gang members, which followed a pattern familiar to caseworkers in the area. The youths would hang out without supervision in their neighborhood, which would invariably lead to criminal activity. Once a youth is started on a life of crime, little treatment is available because probation officers are overloaded with cases. Each officer has a minimum of sixty or seventy boys assigned to him, which, Murrow added, translates to one talk per individual each month.

It was reported that the boy who stabbed Michael Farmer in the attack at Hybridge Park had served a year in state training school and was diagnosed as a "dangerous psychopath" when he was released five months earlier. In spite of the diagnosis, he received no psychotherapy because of the extensive institutional workload in the state. Murrow said that although juvenile delinquency was on the rise at the time, resources had not increased proportionately, and staff shortages were characteristic of the system.

He began the concluding segment by pointing out the irony that, in the richest state in the richest nation, long-term care is not available for nearly 80 percent of delinquent children under twelve years of age. The state did not address this area, although a few private outlets were available, but oversubscribed. He added that one of the boys involved in the Farmer attack had committed five different offenses before the age of twelve. In each case, the child was immediately sent back to the streets unassisted and unsupervised.

A special segment added to the end of the documentary put the blame at the feet of parents unable to control their children and gave statistics showing related cases on the rise. Sixteen major violent incidents had occurred in that same area in the three years prior to the attack. Murrow used another source, a youth worker from the neighborhood, to point to efforts to reorganize the gang after the trial. The Farmer family added their concerns about the welfare of their remaining son, as well as their late son's friend Roger McShane and his prospects for the future, after having testified against gang members.

RESPONSE

New York Times broadcast critic Jack Gould commended the documentary unit for involving participants, calling the program an absorbing hour, with the highlight being the opportunity to hear those involved in the case tell the story from their perspective. On the other hand, Gould took the show to task for not pointing toward solutions to the problem of street gangs, with too much emphasis on negative and seemingly hopeless aspects of delinquency. Certainly the program could be credited with jolting listeners from complacency on the issue, he said, but it provided little in the way of instruction on how the situation could be improved.

Gould pointed out that the program never provided specifics about what actions Youth Board caseworkers employed in dealing with gang crime, adding: "The graphic and grave realities of juvenile crime in street gangs should be reported in all media. But there is something disturbing about a radio program that concludes that society has an awesome problem on its hands and then can only say 'good night.' "[10] The constructive headway made by various organizations in coping with the gang problem was never adequately addressed, according to Gould, and he concluded his critique by asking what reformed gang members might have contributed to the editorial mix to shed some positive aspects on the issue.

The documentary frightened a lot of people and clearly articulated the growing problem of youth violence. Murrow concluded the program by emphasizing that, although the verdict had been rendered and the crime solved by virtue of commitment of fifteen boys to institutions, this was not the end of the story or the cycle of juvenile crime, as those facilities were not properly equipped to rehabilitate youngsters, thus presenting the likelihood that they would eventually return to the community to victimize others.

He reiterated that experts agree on the conditions that produce juvenile delinquency and criminal behavior, but he also implied that these crimes were likely to continue because of apathy on the part of the general public. Certainly, this broadcast helped to raise the levels of awareness and concern of listeners. Beyond that, it helped CBS widen the scope of its documentary efforts. Indeed, for some contributors to this effort, especially writer and producer Jay McMullen,[11] it was a major step in the progression of a career devoted to a wide range of issues with urban, political, and civil liberties themes extending into television.

NOTES

1. Donald G. Godfrey, "CBS World News Roundup: Setting the Stage for the Next Half Century," *American Journalism* 3(3) (Summer 1990): 164–172.

2. Edward Bliss, Jr., ed., *In Search of Light: The Broadcasts of Edward R. Murrow, 1938–1961* (New York: Alfred A. Knopf, 1967).

3. *Great Moments in Radio*, vol. 1 (New York: Evolution Recording, 1974). Sound recording.

4. See Alexander Kendrick, *Prime Time: The Life of Edward R. Murrow* (New York: Little, Brown and Company, 1969); Ann Sperber, *Murrow: His Life and Times* (New York: Freundlich, 1986); Betty H. Winfield and Lois B. DeFleur, *The Edward R. Murrow Heritage: Challenge for the Future* (Ames, IA: Iowa State University Press, 1986).

5. Wayne Phillips, "Truman Disputes Eisenhower on '48," *New York Times*, February 3, 1958, p. 1.

6. Val Adams, "CBS Appeals Action by Union," *New York Times*, February 7, 1958, p. 45.

7. Jack Gould, "TV: Human Document," *New York Times*, February 3, 1958, p. 46.

8. Most of the broadcast script is contained in Robert L. Hilliard, *Writing for Television and Radio* (Belmont, CA: Wadsworth, 1984), pp. 147–163.

9. See "4 Youths Held in Fatal Gang Fight; Police Patrol Scene," *New York Times*, August 1, 1957, p. D 17.

10. Jack Gould, "Radio-TV: Street Gangs," *New York Times*, April 22, 1958, p. 67. A similar case with an entirely different outcome coincided with the broadcast. See "2 Judges 'Spank' Parents of Boys," *New York Times*, April 22, 1958, p. 35.

11. McMullen went on to produce, for example, on "CBS Reports," "Biography of a Bookie Joint," which is discussed later in the book. See Fred W. Friendly, *Due to Circumstances Beyond Our Control* (New York: Random House, 1967), p. 138; and A. William Bluem, *Documentary in American Television* (New York: Hastings House, 1965), p. 107.

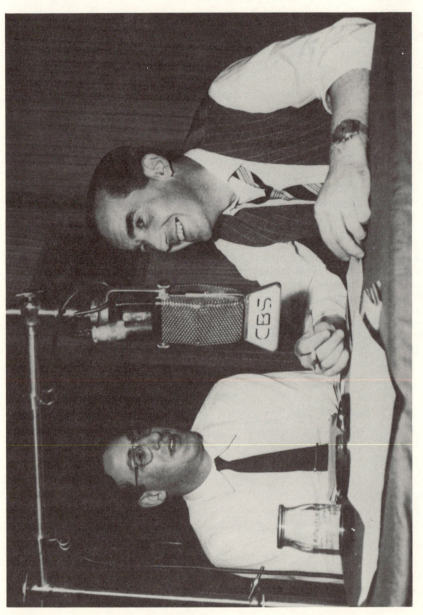

Fred W. Friendly and Edward R. Murrow, broadcasting's most celebrated team, prepare a radio broadcast. Their television work on "See It Now" became equally important. Used with the permission of CBS Inc.

Chapter 4

CIVIL LIBERTIES

At the start of the decade of the 1950s, CBS could be found investigating a wide range of stories related to the general theme of social injustice, some of it institutional in nature, often with incidents and policies related specifically to government policy. One such case involved a twenty-six-year-old Air Force reserve officer who was having his military commission revoked simply because of his close and ongoing relationship with his father and more remote contact with his sister. The rationale for this action related to the young man's security status. As a college student at the University of Michigan, Milo Radulovich was especially concerned about the fallout from this action because of the black mark it would leave on his employment record, especially in his chosen field of meteorology, which frequently relies on government experience as evidence of expertise.[1]

In early correspondence with Radulovich, military authorities made it clear that they were not concerned about the young lieutenant's personal loyalty, but rather his association with Communists in his family. They even testified to his exemplary record of achievement to date, while questioning his relationship with his father, whose views were considered unconventional. The father, John Radulovich, a Serbian who had immigrated to Detroit in 1914, worked as a coal miner and in automobile manufacturing after a stint in the U.S. Army during World War I. The fact that the senior Radulovich subscribed to a Croatian language newspaper, *Slobna Rech*, a publication that supported Prime Minister Tito, and read the *Daily Worker* on a regular basis was cited in documents military authorities used to judge his son. Beyond that, the officer's sister, Mrs. Margaret Fishman, was also accused of pro-Communist activities, including picketing a federal building in 1948, celebrating the anniversary of the *Daily Worker*, and picketing a hotel that refused to admit Paul Robeson, who was accused of supporting various pro-Communist movements.

Radulovich himself denied any connection between his sister's political activity and his own views. He asked why he should be held accountable for his sister's actions, adding: "I can't help it if she goes off the deep end."[2] Without sounding as if he was at odds with his sister on personal grounds, he mentioned that he seldom even had contact with her and that they had never once discussed politics. As for his father, he pointed out that it was not unusual for him to read a wide range of newspapers including anti-Communist publications but that this fact was not considered by military investigators in the case. In spite of the attention and embarrassment the case created in Dexter, Michigan, his hometown, Radulovich vowed to fight the early judgment because he thought it might jeopardize both employment prospects and his goal of eventually doing graduate work in the sciences. He felt that an early discharge due to his classification as a potential security risk would hurt his academic and job prospects.

Just prior to a scheduled hearing held at Selfridge Field, Radulovich received support from some political figures in the area. The preliminary questioning which revolved around the father reflected the view that he was a loyal, hardworking American.[3] Testimony from fellow employees and superiors at the Hudson Motor Car Company, his place of employment, supported his strong standing. In the course of the hearing defense attorneys used excerpts of a speech by Dwight Eisenhower in which he denounced a "book burning" mentality in which contrary thinking is viewed as inaccessible, unrecorded, and concealed from public view and debate.[4] The defense raised objections involving Radulovich's sister, saying the facts had no bearing on this case because she seldom even saw her brother. Attorneys for Radulovich also questioned whether the proceedings abridged the sister's constitutional rights, although the military used this same issue to bar press coverage of the hearing on the grounds of protecting the family, while stressing the fact that the hearing represented an administrative Air Force matter and not a trial.[5]

The outcome of the hearing went against the lieutenant and he was ordered discharged although, as in prior discussions, the Air Force reinforced the idea that Radulovich's personal loyalty was not questioned. His attorney, Charles Lockwood, had earlier characterized the hearings as being based on "unsupported allegations" by "unknown persons."[6] He also pointed out that four similar cases had already been lost by individual service members and that the most that could be done would be to present the strongest possible case by producing the record, then face the inevitable negative consequences. At the conclusion, he termed the proceedings using unsupported allegations and rumor "a farce" and said the "undemocratic" judgment in the case was based on hostility toward his client because of publicity generated by the hearing and his client's earlier unwillingness to accept a secret dismissal without fanfare. Another attorney who had volunteered to represent Radulovich, Kenneth Sanborn, questioned rules of evidence as applied to the case, and Radulovich himself repeated his views that the actions of his father and sister should have no bearing on his military status.[7]

The decision for termination was based on twelve major points, with half of them related to the lieutenant's sister and her support of Communist causes. Two of the charges were tied to his father's reading of newspapers. Radulovich concluded that if he had gone so far as to denounce his relatives, with the word "denounce" being used repeatedly in the hearing, he might have been spared his military commission. Although unwilling to endorse their political views, he was equally adamant about his unwillingness to disown his family, saying: "In America you are supposed to be able to believe what you want to. I don't believe in communism, but I don't think I should sever all ties with my family because they don't think the same as I."[8] Within a week of his making that statement, "See It Now" elected to prepare for broadcast "The Case of Lieutenant Milo Radulovich," which had been carefully followed by Joe Wershba of the CBS staff. Wershba was immediately sent to Michigan and frequently called in with updates on story development. The photographic unit accompanying Wershba was forwarding interview material back to New York headquarters within two days of initiating the project.

Early interviews with Radulovich and his father were very effective in that they reflected the pride both men held in being American citizens and the sorrow and shame of being punished for what amounted to the father's reading habits. One early filmed segment consisted of the father reading from a personal letter he had sent to Dwight Eisenhower in which he implored the president to intercede in the case and provide justice for his son. This emotional plea, along with the lieutenant's well-reasoned arguments on his own behalf, compelled the "See It Now" staff to do additional filming, along with the decision to devote an entire half-hour program to this case, as opposed to the usual ten-minutes-per-story format. Interviews with Radulovich's sister, his wife, those who testified at the hearing, and a cross-section of citizens from his hometown in Dexter, Michigan, all added to the case.

Fred Friendly personally sought out opposing views from Pentagon sources in an attempt to offer another perspective. Edward R. Murrow was subsequently visited by Air Force representatives at CBS, who expressed the hope that "See It Now" would maintain a good relationship with the military and exhibited some skepticism that the story would ever be broadcast. Murrow, on the other hand, was enthusiastic about the report and expressed the opinion that this report would help the series "stake out an important claim that broadcast journalism should occupy."[9] Over thirty thousand feet or about five hours' worth of film had been shot in preparation for the broadcast. In light of this extended effort and enthusiasm, the "See It Now" staff, Murrow and Friendly, sought out special funding for newspaper advertising to support this program and asked the series sponsor, the Aluminum Company of America (ALCOA), for permission to drop the broadcast's middle commercial. ALCOA agreed that would be appropriate in this case, but the network refused additional advertising. Murrow and Friendly then used their own funds to place an ad in the *New York Times* at a cost of $1,500.

The program was completed just shortly before airtime. Although Murrow had no time to rehearse the concluding segment emphasizing the theme of freedom of association, Friendly nonetheless regarded the program as technically flawless. He frequently discussed how the effect of the father's testimony, the criticism by friends and neighbors of the injustice being done, and Radulovich's own presentation of facts in the case helped to visually demonstrate misguided decision-making. The military officials in charge of reviewing the recommendation to dismiss Radulovich, including Secretary of Defense Charles E. Wilson, supported the initial outcome. But Wilson said the difficulty of the case, forcing someone to choose between family and country, was best summarized by Senator Joseph R. McCarthy of Wisconsin. He reiterated McCarthy's growing popularity and position that the government had previously been too soft in dealing with security questions, saying that issues presenting conflict between individuals and national interest should be resolved in favor of the nation.

PRESS RESPONSE

This issue was subsequently adopted by the nation's press and the wider application of the issues in this instance was encouraged in many quarters. The *Detroit News*, for example, immediately referred to the case as one with broad implications that went beyond Michigan, in which the arbitrary power of institutional authority was faced up to by an average law-abiding citizen. Editorial voices were also raised, asking whether selection of military officers would be based in the future on family ties rather than professional qualifications, if the Radulovich case were to stand. The *New York Times* referred to the issue as "a kind of blood taint" representing totalitarian justice. Editorials, while acknowledging the key importance of security in military matters, also argued against guilt by association in a democracy, especially as part of military hearings in which full disclosure of facts was masked, usually under the guise of protecting sources.

The fact that cross-examination of witnesses was prohibited in the case while the "See It Now" crew had interviewed a variety of sources, including townspeople and military veterans, the town marshall, the mayor, and a commander of the American Legion post, who all agreed that an injustice had been done in this case greatly enhanced the effectiveness of the broadcast. The televised treatment was introduced by Murrow, assisted by Joe Wershba, who explained the physical setting for the case and the hearing. Lieutenant Radulovich was then allowed to tell his story and explain his position in his own words. He stressed that his own personal loyalty was not an issue in the case. His defense attorney, Charles Lockwood, offered an overview of the legal maneuvering associated with the case, something he claimed was a farce and travesty of justice. He offered comparisons to Nazi Germany.[10]

The theme of guilt by association was picked up by almost every spokesperson; most expressed some degree of fear that, if upheld, this type of procedure would become more commonplace and threaten the fabric of civil liberties. The mayor of Dexter, Michigan, pointed out what little control we have over the actions of others and that forcing individuals to be accountable for the behavior of relatives or friends set a dangerous precedent. The commander of the American Legion Post in the town, Steve Sorter, referred to the Radulovich hearings as a "purge" and added that any kind of personal animosity held against a person by anyone else could arise when accusations were made, making life uncomfortable and unfair for anyone and everyone.

Factory workers familiar with Radulovich's father pointed out that there is a natural tendency for people of foreign extraction to want to keep up on news from the old country by reading hometown newspapers in the language of that area. Murrow added that Radulovich had refused subscriptions to the *Daily Worker* and only subscribed to the Serbian newspaper because he said he liked the Christmas calendars they published. Radulovich's wife also presented a strong defense of both her husband and his sister. While refusing to discuss her personal politics, she called the Air Force case part of a growing and disturbing trend.

The telecast concluded with Radulovich clarifying his relations with his sister as being very limited, although he again voiced his refusal to denounce his family to keep his military commission. He extended the argument further by asking whether his children would also be asked to disavow relations with him at some future time, in the event that he lost his position. By reviewing the case and reading excerpts from proceeding transcripts, he asked whether it was rumor or hearsay that had doomed his position. He discussed the fact that not one witness came forward and that formal evidence in the military action was unknown to both the lieutenant and his legal representatives.

Murrow talked about the facts in the case, that the lieutenant's sister was never proved to be a member of the Communist Party and that his father's affiliations were never called into question beyond his reading of newspapers from his homeland. He concluded by saying that charges against Lieutenant Radulovich were unproven, that the Air Force accepted a burden of proof to communicate its concerns more fully, and that both national security and individual rights must be maintained at all costs. This position was upheld and supported by most of the major press outlets of the day. The *New York Times* critic, Jack Gould, praised "See It Now" after the program for taking the first step by a major network and sponsor to provide an editorial stand in support of controversy, a stand against what he termed "a curtain of silence which has so often descended on difficult security questions."[11]

Daily Variety, the trade publication, said this was easily the "most important single contribution made to television," adding that it was "a milestone in the realm of pictorial editorialization which brought to the TV medium a new found respect."[12] The public also embraced the position taken in the program. Nearly eight thousand letters and telegrams were received by the network, and the response supported Radulovich a hundred to one. Shortly after the telecast, Air Force Secretary Harold E. Talbott talked to Murrow about the case and soon thereafter decided to reverse the board's decision, which he was invited to explain on a subsequent "See It Now" program.[13]

The secretary of the Air Force offered a detailed accounting of the role of civil liberties in military matters and national security but argued that these concerns did not apply in this case. Radulovich wrote Murrow to credit the CBS program and his commentary for his own success in keeping his position and also for presenting the issues involved in state versus individual rights on a national scale for the American public. "The Case of Lieutenant Milo Radulovich" set the stage for "See It Now" to consider other cases with civil liberties as a theme.[14] Shortly after that, another midwestern forum was selected for the investigation of a similar situation during the fall of 1953, with this one involving the right to assemble peaceably for the purpose of public discussion.[15]

PEACEFUL ASSEMBLY

When the idea of setting up an Indiana Civil Liberties Union was first raised in Indianapolis, an organizational meeting seemed like a natural step; little consideration was given to potential protest by outsiders. The idea that a movement might be started to ban the meeting seemed unlikely. Then the state commander of the American Legion, Roy M. Amos, informed ACLU authorities of a resolution to ban the meeting. This action was reportedly taken so that the Civil Liberties Union might be included under the scrutiny of groups by the Jenner Committee, then examining infiltration of the United States by Communists.[16] When that occurred, founding members, many of whom were attorneys and academic types from the area, started seeing their meeting in an entirely different light. Amos let it be known in correspondence to the committee that his organization would do its best to bar a meeting of the ACLU in Indiana and let others know of their intent. After the decision to revoke the reservation of the ACLU meeting, Indiana law professor Ralph Fuchs, chairman of the new chapter, announced his objective of finding another meeting place for the group in Indiana.

The organization's arrangements committee chair, Martin Larner, said he would also proceed with a meeting agenda that would include a speech by a national ACLU figure, Arthur Garfield Hays, in opposition to the American Legion protests. When a good number of efforts to discover an appropriate meeting place in a variety of locations including hotels and civic meeting and church halls were unsuccessful, the pastor of St. Mary's Roman Catholic Church, the Reverend Victor L. Goosens, offered his church's civic center. The announcement was made by ACLU spokesperson Merle Miller, an attorney, just one day before the meeting was scheduled to take place.

The ACLU chairman, Ralph Fuchs, added that the organization had a wide range of supporters including religious and civic leaders, as well as a number of prominent American jurists. He reviewed words of praise from leading newspapers including the *New York Times*, the *Washington Post*, and the *San Francisco Chronicle*; he also discussed support the organization had received from major political figures including Thomas Dewey, Douglas MacArthur, and President Dwight D. Eisenhower.[17]

On the other hand, the American Legion's right to protest use of the memorial building was defended by the *Indianapolis Star*, as was the memorial's trustees' right to deny access. The newspaper's editorial staff did oppose, however, the Legion's determination to attempt to bar a meeting anywhere in the state of Indiana, saying that peaceful assem-

bly rights should be protected for all citizens, whose rights were equal
to those of the American Legion.[18] As a result, Roy Amos of the Legion
denied that his group opposed the right of the ACLU to meet anywhere,
but he continued to maintain his opposition to its leadership because of
the allegation that the ACLU protected Communists. The spokesperson
for the ACLU, Merle Miller, tried to point out that his organization had,
from time to time, protected anti-Communists as well; and he cited
specific efforts to defend rightist organizations and their spokespersons,
including Senator Joseph McCarthy.

As a countermeasure to the eventual successful effort to find a meeting place on behalf of the ACLU, the American Legion started planning
a meeting of its own with the avowed purpose of debating the merits
of the ACLU's right to meet. Nearly three dozen Legion officers were
extended the invitation to gather with an eye toward putting the meeting of an alleged Communist-front group into perspective, thus questioning the logic of free legal defense for those who were said to be
engaged in treasonable activities.

At this point in the dispute, an editorial appearing in the *Indianapolis
Times* was brought to the attention of the "See It Now" production crew,
as a follow-up to staff member interest in this case and a previous
attempt to ban a book in Indiana, which Edward R. Murrow had
addressed in a radio editorial.[19] His commentary had been reprinted in
the *Indianapolis Times* the day following the broadcast. When the entire
civil liberties dispute over a meeting hall was brought to his attention,
the "See It Now" staff member who had been following the situation,
once again Joe Wershba, was dispatched to Indiana with a film crew to
do preliminary preparation for a possible story on the conditions sur-
rounding the planned meeting.[20]

When he arrived in Indianapolis, Wershba immediately approached
American Legion commander Amos for additional information and
discussed CBS interest in the story. He also mentioned that "See It Now"
was considering documenting the meeting for national broadcast. Amos
expressed his desire to have a film crew also document the opposition
meeting by his organization. The "See It Now" staff member immediately informed the New York office of this development, and another
camera crew was sent to the location. The production crew focused
initially on the basis of the conflict and concentrated their efforts on
getting an overview of the story by conducting interviews with central
characters in the dispute. They discussed the development of the controversy with pro-ACLU business executive W. Roland Allen and questioned the manager of the war memorial, F. J. Brown, on events leading
up to the meeting and the rationale behind cancellation of the group's
reservation to use the hall.

When the "See It Now" treatment of the dispute aired November 24, 1953, just four days after both meetings, the initial interviews with Allen and Brown were shown at the start of the program.[21] Brown, for example, was heard explaining how the American Legion and another group, the Minute Women of Indiana, made initial attempts to bar the meeting, thus creating a controversy that would have been in violation of rules and regulations governing use of the monument. Asked about what he knew of the second group opposing the meeting, Brown said he was aware that the group was a legitimate one, but little else. "See It Now" then provided the viewer with an interview with a past officer of the Minute Women organization, Marguerite Dice, who condemned the use of the building by the ACLU because of her perception that its members were avowed Communists promoting the overthrow of the United States government.

Legion commander Amos said that he regarded the memorial as hallowed ground because it honored the memory of those who had fought communism in Korea and questioned whether it should be used as a forum from which pro-Communist ideas were expressed.[22] The "See It Now" report followed the Amos interview with an expanded commentary on how the ACLU had advanced its efforts to find a meeting place. Murrow provided a checklist of establishments that had rejected the request for a hall and noted that, at one point, an alternative location was found, a Knights of Columbus auditorium. He added, however, that approval for ACLU use of this location was rescinded shortly after the initial acceptance of the meeting.[23] Joe Wershba asked the head of that organization, Donald Latendresse, why the group had pulled out its support. The Knights of Columbus spokesperson indicated that his organization was unaware, when the lease for use of the hall was approved, of the nature and extent of the controversy generated by the meeting.

This group's representative also discussed the membership and makeup of his organization and the desire to avoid internal strife among individuals representing a vast, heterogeneous group of members with varying political positions and views. This informal organizational policy prohibiting the support of controversial meetings was the reason provided for the rejection. In the opening minutes of the broadcast, Murrow reviewed the positions held by the various groups involved and also looked at the newspaper coverage of the controversy by the Indianapolis press. He concluded the opening segment with a chronology of events leading up to the meetings themselves. This was followed by a segment in which the pastor of the church that accepted the ACLU meeting, Father Victor Goosens, offered his preliminary assessment of his involvement in the case.

Father Goosens said he took a very casual preliminary view of the controversy, although he had no basis on which to make a decision concerning the suitability of the organization itself. However, he added that, as the debate developed over time, he could see no reason to believe that the organization was unfit or unworthy of use of an auditorium and that, indeed, he began to feel obligated and even insistent that the organization be allowed to meet, once he was able to get a more thorough picture of the controversy.

In a statement which appeared in the "See It Now" program, Goosens cautioned that the treatment and rights of minorities should be among the most critical concerns of a democracy because quite often political and religious minorities can become the subject of restraint outside the legally constituted branches of government. When this happens, we can all suffer and all of our liberties can come under fire. He mentioned specifically the right to gather in peaceful assembly and engage in free speech as being preeminent concerns, especially in an instance in which one group, regardless of their good intentions, attempts to censor another. Goosens also made a special effort to point out that the experience of the ACLU, which is not traitorous or subversive, could be applied to other circumstances and other groups, thus endangering the exercise of freedom of religion.

In an attempt to offer the viewer an opportunity to judge arguments from both sides of the debate on this issue, "See It Now" used the technical device of intercutting parallel dialogue between the two meetings, with the American Legion gathering at their state headquarters less than half a mile away from the church social center offered to the ACLU organizing group. This was the first time the CBS documentary unit used this technique, which provided the viewer with the illusion of something of a face-to-face debate on various issues, which was accommodated nicely by the format of the American Legion meeting because it consisted of a series of brief testimonials by Legion members condemning the ACLU. This was followed by a general vote of members present offering another indictment by legionnaires of the group.

By way of contrast, the ACLU meeting consisted primarily of an address by organization national director Arthur Garfield Hays, with some supporting statements by chapter chairman Ralph Fuchs and Indianapolis attorney Merle Miller.[24] Father Goosens and three other spokespersons were also included. They voiced some hostility at having been told that they could not meet. Few identifications of speakers were included in the broadcast, with the exception of Fuchs's formal introduction of spokesperson Hays.

Both organizations were included in the edited remarks from the two meetings. Legion commander Amos told his followers that the effort by the ACLU represented a development on the "red firing line" in Indiana.[25] The chaplain of the Indiana branch of the Legion, Reverend Bernard Gordon, went to great lengths to explain that the ACLU meeting, while taking place on church property, should in no way be viewed as an endorsement by the Catholic Church.[26] Speakers at the ACLU gathering were heard denouncing the efforts to prevent their meeting in violation of both American tradition and constitutional rights. Interestingly, Commander Amos expressed some sympathy toward civil rights organizations who had defended veterans whose rights had been threatened. The ACLU's Merle Miller defined and defended his view of "liberal" versus "conservative" thought and described how civil liberties issues in America had the potential of fusing the political philosophies of those who would otherwise be regarded as enemies.

The ACLU keynote speaker, Arthur Garfield Hays, offered evidence that the good work of his organization represented one of the few things which both President Dwight Eisenhower and former president Truman could agree. He also quoted words of praise by Douglas MacArthur for the founding father of the ACLU, Roger Baldwin. On the other hand, a legionnaire was presented in the program offering a magazine advertisement that called for the repeal of the Smith and McCarran Act as evidence of promotion of the Communist cause, which supported a move for censorship of the ACLU.

The ACLU national director presented statistics showing that less than 10 percent of his organization's work was devoted to support Communists, and he questioned the overriding concern with controversial aspects of his work while pointing out that controversy was as American as the Fourth of July. A specific instance in which the ACLU defended a Communist or at least someone expelled from a national organization, the CIO in the late 1940s, was presented by a legionnaire; this was followed in the broadcast by a statement on the importance of freedom of expression by an ACLU member.

The last filmed sequence from the Indianapolis meetings showed the executive committee of the American Legion unanimously supporting a motion to uphold the appeal to censure the ACLU. Edward R. Murrow followed with commentary, pointing out that, although the Indianapolis meetings were concluded, the controversy was spreading all over. The pastor hosting the ACLU meeting, Father Victor Goosens, had the last word, and he also commented on the climate of the country, questioning whether this was a healthy development in light of some people's apparent willingness to take the law into their own hands or ignore the law altogether and deny others the right to free speech and peaceful assembly. In such an instance, Goosens insisted, it is these people who are un-American in their activity.

In the aftermath of the meeting and the broadcast, both sides of the controversy reported an increase of activity and support. The American Legion, for example, said they experienced an overwhelming increase in membership as a result of their stand.[27] The Legion was also quick to mention a change in editorial position by the *Indiana Catholic Record*, a weekly partisan paper, which derided ACLU leadership, saying an organization is only as strong as its leadership, while questioning Arthur Hays's background and motives.[28] Similarly, the deputy attorney general of Indiana, Cale Holder, focused on the Hays speech at the Indianapolis ACLU meeting and concluded that the defense of Communists represented what he called "a vicious racket" that was attempting to cash in on the American people's love of fair play.[29]

In the aftermath of the meeting, Legion commander Amos spoke out again and again on the issues involved in the controversy and charged that after careful study he had determined that the sole reason for the ACLU organizational meeting in the state was to rally support for a Communist member of the Indiana Teachers Association.[30] Amos began to emerge as a spokesperson for the anti-Communist cause in Indiana and was even nicknamed "The Fighting Commander" in some press accounts. He responded by saying, "I love a good fight, particularly against people who are trying to destroy the American system of government." Some newspapers, such as the *Indianapolis Star*, editorialized that the dispute produced healthy results in that it got people discussing a wide range of issues.[31] It also urged the Legion to cease attempts to prohibit ACLU meetings while applauding the fact that the arguments of both parties were out in the open and available for citizens of Indiana to weigh and use to make informed decisions.

OUTCOME

Shortly after the televised debate of issues on "See It Now," the *New York Times* reported that an organized effort was under way by the Veterans of Foreign Wars to launch a similar so-called anti-Communist assault. The fact that the debate around which this national broadcast evolved ever became widely argued is testimony to the growing import and influence of "McCarthyism" as a political factor in 1953.[32] On the other hand, Fred Friendly called the broadcast addressing this dispute both a triumph and the source of accelerated pressure for the network, because even though Murrow challenged critics to point to instances in which he took sides on the controversy, a great deal of opposition emerged.

A public relations officer for the American Legion, Jack Cejnar, claimed that the entire dispute had been manufactured by Murrow as part of a calculated campaign of propaganda.[33] He based his argument on remarks by CBS producer Joe Wershba, who, Cejnar maintained, derided the Legion meeting to others while he was in Indianapolis. Wershba, who directed "See It Now" filming and most of the editing of the program, denied the charge, saying that the techniques employed in this telecast were consistent with the series' usual approach and policy.[34] Beyond that, other sources expressed the view that letting participants speak for themselves as in this instance was, perhaps, the most judicial approach one could employ.[35]

One witness to the ACLU meeting, Thomas Flaherty, working on behalf of the House Un-American Activities Committee, expressed a great deal of skepticism that the two-hour meeting could be adequately represented in a distilled, fifteen-minute format for broadcast.[36] The capsulization due to editing became a major source of criticism by the Legion, and their group publication, *American Legion Magazine*, among others, used this topic as a prime means of attacking the program.[37] A major daily newspaper, the *Indianapolis Times*, also accused the CBS staff of bias, saying in an editorial that someone on Murrow's production crew went to great pains to show only the bad side of the Legion participants, while ACLU members always looked good on camera.[38] As an example of bias, the *Indianapolis Times* cited a well-reasoned, very articulate speech delivered at the Legion meeting by Cale Holder that was edited out and not used for the broadcast. On the other hand, an alternative participant who had a great deal of trouble presenting his ideas was included in the final telecast as it aired nationwide. The technique of intercutting filmed sequences, as well as the technical aspects of the manner in which the two meetings were filmed, also became the source of concern. In his book *The Left-Leaning Antenna* (1971), for example, Joseph Keeley pointed out that harsh lighting made the legionnaires look bad. At one point the CBS film crew focused on a member of the organization's color guard in whom, according to Keeley, "When the colors were advanced, one sensed a disturbing resemblance to Hitler leading the corporal's guard of storm troopers—possibly because the sound of the heels was amplified."[39]

When the cameras switched to the civil liberties meeting, on the other hand, the author claimed that members of this group came across visually as thoughtful, articulate, and concerned citizens. Their voices were well modulated and pleasant in contrast with the legionnaires' voices, which sounded harsh and irritating. The bottom line on Keeley's appraisal of the broadcast was that the visual impact of the documentary was so overwhelming that the arguments forwarded by both groups were secondary, with the ACLU the obvious winner. Prominent critic Gilbert Seldes said the editorial results of intercutting shots gave the illusion of debate and had the effect of impartial reporting.[40] But the selection of shots and spokespersons left questions as to whether the "See It Now" staff had been judicious in its treatment of both groups.

Much as in other key CBS broadcasts, it is difficult to determine the extent to which the "See It Now" staff's enthusiasm for free speech in support of the ACLU influenced their preparation of the program. Statements by the crew on the intent of the broadcast are best regarded as attempts by journalists to retain their credibility and perhaps save face. The "See It Now" goal was to lessen the impact of the Legion and discredit the organization by exposing their intentions to a more discriminating public view. The goal of the broadcast developed out of a growing concern by "See It Now" for violations of civil liberties.

The fact that "See It Now" may have overstepped the mark with regard to objectivity certainly created disenchantment for Legion supporters and other conservatives. Even though both organizations were represented, public criticism showed clearly that the Legion felt compromised by the CBS treatment in this case. The broadcast showed the complexity of the medium and called into question the judgment of some CBS staff members. In the Radulovich broadcast, a case was carefully built with more limited source material to support a point of view in favor of the young lieutenant, and that case was resolved right away. The dispute over the ACLU meeting place itself was resolved after twenty years when the war memorial was ruled state property by the Supreme Court. In the aftermath of that ruling, the Indianapolis ACLU met in that building on October 13, 1973; and Fred W. Friendly expressed his regret that Edward R. Murrow did not live to gavel that meeting to order.[41] He did live to face an even more formidable task in the form of a direct assault on the source of much of the anti-Communist resentment.

NOTES

1. "University of Michigan Student Fights Expulsion from Air Force," *Detroit News*, September 23, 1953, p. 1.

2. "Air Force Will Fight Ouster," *New York Times*, September 24, 1953, p. 23.

3. "Student Gets Ferguson Aid in Air Force Ouster," *Detroit News*, September 24, 1953, p. 1.

4. "Eisenhower Quoted to Security Panel," *New York Times*, September 30, 1953, p. 25.

5. "Lieutenant's Kin Guarded after Threats," *Detroit News*, September 28, 1953, p. 1.

6. "Accused Reservist Is Ruled Bad Risk," *New York Times*, October 14, 1953, p. 17.

7. "Officer Maps Appeal to Ike on Air Force Ouster," *Detroit News*, October 14, 1953, p. 1.

8. Ibid.

9. Fred W. Friendly, *Due to Circumstances Beyond Our Control* (New York: Random House, 1967), p. 4.

10. Edward R. Murrow and Fred W. Friendly, eds., *See It Now* (New York: Simon and Schuster, 1955), p. 37.

11. "Video Journalism: Treatment of Radulovich History by 'See It Now' Is Fine Reporting," *New York Times*, October 25, 1953, p. 13. See also "Guilt by Kinship," *New York Times*, October 21, 1953, p. 28.

12. See "Edward R. Murrow, of the 'See' around Us," *Variety*, January 6, 1954, p. 196; "The Hue and Cry: TV's Hope for a Brighter Tomorrow," *Variety*, January 6, 1954, p. 86; and "The Case of Lieutenant Radulovich," *Variety*, October 28, 1953, p. 25.

13. Murrow and Friendly, *See It Now*, p. 42.

14. "Eyes of Conscience," *Newsweek*, December 7, 1953, p. 65.

15. The complete text of this broadcast is contained in Murrow and Friendly, eds., *See It Now*, pp. 44–53. An edited version was telecast as part of the "CBS News Retrospective," July 15, 1973. For additional details, see Michael D. Murray, "To Hire a Hall: 'An Argument in Indianapolis,' " *Communication Studies* 10(2) (Spring 1975): 12–20.

16. "Civil Liberties Union Is Refused War Memorial for Meeting," *Indianapolis Star*, November 17, 1953, p. 1; and "Liberties Group Hails War Memorial Ban," *Indianapolis Times*, November 17, 1953, p. 1.

17. See "Ike's Praise Cited by Barred Group," *Indianapolis Times*, November 18, 1953, p. 3.

18. "Civil Liberties Unit to Meet in Church," *Indianapolis Star*, November 19, 1953, p. 26. Also, "The ACLU Has Rights, Too," *Indianapolis Star*, November 20, 1953, p. 29.

19. "Civil Liberties, Unlimited," *Indianapolis Times*, November 19, 1953, p. 22; and Ted Knap, "Murrow to Televise Civil Rights Dispute," *Indianapolis Times*, November 20, 1953, p. 1. Most national and regional newspapers did not comment on the dispute. See Alexander Kendrick, *Prime Time: The Life of Edward R. Murrow* (Boston: Little, Brown, 1969), p. 39.

20. "Once Upon a Time, Madam, There Just Were No Communists," *Indianapolis Times*, November 14, 1953, p. 1.

21. See, "Edward R. Murrow Airs Dispute on 'See It Now,' " *Hoosier Legionnaire*, December 1953, p. 4.

22. Murrow and Friendly, *See It Now*, p. 46.

23. "Executive Committee Unanimously Backs Amos," *Hoosier Legionnaire*, December 1953, p. 4. Also included in this publication is the text of Hays's address, "Communists Being Given Undeserved Reputation," at the ACLU meeting. It was published again later in the *Indianapolis Times*, May 26, 1954, p. 1.

24. "ACLU Prefers Few Reds to Intimidation," *Indianapolis Star*, November 21, 1953, p. 1.

25. Murrow and Friendly, *See It Now*, p. 50.

26. The Reverend Goosens, who allowed use of the social center, was later asked by his superior, Archbishop Paul C. Schulte, to check with his office before allowing outside groups use of church premises. See "Schulte Hits at Use of Center by Civil Liberties Union," *Indianapolis Times*, November 24, 1953, p. 1; and "Eyes of Conscience," *Newsweek*, December 7, 1953, p. 66.

27. "Veterans Rally to Legion Stand on ACLU," *Hoosier Legionnaire*, December 1953, p. 4.

28. "An Organization Is No Better Than the Men Who Lead It," *Indiana Catholic Record*, November 27, 1953. Reprinted in the *Hoosier Legionnaire*, December 1953, p. 4.

29. "Holder Replies to ACLU Chief's Speech, Rips 'Fact Discrepancies,' " *Indianapolis Star*, November 22, 1953, p. 1. See also Jim Jordan, "Legion Brands Civil Liberties Union 'Vicious Racket,' " *Indianapolis Times*, November 22, 1953, p. 4.

30. "Legion Hits ACLU as Wyatt Backer," *Indianapolis Star*, November 23, 1953, p. 11.

31. "Let the Facts Speak," *Indianapolis Star*, November 24, 1953, p. 22.

32. See "Truman Accuses Brownell of Lying; Sees Office Debased in White Case; Says G.O.P. Embraces 'McCarthyism,' " *New York Times*, November 17, 1953, p. 26. Also, "McCarthy Accuses Truman in Reply," *New York Times*, November 25, 1953, p. 1.

33. See "How Americans Protest," ACLU Commemorative Publication, August 1963.

34. Personal interview with Joe Wershba, November 9, 1973.

35. "Eyes of Conscience," *Newsweek*, December 7, 1953, p. 65.

36. "Holder Replies to ACLU Chief's Speech, Rips 'Fact Discrepancies,' " *Indianapolis Times*, November 21, 1953, p. 2.

37. See also "Midwinter Conference to be Held in January," *Hoosier Legionnaire*, December 1953, p. 6.

38. "ACLU Aimed at Jenner," *Indianapolis Times*, November 30, 1953, p. 10.

39. Joseph Keeley, *The Left-Leaning Antenna: Political Bias in Television* (New Rochelle, NY: Arlington House, 1971), p. 36.

40. Gilbert Seldes, *The Public Arts* (New York: Simon and Schuster, 1956), p. 219. See also "Murrow: The Man, the Myth and the McCarthy Fighter," *Look*, August 24, 1954, p. 27.

41. Fred W. Friendly, " 'Argument in Indianapolis' or the Longest Scheduled Meeting in American History," reprinted in *To Hire a Hall*, Indiana Civil Liberties Union, October 1973, p. 2.

Chapter 5

COMING OF AGE

The procession of civil liberties broadcasts leading up to the confrontation with Senator Joseph McCarthy culminated in two key telecasts: one, regarded as the prototype of a gutsy, no-holds-barred indictment, focused on the senator through a wide-ranging examination of his techniques; the other, a more subtle firsthand account of committee hearings, held his behavior in a single case up to scrutiny. Interestingly, although the "See It Now" staff regarded the second broadcast as the more significant of the two, it is sometimes forgotten, because of the unusual nature of the first program. Preparation for that initial broadcast was conducted over an extended period of time, with "See It Now" collecting film footage on McCarthy early in 1953. The second telecast offered a thorough look at the senator's methods in a single hearing, which occurred after the initial broadcast report on the senator was completed.

The questions remain of how a junior senator was able to captivate a large number of voters, generate so much interest in a cause, and create such havoc in political circles, the military, and the public sector. Speculation on these points has been the source of considerable interest. McCarthy's career as chief investigator of Communist subversion began right after his fellow Republican Dwight Eisenhower was inaugurated in 1953. But the impetus for the movement was started at least three years earlier, when a former State Department official, Alger Hiss, was indicted for perjury. The charge carried an implication that Hiss had handed over confidential information to Communist governments, a belief promoted by various members of Congress who insisted on investigations of abuses.[1]

At the forefront of this movement, McCarthy insisted that Communists were working in government and cited an exact number of 205 in sensitive positions in U.S. agencies. These charges flourished in the era of the atom bomb and the Korean War. Broadcasters were confronted with blacklists during the Cold War that discouraged involvement with some of McCarthy's backers, also responsible for blacklist documents.[2] McCarthy's committee, the Permanent Subcommittee on Investigations, a frequent platform for attacks on those accused of infiltrating and undermining government and military operations, specifically probed alleged subversion of the International Information Administration, the nation's anti-Communist propaganda agency in charge of the Voice of America. This investigation included an in-depth interview with the deputy chief of that agency, Reed Harris.[3]

McCarthy utilized nationally televised hearings in this case to bolster his public standing by accusing Harris of a variety of alleged transgressions, beginning with his leftist affiliations while a student at Columbia University and his authorship of a book in which the value of American institutions including college athletics was called into question. Harris denied Communist ties and clarified the point that he had resigned from Columbia University, not been forced out of the school as McCarthy implied. He also pointed to the limited impact of the book, entitled *King Football*, because of its low sales and the lack of interest in it. McCarthy failed in his attempt to relate Harris's activities in government service, including the curtailment of broadcasts, to aid to the Communist cause.

Television viewers were introduced to a forceful interrogator, however, someone who, as McCarthy had done throughout his political career, came across as a hard-nosed combatant who would stand up for American rights. At the same time, some observers expressed concern not only about McCarthy's methods but also his apparent easy access to the medium of television. The *New York Times* television critic Jack Gould, for example, noted McCarthy's behind-the-scenes maneuvering and deal-making with television programmers to insure that he came across with maximum impact. At the same time, Gould noted that the American Broadcasting Company cut off Reed Harris's rebuttal to charges by McCarthy, for example, so the public heard most of the allegations but were left with an unfocused response.[4]

McCarthy's method of advanced bargaining with television executives over time allotments and placement of breaks in coverage for announcements was duly noted by elements of the press and outside groups, who charged that McCarthy was creating a "show trial" atmosphere and waging psychological warfare through his use of television.[5]

Although Democratic members of Congress expressed concern over McCarthy's methods, few sought to test his influence even after his repeated attacks on the former Democratic administration of Harry Truman. Members of his own party seldom challenged the crusade against Communist subversion, as this had been an ongoing theme in political circles, until much later when McCarthy started directly attacking the effectiveness of the Eisenhower administration.[6]

Asked at a press conference whether he felt McCarthy's Voice of America investigation was achieving goals of denigrating the internal threat of communism, Dwight Eisenhower responded by denying knowledge of McCarthy's objectives and stating his assumption that the senator had the support of Congress or else it would not support his activities.[7] Indeed, shortly after that statement, three Democratic committee members, Stuart Symington, John McClellan, and Henry Jackson, resigned from that committee to protest McCarthy's public posturing that he had sole hiring and firing authority over committee staff. By that time McCarthy had begun threatening an investigation of the Central Intelligence Agency while attacking the work of Secretary of State John Foster Dulles.

McCarthy also started investigating civilian employees of the U.S. Army Signal Corps Center at Fort Monmouth, New Jersey, where he said he uncovered subversion among those handling secret documents. Hearings in this area were closed to the public by McCarthy, who periodically emerged with charges of espionage at the Signal Corps facility. To complicate the scenario further, U.S. Attorney General Herbert Brownell seemed to indicate Communist influence in the handling of another staff member from the Truman administration. This resulted in Harry Truman's direct televised response, in which he denied the charges and warned the nation of the threat of what he termed "McCarthyism."

McCarthy reacted quickly on television, with a further charge against Truman and Democratic members of Congress, as well as an indictment of the Eisenhower administration for its failure to take action against Communists in government. By the time the 83rd Congress was due to convene the following year, McCarthy had switched gears and was attempting to lure Democratic committee members back into the fold in an effort to gain needed appropriations for committee activity. After the funds were approved, he reversed direction once again and began an unprecedented attack on both the previous administration, labeling it "twenty years of treason," and the U.S. Army. His military tirade revolved against the promotion and honorable discharge of a military dentist, featuring McCarthy's public grilling of Brigadier General Ralph W. Zwicker, commandant of Camp Kilmer where the army dentist had been stationed.

The exchange with Zwicker centered on whether the honorary discharge should have been awarded in this case and included direct assaults on both the general's decision-making and his intelligence. In attempts to clarify McCarthy's questions, for example, the senator responded by saying that "a five-year-old child" could understand his line of questioning. The interrogation concluded with McCarthy suggesting that the general be removed from his command.[8] McCarthy's behavior at the hearing and questioning of Zwicker, a highly decorated combat veteran, resulted in a direct confrontation with Secretary of the Army Robert Stevens, who insisted that Zwicker would not, under his order, appear before additional sessions of McCarthy's committee. Stevens said that in the interest of security and morale he could not permit military officers to be unfairly subjected to unwarranted criticism. Then McCarthy called for Stevens himself to appear before the committee.

McCarthy repeated his attack on General Zwicker in a speech on George Washington's birthday in Philadelphia, while the senator's chief assistant, Roy Cohn, said the case represented either stupidity or treason on the part of the army. He promised that someone would be punished as a result. Secretary Stevens repeated his support for the nation's military officers in a speech at the Freedom Foundation in Valley Forge. With congressional elections on the horizon, McCarthy and Stevens met privately in the nation's capital and worked out a compromise or "memorandum of understanding." They agreed mutually on the need to root out Communists in government, and those involved in the Zwicker case were to be made available to the McCarthy committee.[9]

Stevens's committee appearance was canceled and Zwicker's second appearance postponed. The agreement was interpreted by the press as capitulation to McCarthy, but Stevens insisted that it was in the interest of army morale to avoid further public confrontation and attacks on officers, although McCarthy charged that this was not part of the agreement.[10] President Dwight Eisenhower began a subsequent news conference by stating that some investigating committees of the government had appeared to disregard rules of fair play. He praised General Zwicker by name and stated that he would not tolerate humiliation of an officer, although he stopped short of condemning McCarthy directly.[11]

Privately, according to a well-known quote from his press secretary, James Hagerty, the president vowed not to "get into the gutter" with McCarthy. Hagerty scheduled another press conference for Stevens including a statement, endorsed by the president, in which the army secretary repeated that he would not accede to military personnel being humiliated or browbeaten in a public forum.[12] McCarthy again responded with a denial that the agreement with Stevens extended to appearances by officers before his committee; Senator Karl Mundt, who helped draft the agreement, conceded Stevens's position. This was interpreted as a sign that some chinks in McCarthy's armor might be starting to appear, an indication that pacification toward his activities may terminate.

At about the same time, Edward R. Murrow, at the end of a broadcast report entitled "Anatomy of a Symphony Orchestra," announced his intention for "See It Now" to address the public climate of unreason and fear in an upcoming telecast. Shortly afterwards, Adlai Stevenson challenged the Republican administration in a nationally televised speech in which he confronted Dwight Eisenhower with accepting McCarthyism as a partisan formula for success which he said represented a political party at odds with itself. McCarthy fumed over this attack by the Democratic presidential hopeful and demanded television time to respond.[13] Vice President Richard Nixon, who had successfully used the young television medium on a number of occasions, including the well-known response to accusations of accepting illegal campaign contributions in the "Checkers Speech," was selected to respond to Stevenson. Conservative Republican senator Ralph E. Flanders then took the floor of the Senate and lambasted McCarthy, accusing him of trying to establish his own political party, "McCarthyism."[14] That evening, Edward R. Murrow followed through on his promise to address the issue and climate of fear in a "Report on Senator Joseph R. McCarthy."

THE McCARTHY TELECAST

The opportunity to chronicle McCarthy's activities was accomplished fairly easily because of an agreement "See It Now" had with the Hearst-owned "News of the Day" for use of footage shot by newsreel photographers on a regular basis. The Hearst Library file contained footage of all major McCarthy hearings such as the one containing the Reed Harris testimony. Joe Wershba and Palmer Williams of "See It Now" occasionally extracted for duplication footage to be used as a supplement to what CBS was shooting in their coverage of the senator's story. By the time Murrow decided to address the McCarthy issue, over 1,500 feet of film on the senator had been amassed and edited.[15] By this time, the "See It Now" staff consisted of twenty-eight members, with four full-time camera crews, each with a photographer and sound specialist.

Fred Friendly and Murrow shared production and administrative chores, and associate producer Palmer Williams was in charge of the budget. Reporting duties were handled by Murrow, Ed Scott, and Joe Wershba. The "See It Now" staff was eager to proceed with the broadcast, and timing became a crucial element in strategic planning. Joe Wershba, a key player in the documentary unit's planning and a former newspaperman who had covered McCarthy since the late 1940s, discussed how attacking the senator during a period in which he was unencumbered with other matters would invite an immediate response when "McCarthy would be free to dispose the enormous power of his Senate committee to come down on Murrow like a ton of bricks."[16] On the other hand, if McCarthy struck CBS and Murrow first, any response would be viewed as reprisal. According to Wershba, McCarthy's success often rested on his ability to anticipate personal attacks and strike first or, as the reporter added: "The tragedy of many McCarthy victims was that they never knew what hit them."[17] With this in mind, "See It Now" took advantage of the barrage of criticism suddenly leveled at McCarthy to lessen the chance of a quick and unencumbered response.

The staff of "See It Now" was highly organized and united in their effort and involvement in this particular broadcast, and the nature of the telecast undoubtedly enhanced their cohesiveness and determination. The possible consequences and implications of participating in the effort were reinforced by Fred Friendly when he gathered the staff together and asked them if there might be anything in their backgrounds that could be held up to criticism and reflect badly on the program. Even though it was generally understood that Murrow would receive the brunt of the attack, Friendly felt that this meeting was a necessary precaution. Some members of the staff expressed reservations about the timing of the program and questioned whether the footage was as compelling as that which preceded it, Radulovich or the Indianapolis meeting hall dispute.

Murrow personally asked each staff member about feelings toward the program as designed. He questioned reporters, film editors, projectionists, and even the office staff members. Most of the staff, editors especially, were convinced of the effectiveness of the film, although the reporting staff expressed reservations. Asked what he would say in the broadcast, Joe Wershba recalled that it may have been the first and last time Murrow ever preached to the staff asking how the entire nation could allow one individual to terrorize it with impunity. This created a silence which was broken by laughter when Wershba stood up and said: "Mr. Murrow, it has been a privilege to have known and worked for you."[18]

Palmer Williams, who received his film training during World War II and at the army's Signal Corps headquarters at Fort Monmouth, which had received so much of the heat from McCarthy's recent probe of the military, described his feelings toward the senator as resentful and wary of the awesome power being exercised by the Senate Investigating Committee. Interestingly, the "See It Now" resources would also be directed toward a Signal Corps employee, Annie Lee Moss, a forty-nine-year-old black woman. In the midst of Senator McCarthy's heated dispute with the secretary of the army, Moss was accused of subversive activity in the handling of coded messages, a charge she thoroughly denied. Meanwhile, the network's refusal to let McCarthy respond to Adlai Stevenson and an unanticipated anti-McCarthy Senate speech by a conservative Republican took the wind out of the senator's sails, and the CBS documentary unit pounced on the opportunity to deliver a crucial first blow.

The actual production work was completed during the week following Murrow's announcement of the upcoming program. CBS management was told of the telecast five days before broadcast, and a request for special advertising funds was made but rejected, just as previously with the Radulovich broadcast. As in that case, Murrow and Friendly used their personal finances for an advertisement in the *New York Times* that was simple in format and copy, announcing the time, 10:30 P.M. eastern standard time, and the local outlet, Channel Two in New York. In the production of this particular program, Edward R. Murrow insisted on dictating the content word for word while the staff worked to compile footage of McCarthy in dramatic moments addressing critical issues.[19]

This format, while allowing McCarthy to speak for himself, in a sense, was viewed by some as a questionable technique that invited underhanded efforts to choose especially damaging visual sequences, placing McCarthy in a particularly bad light. The total of seven filmed sequences used in the program showed McCarthy speaking at various public and private functions and in committee hearings including the Reed Harris interrogation. The hearing footage was supplemented by statements by Army Secretary Robert Stevens and President Dwight Eisenhower. Also presented was an audio tape of a well-known McCarthy speech from Wheeling, West Virginia, in which he first made major charges of subversion in government.

The telecast began with a brief introduction by Murrow, who attempted to show contradictions in McCarthy's public statements on various issues, such as his pledge of cooperation with Dwight Eisenhower. McCarthy is shown in a contradiction when he appears at a Milwaukee speech decrying a fight between America's two political parties and, on another occasion, condemning the Democratic Party for what he terms "twenty years of treason." The then presidential candidate Dwight Eisenhower appears in an early filmed sequence in Green Bay, Wisconsin, promising to deal forthrightly, if elected, with charges of subversion in government. McCarthy is seen praising Eisenhower and pledging support, then, in outspoken fashion, condemning the military hero on the importance of the issue of communism in government.

Murrow labeled McCarthy a "one-man committee" in hot pursuit of "fifth amendment Communists." He reviewed State Department charges as a prelude to addressing the case of General Ralph Zwicker and his treatment at McCarthy's hands. "See It Now" included filmed sequences with Army Secretary Stevens condemning the senator's behavior in attempts to humiliate army officers and juxtaposed these sequences with McCarthy's condemnation of elements of what he termed the "left-wing" press. Murrow then presented excerpts from editorials of the nation's leading newspapers questioning methods in the Zwicker hearing and condemning McCarthy. These were, Murrow said, the distinguished papers that McCarthy labeled radical "left-wing" publications.[20]

As a follow-up, the program offered two illustrations of McCarthy's methods, characterized by personal attacks on the Voice of America official Reed Harris and presidential candidate Adlai Stevenson. Murrow tagged the attack on Stevenson as exemplary of the half-truths used by McCarthy, focusing on his effort to associate Stevenson with a rural setting in Massachusetts alleged to be a center for Communist activity. The coverage on the Zwicker case was also reported in depth by the "See It Now" staff. Joe Wershba later reported words he exchanged with McCarthy on his way into the hearing: "When McCarthy saw me he came over, put his arm around me and said: 'How's Ed?' " The seasoned reporter responded with "Ed's fine," and added, "Joe, we have cameras in there. I want you to be very good today." "He was very good, he murdered Zwicker and I think he helped finish himself that day," Wershba added.[21] The sequence in which McCarthy repeated a direct indictment of General Zwicker was also included.

As for the attack on Democrat Adlai Stevenson, the "See It Now" staff felt that those allegations could be easily refuted with the facts. McCarthy's investigative methods also came under scrutiny with his badgering of Reed Harris in testimony before the committee and attempts by Harris to refute charges that his book was subversive. Harris offered his defense, and McCarthy focused on his legal support by the ACLU, which the senator also labeled as subversive. Murrow cited letters of commendation to the ACLU by patriotic American leaders of both parties including both Presidents Truman and Eisenhower. In a concluding segment, Murrow questioned whether Americans had not invited McCarthy's abuses through acquiescence to his methods and message. In that sense, this CBS program was a call to stand up against demagoguery. At the same time, Murrow asked whether McCarthy was indeed giving more comfort to the nation's enemies by destroying American traditions of due process and fair play. The fact that Murrow never feigned objectivity in his report led to a great deal of popular criticism of the "See It Now" effort.

REACTION

The broadcast was clearly one-sided, with no effort to allow McCarthy an opportunity to respond at the time as part of that telecast. Some journalists such as Gilbert Seldes suggested that the first blow can often inflict an injury so serious that one can seldom recuperate.[22] A lack of consistency between the initial attack and subsequent rebuttal also indicated an unusual level of bias in this case. "See It Now" was hoping to avoid accusations of a serious one-sided attack, while placing the Zwicker accusations at the start of the program as a strategy to establish the senator's violent streak early.[23] Even though reply time was allotted to McCarthy, Murrow's public stand in the case was a quote by Winston Churchill asking whether one should give equal time to Judas Iscariot.

A great deal of the impact of the telecast has been attributed to the delivery of Edward R. Murrow. Former CBS News director William Small has pointed out television's ability to impart respectability on content and asked, in this case, because of Murrow's bold indictment, whether the senator did not deserve such treatment.[24] Remember, too, that in this broadcast Murrow announced his intention of reading carefully from script to insure accuracy, thus reinforcing the seriousness of the accusations, and to make no mistake about what was being said. The choice of key sequences showing McCarthy on the stump was criticized by some as direct evidence that "See It Now" was attempting to distort the case and public persona of McCarthy, showing him at his worst moments.

Various elements of the press, even some liberal commentators, said certain segments of McCarthy were unrepresentative and gave a false impression. John Crosby, who praised the intent of the broadcast, observed that in some instances McCarthy was "caught huffing and chuckling in a way that sounded as if he were just a little nutty."[25] Writing in *Commonweal*, John Cogley said the broadcast set an unusual standard and suggested that other broadcasters might have shown McCarthy in an entirely different and perhaps more positive set of circumstances. The *Saturday Review*'s Gilbert Seldes commended Cogley for a perceptive analysis of the program and indicted it as an "attack" rather than a "report" on the senator in which, he said, an image had been established which no follow-up or response could eradicate or replace. Interestingly, the staff of that publication added a note that this program and its appropriateness had stirred great internal editorial debate.

Time magazine called it a "hard hitting attack that made such a bang as television has rarely registered"[26] while the trade publication *Broadcasting* labeled it "the greatest feat of journalistic enterprise in modern times."[27] A *St. Louis Post-Dispatch* editorial lauded Murrow and noted: "No one needs to fear television and radio so long as the demagogues are matched and more by honest men who care about the fate of their country."[28] Jack O'Brian of the *New York Journal American* called Murrow a "pompous portsider" and suggested that Murrow be fired. Fulton Lewis, a well-known broadcaster himself, also blasted Murrow, offering Senator McCarthy time on his radio program to respond to the charges.[29] The fact that the broadcast appeared on the surface to represent the efforts of one man, Murrow, against another was thought to create a dangerous precedent and potential for misuse of the medium among some who observed that "impulsive and irresponsible imitations of 'See It Now,' whether 'pro' or 'anti' the Senator or anyone else, could lead to great harm."[30]

On the other hand, Jack Gould praised Murrow for his willingness to admit that this was certainly not objective reporting, since no pretense of impartiality was made, and to understand that given McCarthy's methods, ruthless and devoid of democratic processes, an objective, balanced effort would have been pointless and ineffective. Fred Friendly cited the daily opportunities McCarthy had to present his story to a national audience with the power of the United States Senate to back him up, as well as a cadre of columnists extolling his virtues in the press every day, as justification for the strong, one-sided editorial stand against him. He also denied charges that intentional selection of derogatory filmed sequences were chosen for effect, calling it a "mockery" that critics would suggest that certain sequences were used simply because McCarthy looked particularly bad.

In fact, Friendly offered the view that the first edits of the sequences were done on paper with little initial regard for visual elements. Murrow made similar denials on that score, as did Palmer Williams. Joe Wershba pointed out that it is frequently the visually unusual that creates interest in television. He said that one particularly damaging sequence was used because it contributed to the story, adding: "If you get up and read a paper for a half-hour, or what McCarthy did in his reply, you put a lot of people to sleep."[31] The fact that most of the visual reporting on McCarthy was kept to medium shots or extreme facial close-ups also is consistent with published accounts of the methods used by "See It Now" on most stories focusing on individuals.[32]

Fred Friendly credited management endorsement for much of the success of this broadcast, noting that William S. Paley telephoned Murrow and pledged support before the program. Of course, later on, the network's role in the "See It Now" operation became a much-speculated-on relationship. The sponsor, ALCOA, clearly had limited interest, although they had requested advanced notification on controversial topics to insure proper response and involvement with newspaper inquiries on programs they endorsed. Murrow's view on the relationship was often summed up in the quote, "They make aluminum and I make film."[33] All sources agree that ALCOA was probably the least involved in the series except in financial matters and as another source of complaint when the series stepped on too many toes, although the company conceded that the direct response to the sponsor for this broadcast was four-to-one in favor of "See It Now."

Beyond that, the overall response from the public was overwhelmingly positive. Four hours after the telecast, CBS reported that it had received 2,365 telephone calls, with all but 151 favorable to the network. CBS also received close to three thousand telegrams and only eighty-six were critical. The national count of over eleven thousand calls was measured against slightly less than eight hundred protests, and that number included four hundred calls complimenting the broadcast in the senator's home state of Wisconsin, where no negative feedback was recorded at WCAN-TV, the CBS affiliate in Milwaukee. CBS sources reinforced the fact that many of those who called or wrote the network said that this was the first time they had ever responded personally to a network telecast.[34]

Feeling the heat, McCarthy responded to the program by saying he did not see it, insisting that he never viewed broadcasts by what he called the "left-wing bleeding heart element of radio and television," but adding that he would respond to Murrow and charges that he called the ACLU subversive, an assertion he denied. He also alluded to allegations concerning Murrow's background as evidence of why the broadcaster would conduct a campaign against him: "Maybe he feels that, having been on the advisory council of Moscow University, he should worry about the exposure of some of his friends."[35] McCarthy also followed up with a telegram stating that although he did not see the program he expected time to reply. Murrow responded by setting forth CBS guidelines for any response that prohibited substituting others in McCarthy's place, as McCarthy indicated a desire to have conservative columnist William F. Buckley respond to the broadcast.

FOLLOW-UP

McCarthy, in the midst of his first serious public challenges, vowed to expose "known Communists" in government including a civilian employee of the U.S. Army Signal Corps, who he claimed engaged in handling "top secret" messages while being listed as a member of the Communist Party by the Federal Bureau of Investigation. The accused, Annie Lee Moss, declared that she had never been in a code room in her life and denied knowledge of communism. A Republican House member said a public hearing was not warranted due to insufficient evidence.[36] McCarthy began proceedings on the case, and Joe Wershba insisted on documenting the hearing because he felt that this woman was destined to be overwhelmed by the power of the McCarthy committee and to submit to the accusations.[37] The army reported that although Moss had a security clearance she did not handle secret documents or have access to classified documents. McCarthy called this a cover-up, with military officials aware of her status both in a sensitive job and as a Communist Party member. McCarthy went on to predict that when she appeared before the committee she was likely to perjure herself and be indicted. The senator maintained that he could produce a leading Communist official with evidence to document his stand against Mrs. Moss.

When she was first called before the committee hearing, it was reported that Mrs. Moss was ill with a cold and nervous over the impending committee interview. McCarthy, acknowledging the prospect for complications due to the illness, allowed her to put off an appearance but at the same time again predicted that perjury would result if she kept denying her Communist ties to the press. Mrs. Moss denied having access to the code room while recovering from her illness, while Army Secretary Stevens and McCarthy met to discuss the General Zwicker case. The day after that meeting, Moss was released from her job at the Army Communications Center and she was immediately called before the McCarthy Committee to appear on March 11.[38]

A "See It Now" field crew consisting of Joe Wershba and Charles Mack recorded her defense at the hearing, which lasted two hours while another classic civil liberties struggle evolved before the cameras. The hearing began with McCarthy questioning Moss on the nature of her position. He asked specifically how someone classified as a cafeteria worker could gain access to a military code room. Moss denied that she had access to or knowledge of secret codes, and her lawyer interrupted with objections as a follow-up to earlier intervention in which he complained about McCarthy's public comments regarding Moss's status before the hearing even began. McCarthy insisted that Moss speak for herself and clarified that he did not view her as a major player in the Communist cause but as a symbol of wide-scale abuse and Communist activity, a charge Moss vehemently denied. At this point, McCarthy retreated from the hearing room to work with Fulton Lewis on a radio response to accusations being made against him.

As McCarthy left the hearing room, "See It Now" cameraman Charles Mack filmed McCarthy's exit, then focused on the senator's empty seat in the chamber. McCarthy's young assistant, Roy Cohn, remained to help complete the questioning. At this point, one of the Democratic members of the committee, Senator Stuart Symington of Missouri, inquired about Mrs. Moss's dealings with alleged Communist contact Robert Hall, a correspondent for the *Daily Worker* in the nation's capital. Mrs. Moss admitted an acquaintance with someone named Robert Hall, insisting that this was a black friend of hers, with no contact to Communist causes.[39] The counsel for Democratic members of the committee, Robert Kennedy, clarified to minority committee members that the journalist described at the hearing was a white man. Democratic committee member John McClellan pointed out what appeared to be obvious—that two different people were being described.

Senator Symington sought additional information from Mrs. Moss regarding her employment status with the army. She responded that she had been suspended from her job and was asked to read the suspension notice aloud in the hearing room. She had great difficulty doing that, and Symington clarified her financial situation and the job displacement that was threatening her status and creating the likelihood that she would have to go on welfare. Roy Cohn interrupted the questioning and presented information regarding Mrs. Moss's relationship with another known Communist based on information from FBI sources.

Mrs. Moss admitted to knowing the woman but said she was unaware of any Communist affiliation on her part. Senator Symington offered a line of questioning earlier in which Moss denied knowledge of the Communist Party and said that she had never in her life spoken to a Communist. Cohn said that according to witnesses Moss had such relationships and was also a dues-paying member of the Communist Party. Senator John McClellan castigated Cohn for his cross-examination and said that Mrs. Moss had come before the committee voluntarily and had lost her job. Expressing a desire to get to the heart of the matter, McClellan offered the view that corroborating evidence rather than hearsay needed to be presented. He also expressed the desire to interview witnesses under oath.

On a couple of occasions, McClellan's statements were interrupted by applause in the hearing room. Republican Senator Mundt, who presided in McCarthy's absence, ruled that Roy Cohn's statements be stricken from the record. McClellan shot back that the statements could not be stricken from the public mind or the press and that the policy of convicting people through rumor and hearsay was out of line. In closing and in an attempt to clarify what had transpired, Senator Symington asked Mrs. Moss if sources identifying her as a Communist could be somehow mistaken. She offered the view that the fact that there were three individuals in the Washington, D.C., area with the same name, Annie Lee Moss, might have caused the confusion.

Symington pledged support and said he not only believed Moss but would offer her a job when the controversy subsided. Another witness appeared at that hearing, but Moss's testimony convinced Joe Wershba that he had invested "See It Now" resources well that day. The broadcast of those findings took place just six days after the hearing itself and only nine days after the direct broadcast attack on McCarthy himself. This time, however, Murrow kept himself in the background and only interrupted the film on occasion to clarify the circumstances under review. These included confusion over the identity of Robert Hall, testimony by a witness against Moss, and a description of her efforts to read excerpts from her suspension notice, which Murrow described as being "uncoded."

In terms of editorial content, Murrow again took responsibility for the broadcast early in the program, then adopted the position of Senators Symington and McClellan, clarifying that he did not know whether Mrs. Moss was a Communist or not but agreeing that she should have an opportunity to face her accusers. He followed this assertion with a film clip of Dwight Eisenhower from a famed speech, later labeled the "Code of Abilene" address, in which the president discussed his personal philosophy, based on the code of the West under which he was raised as a boy. Some historians, including Eric Barnouw, have speculated that this speech, delivered on national television November 23, 1953, upon his acceptance of an award from the Anti-Defamation League of B'nai B'rith, was set up to address the issue of McCarthyism, making the same general claim regarding the right of any citizen to look his or her accuser in the eye.[40] Murrow concluded this telecast by commending President Eisenhower on this powerful condemnation on behalf of a principle of American law and justice.

Fred Friendly said that his partner viewed this broadcast as possibly the most "unpremeditatedly analytical report ever done by his documentary unit."[41] Unlike the McCarthy broadcast, CBS management did not provide the specific details of the audience response but later reported an "enthusiastic audience reception," saying that the count of letters received on the program ran nine-to-one favorable to the program. One journalist, Marya Mannes, writing in the *Reporter*, called the earlier broadcast on McCarthy a "biased attack" but said that after seeing the proceedings in the Moss case, she was convinced that ordinary citizens would be compelled to line up in opposition to McCarthy.[42] Many of the press accounts described Mrs. Moss as a soft-spoken, rather ill-informed, and now unemployed widow.

John Crosby of the *New York Herald-Tribune* said Moss's appearance turned the tables and was damaging to McCarthy because her presence showed the senator himself as "a subversive who is trying to undermine the very cornerstone of our country."[43] Other sources compared her plight to that of a McCarthy staff member, for whom the senator reportedly sought preferential treatment; later the staff member's situation became an issue in the televised Army-McCarthy hearings. A *St. Louis Post-Dispatch* editorial called these comparisons "too much for a democracy to suffer."[44] Moss was called upon after the hearing to comment once again on the charges, and she offered only bewilderment, citing her personal pride as a lifelong Democrat because of the stand Democratic members of the McCarthy committee took on her behalf.

Meanwhile, "See It Now" staff members, led by Fred Friendly, asserted that neither Murrow nor Democratic members of the committee believed that some of the charges against Moss were not true, only that the hearing process was flawed and that she had a right to stand up to her accusers. Two weeks after the March 27 "See It Now" broadcast, Moss was restored to her position with the Signal Corps; but shortly after that, on August 4, 1954, she was suspended a second time pending further investigation. A security hearing board reviewed the charges a second time in January 1955 and she was reassigned by order of Defense Secretary Charles E. Wilson to a "nonsensitive" office of the army chief of finance.

Much later, on September 19, 1958, the Subversive Activities Control board conducted an investigation in which FBI documents were used to show that an Annie Lee Moss had been a member of the Communist Party. Some sources, including McCarthy assistant Roy Cohn maintained that this was the same person who had appeared at the hearing.[45] Fred Friendly said later that the broadcast hearing showed the disproportionate power wielded by McCarthy against individuals and pointed out that, had the Moss hearing taken place earlier, the "See It Now" program on McCarthy might not have been necessary. He also asserted that McCarthy accepted Murrow's invitation to reply to the earlier program the same day the Moss telecast aired.

McCARTHY'S DOWNFALL

The nation's press began to document McCarthy's declining popularity among the citizenry, including former supporters. Attacks on the

Eisenhower administration, as well as challenges to the patriotism of Democrat Adlai Stevenson, hurt his public standing; and he struggled to keep up with speaking commitments in spite of ill health. He used one occasion to challenge Murrow again, accusing him of having participated in Communist programs at Moscow University, and he once again attacked both the Democratic Party and the American Civil Liberties Union. The head of the ACLU responded by citing support by President Eisenhower for the organization and charged that McCarthy had become confused in distinguishing Communists from patriots.

Adlai Stevenson announced that he would no longer respond to McCarthy or "stoop to the Senator's level,"[46] although later, after learning that the Young Republicans of New York had repudiated McCarthy for "irresponsible and reckless conduct," Stevenson quipped in a speech at Harvard that he would have to agree with the Young Republicans.[47] McCarthy then lashed out at the nation's press for providing the American people with the view that he was in conflict with President Eisenhower. He also mentioned his confidence in light of impending military investigations concerning the report of special treatment of his staff and vowed to expose a Communist conspiracy against him among elements of the left-wing press.

Responding negatively to a demand by Senator Stuart Symington that he resign from his subcommittee assignment while the army conducted its investigation, he vowed to continue his fight against individual Communists and traitors. Symington said McCarthy's position at the helm of this body placed him in the role of accuser, prosecutor, and judge and was clearly inappropriate. On March 27, 1954, Republican National Chairman Leonard W. Hall asserted that McCarthy's influence had diminished and the army soon announced the appointment of attorney Joseph N. Welch to handle the investigation of the senator. Meanwhile, McCarthy prepared his response to the Murrow broadcast, which was filmed at Fox Movietone Studios in New York, with the assistance of Hollywood producer Louis B. Mayer and columnist George Sokolsky. He promised to show that Murrow was lying about him and, in doing so, helping the Communist cause.[48]

The McCarthy film reply arrived at CBS just hours before the scheduled broadcast with just enough time for a single preview, which was required by network policy and which resulted in the deletion of two sentences regarded as potentially libelous. An agreement was reached with McCarthy representatives on this issue, and Fred Friendly followed up with statements regarding the poor production quality. He said that the "See It Now" staff was frankly surprised by the program. The content of the broadcast was a frontal assault on Murrow, whom McCarthy called symbolic and "the cleverest of the jackal pack" of those exposing Communists. McCarthy also included a listing of allegations concerning Murrow's activities and associations with Communist groups and individuals.

The film concluded with additional attacks on Murrow, but McCarthy first charged that Communist infiltration of government scientific circles had delayed development of the hydrogen bomb. This accusation, which was immediately refuted by a variety of sources including both President Eisenhower and former president Truman, further eroded McCarthy's public position. Critic Gilbert Seldes termed McCarthy's response to Murrow "a feebly handled newsreel talk."[49] CBS followed the McCarthy film with a statement of support for Murrow and his devotion to the nation and its founding principles of equal justice and fair play. While support for Murrow right after the McCarthy program eclipsed that for the senator in terms of the total number of telephone calls, the network reported a surprising response favoring McCarthy of nearly three thousand, while close to five thousand were recorded in support of Murrow.

Jack Gould of the *New York Times* had predicted that Murrow would pay a temporary price for "mousetrapping" the senator, but President Eisenhower publicly announced his friendship and support for Murrow the day after the broadcast and shortly thereafter approached Murrow at a White House dinner at which the president jokingly rubbed Murrow's back: "Just to see if any of the knives were sticking out."[50] Meanwhile, Murrow continued to deny assertions that he had been on a personal crusade to "get" Senator McCarthy amid a number of honors following the broadcast. The next year Murrow received nearly every distinction for broadcast excellence including a Peabody and Overseas Press Club Award, while McCarthy appeared to switch field once again and was quoted as having said that he wished every radio and television commentator were as fair as Murrow.[51]

The televised Army-McCarthy hearings that followed are commonly accepted as the decisive blow to Senator McCarthy, but most sources also credit Murrow, Friendly, and the whole CBS "See It Now" team both for the strong stand in the first broadcast and for the Moss program, which clearly demonstrated a gross violation of rights against a U.S. citizen. A disregard for due process was self-evident to viewers, just as in his later television performance, in which McCarthy would also hurt and discredit himself in cross-questioning by army attorney Joseph Welch. Coincidental assaults on McCarthy by Adlai Stevenson and Senator Ralph Flanders also undoubtedly altered perception of McCarthy and facilitated change for a new public view of the senator.

In the years that followed, Edward R. Murrow experienced a number of strains with CBS management, often related to his strong independent stand on controversial issues. Certainly the McCarthy broadcast would be remembered as contributing to this impression, as well as some other broadcasts that would create problems for other politicians, government agencies, and the network itself. The most widely regarded, yet controversial, of these programs involved the farming industry and its methods of harvesting crops.

NOTES

1. The best account of the Murrow vs. McCarthy broadcast is contained in Fred W. Friendly, *Due to Circumstances Beyond Our Control* (New York: Random House, 1967). See also, Michael D. Murray, "Persuasive Dimensions of *See It Now*'s report on Senator Joseph R. McCarthy," *Communication Quarterly* (Fall 1975): 13–20. All of the Murrow biographies also cover the broadcast. See, for example, Ann Sperber, *Murrow: His Life and Times* (New York: Freundlich Books, 1986), pp. 414–471.

2. See John Cogley, *Report on Blacklisting* (New York: Fund for the Republic, 1956); John Henry Faulk, *Fear on Trial* (New York: Simon and Schuster, 1964); and Robert K. Murray, *Red Scare: A Study in National Hysteria* (Minneapolis: University of Minnesota, 1955).

3. See "Voice Aide Sees McCarthy Aiming at 'My Public Neck,' " *New York Times*, March 4, 1953, p. 1; and "McCarthy Methods Scored at Inquiry," *New York Times*, March 5, 1953, p. 9.

4. "Reed Harris Cut Off in Middle of Rebuttal to Charges in 'Voice' Inquiry Called Disgraceful," *New York Times*, March 6, 1953, p. 34; and "Televised Hearings: The Public Is Entitled to This Service but TV Methods Could Be Improved," *New York Times*, March 8, 1953, p. X11.

5. "Mundt Says 'Voice' Is 'Justified Idea,' " *New York Times*, March 9, 1953, p. 18.

6. "Dulles Welcomes Congress Inquiries on Staff Loyalty," *New York Times*, February 28, 1953, p. 1; and "McCarthy Poses an Administration Problem," *New York Times*, February 22, 1953, p. E3.

7. "The Investigators: Administration 'Panic,' " *New York Times*, March 1, 1953, p. 1B.

8. Quoted in Roberta S. Feuerlicht, *Joe McCarthy and McCarthyism: The Hate That Haunts America* (New York: McGraw-Hill, 1972), p. 119. The text was published in its entirety in the *New York Times*, February 23, 1954, p. 16. See also "Zwicker Denounces McCarthy's Tactics," *New York Times*, March 4, 1954, p. 1.

9. Fred J. Cook, *The Nightmare Decade: The Life and Times of Senator Joe McCarthy*, (New York: Random House, 1971), p. 468.

10. "President Chides McCarthy on 'Fair Play' at Hearings; Senator Defiant in Retort," *New York Times*, March 4, 1954, p. 1.

11. Emmet John Hughes, *Ordeal of Power* (New York: Atheneum, 1963), p. 124.

12. Quoted in "American Masters," "Edward R. Murrow: This Reporter," PBS Television broadcast, July 30, 1990.

13. "Charges President Eisenhower Has Accepted 'McCarthyism,' " *New York Times*, March 7, 1954, p. 6; and "Stevenson Says President Yields to McCarthyism," *New York Times*, March 7, 1954, p. 1.

14. "McCarthy Rakes Networks for Refusing Him Time to Reply," *St. Louis Post-Dispatch*, March 9, 1954, p. 2A; and "McCarthy 'Doing Best to Shatter' G.O.P. Flanders Says in Senate," *St. Louis Post-Dispatch*, March 9, 1954, p. 1.

15. Joe Wershba, personal interview, November 9, 1973.

16. Ibid.

17. Fred W. Friendly, *Due to Circumstances Beyond Our Control* (New York: Random House, 1967), p. 30.

18. Ibid.

19. Joe Wershba, "The Broadcaster and the Senator," undated manuscript, later published in abbreviated form as "Murrow vs. McCarthy: 'See It Now.' " *New York Times Magazine*, March 4, 1979.

20. These newspapers included the *New York Times, New York Herald-Tribune, Chicago Tribune, Milwaukee Journal, Washington Star*, and *St. Louis Post-Dispatch*.

21. Joe Wershba, personal interview, November 9, 1973.

22. Gilbert Seldes, "Murrow, McCarthy and the Empty Formula," *Saturday Review*, April 24, 1954, p. 27.

23. Friendly, *Due to Circumstances Beyond Our Control*, p. 36.

24. William Small, *To Kill a Messenger: Television News and the Real World* (New York: Hastings House, 1970), p. 27.

25. "Salute to a Brave Man," *New York Herald Tribune*, March 12, 1954, p. 19.

26. "The Baited Trap," *Time*, March 29, 1954, p. 77.

27. "Murrow Wins the Nation's Applause," *Broadcasting* 46 (March 15, 1954), p. 7.

28. "When Television Came of Age," *St. Louis Post-Dispatch*, March 21, 1954, p. 2E.

29. "One Last Word," *New York Herald-Tribune*, March 15, 1954, p. 17. See also "McCarthy Says Five Radio Stations Have Offered Him Free Time," *St. Louis Post-Dispatch*, March 11, 1954, p. 11.

30. "TV and McCarthy: Network's Decision and Murrow Show Represent Advance for Medium," *New York Times*, March 14, 1954, p. X13.

31. Joe Wershba, personal interview, November 9, 1973.

32. "Edward R. Murrow of CBS: 'Diplomat, Poet, Preacher,' " *Newsweek*, March 9, 1953, p. 40.

33. Murray Yeager, "An Analysis of Edward R. Murrow's 'See It Now' Television Program," Ph.D. diss., University of Iowa, 1956, pp. 55–59. Also personal correspondence with John L. Fleming, vice president, Aluminum Company of America, April 5, 1974.

34. "Praise Pours in on Murrow Show," *New York Times*, March 11, 1954, p. 19; and "Wires, Calls to Murrow Strongly Anti-McCarthy," *New York Herald Tribune*, March 11, 1954, p. 3.

35. "Senator Attacks: Hits Back at Stevenson, Murrow and Flanders in Radio Broadcast," *New York Times*, March 12, 1954, p. 1; "McCarthy in Broadcast Calls Critics Untruthful," *New York Herald-Tribune*, March 12, 1954, p. 1.

36. "McCarthy Says Red Decodes Secrets, But Army Denies It," *New York Times*, February 24, 1954, p. 1.

37. Joe Wershba, personal interview, November 9, 1973.

38. A complete transcript of the hearing is contained in the subcommittee record, 83rd Congress, 2nd Session, pursuant to Senate Resolution 189. A transcript of the "See It Now" broadcast of the edited version of the hearing is contained in Edward R.

Murrow and Fred W. Friendly, eds., *See It Now* (New York: Simon and Schuster, 1955), pp. 54–67.

39. See "Mrs. Moss Confused but Feels No Anger," *Washington Post*, March 14, 1954, p. 1.

40. See Eric Barnouw, *The Image Empire* (New York: Oxford University Press, 1970), pp. 13–21. See also "Murrow Contrasts Talk of Ike with Moss Probe," *Washington Post*, March 17, 1954, p. 4; and "Murrow Presents Report on Mrs. Moss," *New York Times*, March 17, 1954, p. 21.

41. Friendly, *Due to Circumstances Beyond Our Control*.

42. Marya Mannes, "The People vs. McCarthy," *Reporter* 10 (April 27, 1954): 26.

43. "The Aroma of Decency," *New York Herald Tribune*, March 19, 1954, p. 19.

44. "The Fire Begins to Turn," *St. Louis Post-Dispatch*, March 12, 1954, p. 2C.

45. Roy Cohn, *McCarthy* (New York: New American Library, 1968), pp. 122–124. This view has been repeated several times by noted conservatives, such as prominent columnist and public broadcaster William F. Buckley.

46. " 'I Will Not Stoop to McCarthy Level,' Stevenson Retorts," *Detroit News*, March 21, 1954, p. 40.

47. "Stevenson Scorns McCarthy Charges," *New York Times*, March 21, 1954, p. 1.

48. "McCarthy Pledges Press 'Exposure,' " *New York Times*, March 21, 1954, p. 1.

49. "Murrow, McCarthy and the Empty Formula," *Saturday Review*, April 24, 1954, p. 27.

50. Alexander Kendrick, *Prime Time: The Life of Edward R. Murrow* (Boston: Little, Brown and Company, 1969).

51. "Edward R. Murrow of CBS," p. 40.

Chapter 6

MUCKRAKING

CBS Television entered the evening news field early, with Douglas Edwards at the helm, beginning in 1948. Edwards, who became a fixture at CBS Radio after Walter Cronkite took over television anchor duties in 1962, still continued to deliver daytime reports on television well into the 1970s. But these early network news reports relied heavily on newsreel companies to provide what little video there was to spice up the short, fifteen-minute programs, a strategy documentary producers often incorporated into their operations, as in the McCarthy broadcast. The emphasis in television programming continued to be on entertainment, with comedy figures transposed from radio to television, but gradually some public affairs inroads were made. The news/talk series "Face the Nation" premiered in 1954 on CBS, an alternative to NBC's "Meet the Press." Some major assaults on the broadcast industry, including the payola scandal and blacklisting, forced the networks to reexamine both their means and methods. One blacklist victim, CBS Radio employee John Henry Faulk, went to court to clear his name in a protracted legal battle that he eventually won.

Partisan uses of television were clearly on the rise, as was the awareness that television could be utilized to boost political ambitions, even before McCarthy caught the nation's fancy. Staunch conservative Richard Nixon defended attacks on his credibility as Dwight Eisenhower's vice presidential running mate in the televised performance dubbed the "Checkers Speech," reflecting his statement about a dog he had been given, which he declared he would keep in spite of any criticism. His talk, which defended the use of funds by contributors, was broadcast over both CBS and NBC and is credited with having saved Nixon's place on the Republican ticket. The inauguration of Eisenhower was also covered live by CBS News. His press conferences were also the first to be offered over network television, although they were later criticized for having been staged, with the president coached by former television actor Robert Montgomery. The credibility of the medium, its methods, in all its various aspects and areas was beginning to come under more careful scrutiny.

Frank Stanton sought to maintain quality documentary efforts while regulating Edward R. Murrow's involvement because of his star correspondent's ever-increasing, open criticism of the commercial values and practices of the broadcast industry. While Murrow's role was diminishing, his sidekick, Fred Friendly, was being recruited to produce the new network documentary effort, "CBS Reports," with the understanding that Murrow would be an occasional contributor, sharing reportorial duties with the likes of network anchormen Walter Cronkite, Howard K. Smith, Harry Reasoner, and others. Friendly speculated on how this new relationship and expanded role would change his partnership with Murrow but reasoned that, with the assistance of Stanton, the concept would enhance the efforts the two began years earlier. It might also open up the door to other talented people at the network.

It was well known that pressure and concern regarding various "See It Now" projects were growing among sponsors and government insiders. It might be time to reinforce the potential commercial and image-building value of this type of effort and minimize the prospects for conflict with government and commercial interests. The end of "See It Now" was foreshadowed by a "See It Now" report, for example, entitled "The Farm Problem: A Crisis of Abundance," which, according to Friendly, not only resulted in a public outcry but provided an impetus for considerable internal debate at CBS.

The telecast centered on challenges to the small farmer and a comparison to a growing number of large mechanized growers. The problems of corn, wheat, hog, and dairy farmers were examined with an emphasis on the difference between the farmer's investment and the return on labor. Also coming under close scrutiny was the development of a tremendous surplus of farm products, representing a national problem. Jack Gould of the *New York Times* again credited "See It Now" for its careful analysis of each farmer profiled in the program, which personalized the issue to a great degree. Gould said that the appearance of the farmers themselves, their weather-worn faces and quiet humor in the face of severe personal hardship, made a pithy and succinct statement of their dedication and determination and added a personal touch.[1]

Gould also cautioned that the program seemed incomplete, as it did not investigate the middleman in the farm labor equation. The roles of food distributors and packing facilities were criticized, for example, without being fully explored in the telecast, thus providing an incomplete picture in which consumer and farm prices were discussed in depth, with little attention to other important elements of the story. The secretary of agriculture at the time, Ezra Taft Benson, appeared toward the end of the program and took issue with the overall impression that the survival of small farmers was in question. Benson had been Murrow's guest and said the program was too negative and portrayed an inaccurate picture of the small family farmer.

The day after the broadcast, Benson insisted that the program presented a distorted image of the farm problem, giving the average American the inaccurate view that the small family farm was growing near extinction, a contention he termed "demagoguery at its worst." Speaking from Johnstown, Pennsylvania, Benson maintained that he was just about to respond to the program's errors and present a more factual basis for the small family farm issue when time ran out. The Republican Party requested and received response time from CBS to address these views.

Secretary Benson responded to critics by calling their thinking "frantic"[2] and indicating that they were helping to create difficulties for American farmers. He urged viewers to respond quickly by requesting Congress to act on a new farm bill that would pay farmers to reduce their production.

Benson referred to the old method of compensating farmers as a form of price fixing. He called his appearance on CBS an opportunity to present the truth at a time when partisan politics was producing the feeling that some immediate action, any action, must be taken to stem the tide of panic in some quarters. He said that that kind of sloppy thinking resulted in additional problems in which farm issues were placed on what he termed "the political auction block."[3] The fact that so many last-minute, potentially dangerous amendments had been attached to the bill was evidence of panic, which he said would not assist the farmer. The response time given by the network to the Republicans to rebut the initial documentary not only irritated Murrow but, because of the nature of the partisan response, also resulted in a Democratic rebuttal. Senator Hubert Humphrey of Minnesota and New Mexico's Clinton Anderson were provided network air, free of charge, measures that Murrow also regarded as unnecessary.

ALTERNATIVES

"See It Now" continued to produce programs of high quality during the summer of 1955 that frequently addressed specific controversial issues such as the fight for civil rights, an interview with scientist J. Robert Oppenheimer, and a report on the relationship between cigarette smoking and cancer.[4] The cancer issue was also addressed by CBS in an interview with Dr. Tom Dooley on a "See It Now" program entitled "Biography of a Cancer," which for obvious reasons also raised eyebrows in certain circles, especially among tobacco growers.

Political issues continued to dominate the "See It Now" landscape. For example, in October of 1955, Murrow and Friendly offered viewers an informative look at the office of the vice presidency, using old prints, early documents, and newsreel footage to show the sometimes haphazard way the second in command in the United States has been chosen and the frequency with which vice presidents succeed to the highest office. Murrow cautioned that ten out of thirty-five vice presidents to that date had been called to become the nation's chief executive.[5] The program concluded with interviews with former vice presidents Harry Truman, Alben W. Barkley, and Henry A. Wallace.

This Truman interview is often cited for its show of candor by a chief executive. Excerpts from it are included in Murrow video biographies, with one segment focusing on how previous chief executives such as Andrew Jackson might view Truman's service in the office of vice president. "See It Now" was credited in this particular program with a very careful, conscientious, and even somewhat studious approach to a complicated topic that did not ordinarily lend itself to dynamic presentation, further demonstrating, as Jack Gould added, the usefulness of television in educating a nation.[6] But response to the earlier farm program lingered, and the aftermath of that documentary illustrated a growing division between network management and program producers, as illustrated by agreements to turn over airtime to outsiders for response.

This rising conflict, which eventually led to Murrow's resignation from the CBS board of directors, also contributed to the demise of "See It Now" and the movement by the network to work additional talent and programming into the documentary mix. To this end, Dr. Frank Stanton announced the start of "CBS Reports" in a speech at his alma mater, Ohio State University, on May 6, 1959. The new unit produced its first installment, "Biography of a Missile," with Murrow still performing reporter duties on October 27, in spite of repeated attempts to assert his privilege to comment on network decision-making. One such case involved his advisement to all networks to avoid playing up a visit by Soviet premier Nikita Khrushchev.[7]

Harry S. Truman discusses the role of the vice presidency with Edward R. Murrow. Murrow's interviews as part of the "Person to Person" series attracted a big audience. Used with the permission of CBS Inc.

By the fall of 1960, another farm-related broadcast, but now a "CBS Reports" investigation, sounded an additional major alarm in the farm community; and Murrow once again found himself in the middle of a protracted controversy. Like its predecessor broadcast on an element of the agricultural industry, "Harvest of Shame" included government participation in telling the story of conditions on the farm, but this time the cameras focused on migratory laborers and the conditions they faced. In the muckraking tradition of America's newspaper and magazine press, Murrow and reporter/producer David Lowe, in his first assignment for this series, offered a vivid and sad tale of exploitation and deprivation.

Lowe's experience in covering this story, as in other programs he would produce on such topics as racial prejudice, gun control, and the funeral business, created a climate for reform and soul searching but also resulted in a great deal of defensiveness and criticism. In the case of one program, "The Great American Funeral," the concern was expressed by some that the in-depth study of morticians, their folkways, and their business practices was simply a blatant effort to hurt free enterprise.

Lowe once explained his motivation and methods in a *New York Times* feature story entitled "Where Angels Fear to Tread,"[8] in which he said that a documentary program that steps on no toes is likely to be regarded as a failure. By that standard his efforts on the agricultural scene were a resounding success and certainly helped to stimulate others. Those with whom he worked at CBS shared his enthusiasm, especially in exploring the area of migratory farm laborers working under conditions that Edward R. Murrow described as wronging the dignity of man. All told, at least a half-dozen major television documentaries and segments of "60 Minutes," "20/20," and "Prime Time Live" on ABC have examined the plight of migratory farm labor since the "Harvest of Shame" investigation, which set the standard and became a prototype. It included key elements such as transportation and methods of hiring, standards of living for workers, educational opportunities for their children, and working conditions of the laborers themselves.

All of these areas were thoroughly investigated in this classic "CBS Reports" program, and many became subjects of close scrutiny by critics, the most serious involving charges of misrepresentation and a tendency to paint a picture at odds with reality. Program producer David Lowe said that those usually most outraged by a documentary are those whose pocketbooks are most likely to be damaged as a result, and this broadcast was certainly no exception. The farm bosses and growers maintained that the worst possible examples of worker abuse were analyzed and held up for public scrutiny, as if they were representative. Workers who toiled unusually long hours for almost no pay, people who had exceptionally large families and left their children to fend for themselves, were said to have been especially sought out and featured in the program.

One laborer who worked from sunup to sundown and had fourteen children used the poor return on crops as the rationale for limited compensation. David Lowe visited with some of her children living in a run-down shack without adult supervision in which stale beans qualified as lunch. This interview took place among household items destroyed by vermin traversing the same living quarters. Migrant living conditions were also graphically illustrated with comparisons to race-horse stables located near migratory farm labor camps, with emphasis on the fact that the animals were treated royally by their owners. Murrow quoted from a government report that cited, as another severe limitation for migrants, the lack of hot water for bathing.

These hard facts were presented along with statistics on bus accidents in which poorly maintained vehicles transporting both adult laborers and their children accounted for the annual deaths of many migrants on American highways. They fared poorly, according to Murrow, by comparison to the transport of produce to market, which was regulated by the federal government.

All of this scored a very sour note with reviewers who were served up this broadcast stew the day after Thanksgiving, making the subject all the more meaningful and painful. Comparisons to slavery and the attitude that workers are merely "rented" under unfair labor practices with little consideration for their personal well-being were presented along with inquiries regarding payments to middlemen in the process of harvesting food and getting it to market. Expressions of obvious disregard for workers were played up at the expense of managers at almost every level, including low-level crew leaders, those responsible for recruiting workers, up to the president of the American Farm Bureau Federation lobby, who was heard commenting on the relatively positive outcome of having these workers employed and with some income, if only for a short time each year.

One farm manager was asked to describe the migratory existence. He commented that he thought they must "have a little bit of gypsy in their blood because they like it; in fact, they love it, some of them wouldn't have it any other way, some don't know any better." In response to a follow-up question, the manager admitted that the migrant laborers made a poor living and attributed this to the variable prices their picking produced, as well as the fact that few among them understood the process of getting goods to market. The migratory pattern that required frequent movement and constant upheaval and its effect on farm families were scrutinized, including abuse of children who seldom had time to get acquainted with a classroom or teacher before being uprooted to move on with their family to another location.

The excuse Lowe provided for this strong network treatment of the problem, which some authorities in the U.S. Labor Department viewed as underhanded, was that he had come upon an area so tainted with ugliness that it demanded the strongest stand possible. Secretary of Labor James Mitchell was seen in the documentary not only condemning the way migrants were treated but also vowing to dedicate his time, in or out of public office, to trying to resolve this complicated and unjust situation.

As in some earlier programs, Murrow concluded the broadcast with an appeal to the American people for legislation to assist their fellow citizens: "The people you have seen have the strength to harvest your fruits and vegetables. They do not have the strength to influence legislation. Maybe we do. Good night and good luck." Ironically, once Murrow resigned from CBS on January 31, 1961, shortly after this documentary, to join the Kennedy administration as head of the U.S. Information Agency, he came under fire in confirmation hearings for stressing what was termed "the seamy side" in this program. He then switched gears and attempted, to no avail, to block distribution of this same film overseas,[9] taking the tack that it was a film produced for American consumption, about a complicated American problem.

The muckraking at CBS was not limited during this period to rural problems. Jay McMullen, who was responsible for production in the earlier "Who Killed Michael Farmer?" radio documentary, was equally astute in covering the local urban crime scene for "CBS Reports." This examination of betting operations in a Boston gambling parlor, "Biography of a Bookie Joint," sent shock waves through eastern politics at a time when accusations regarding internal corruption and double-dealing had already hit the front pages of most American newspapers.

The documentary was not shown in Boston at the time the rest of the country viewed it, because legal proceedings in the case were already under way. Walter Cronkite handled announcing chores for the program, but Jay McMullen's approach was to let the cameras do the talking as he filmed bookies, bettors, and even some Boston police officers leaving a bookie establishment that posed as a key-making shop.

Unlike most criminal fiction portrayed on television, this documentary focused on the details of the betting operation itself, including some suspense, with shots of bookies burning betting slips, and an overall explanation of the futility of efforts to shut them down. Police apathy and the inability of citizen groups to take meaningful action led into the federal raid documented as part of the program, with Walter Cronkite's

Before becoming executive producer in charge of "60 Minutes," Don Hewitt established a reputation for being in the right place at the right time. This included the assignment of directing the first of the so-called "Great Debates." Here he is flanked by candidates John Kennedy and Richard Nixon. Courtesy of Don Hewitt.

aside that the effort represented an attempt to address a national rather than a local problem. The program came under the scrutiny of the Federal Communications Commission (FCC) when the Speaker of the Massachusetts House of Representatives, John F. Thompson, complained that the documentary was unjust in its characterization of the Boston situation.

The FCC, however, disagreed in the case and took the position that this program and an NBC "White Paper" entitled "The Battle of Newburgh" were both unbiased and balanced, based on staff reviews of both documentaries. This led *New York Times* critic Jack Gould to ask whether the backing of the FCC was appropriate or whether the networks would have complained about government encroachment in the case if they had not come down on the side of the broadcasters. The fact that the networks were silent in the face of unanticipated praise led Gould to ask whether the legal and publicity departments of the networks had been caught off guard in this rare instance, apparently forgetting to take precautions "in the event that they were loved."[10]

NEWS COVERAGE

CBS gained respect by hosting the first of television's "Great Debates" between presidential candidates Richard Nixon and John Kennedy during the 1960 election, and the network also preempted entertainment programming in 1962 to cover aspects of the Cuban missile crisis. This televised event pitted Kennedy against Soviet premier Nikita Khrushchev, with the youthful American president emerging as a television good guy, or at least the winner of this confrontation. Just three months prior to Kennedy's assassination in 1963, CBS expanded their national evening newscast to a half hour, and that inaugural broadcast featured a JFK interview conducted by Walter Cronkite and focusing on Vietnam involvement. Cronkite is remembered for his emotional announcement of the assassination, with Dan Rather reporting for CBS from the scene of the event in Dallas. Regular programming was suspended during the Kennedy funeral, and the social and foreign policy goals Kennedy sought were explored in subsequent programming, not the least of which included Vietnam and domestic violence following a series of assassinations.

The News Election Service was formed to pool network and wire service resources in 1968. Violence broadcast during the Democratic National Convention in Chicago that same year included a physical assault on Dan Rather, leading Cronkite to indict those responsible, whom he labeled "a bunch of thugs." The need to investigate what was

An off-the-monitor shot from the "Great Debates." Studies showed that those who watched the debates on television were more favorably disposed to John Kennedy. Copyright © Burton Berinsky.

going on in American society in the 1960s or, perhaps better stated, what went wrong, became a preoccupation in television news.

During that decade, the network was once again investigating the treatment of underrepresented Americans in another dynamic "CBS Reports" program, "Hunger in America," with reporters Charles Kuralt and David Culhane. The idea for this program reportedly originated with the late Senator Robert F. Kennedy.[11] But rather than focus on a hunger problem in the farm community, program producers Peter Davis and Martin Carr also looked at ethnic groups: Mexican Americans and Navajo Indians. Charles Kuralt observed as part of his introductory segment that one fourth of the Mexican Americans living in San Antonio, Texas, were hungry all of the time; in a key graphic segment later challenged for authenticity, a baby was shown dying of starvation.[12]

The program went on to show that poor diets contributed to malnutrition among various groups, including Indians in Arizona and tenant farmers and sharecroppers of the rural South, while hogs were being slaughtered under federal programs that assumed that there was no market for them. Some of the more astounding elements of the report included a claim by an eleven-year-old Mexican American girl that she sold herself for food. Overall, the program indicated that 10 million people in the United States went to bed hungry every night and that Navajo Indian babies died because their diets did not include any fruits, vegetables, or meat. Beyond that, the program asserted that the Department of Agriculture, which administered the food surplus program on behalf of the government, had been turning back over $400 million that could have been used to feed the hungry. Of the food provided through government programs, the documentary charged that a starchy diet was provided, one that was good for less than half of the body's needs.

The public reaction to this program was astounding, even by comparison to previous network documentaries. Over five thousand letters were received at CBS and, interestingly, many included cash donations. As one might have expected, Secretary of Agriculture Orville Freeman took strong exception to the claims in this documentary. He accused CBS in the strongest possible language of not only shoddy journalism but also gross distortions and errors of fact, adding: "The program presented to millions of viewers a distorted, oversimplified and misleading picture of domestic hunger . . . and it served to further disillusion, disappoint and disenchant those hungry people who now have been told that no one cares."[13] He demanded equal time from CBS and wrote directly to Frank Stanton to make that request, sharing the letter's contents at a press conference. Freeman charged that only 890 counties lacked the federal food surplus program, although CBS listed 1,000 counties in the program. He also provided background on various types of foods added to the distribution program of his department and discussed how money turned back to the government was used to fight poverty in other ways.

The producer of the program, Martin Carr, denied any attempt to sensationalize the story and even mentioned some segments that had been edited out because of dramatic impact. For example, he said a sequence that reporter David Culhane had worked on, in which a Mexican woman wept openly because of having to abandon her children to beg for food, was left out of the final cut of the documentary because of its emotional content. Producer Carr added: "We didn't start out by saying we want to take pictures of babies dying. But in television you go out and film what you see."[14] Frank Stanton defended the documentary and implied that Secretary Freeman's complaint seemed to focus on blame for abuses as opposed to inaccuracies in the program. The then CBS News president, Richard Salant, also publicly supported the program, expressing confidence in its accuracy in a statement he read personally on the "CBS Evening News with Walter Cronkite." In spite of its insistence to stand firm in the matter, the network repeated the program on June 16, 1968, and gave Secretary Freeman an opportunity to provide a short addendum addressing steps taken to improve the status of federally funded food support.

The charge of distortion was taken up by U.S. Congressman Henry B. Gonzalez from San Antonio, Texas, who asked the Federal Communications Commission to rule on it as a CBS attempt to mislead viewers and "slant the news," particularly in the case of the baby depicted dying of malnutrition in a San Antonio hospital.[15] The FCC found that although malnutrition was found to be prevalent in the hospital ward, with the CBS film crew influenced by statements to that effect, the baby shown in the film died because of premature birth, not starvation. This resulted in a double-edged statement by the FCC, clarifying their role in such cases as appropriately not censoring broadcast content and, at the same time, charging CBS with recklessness and indifference to the truth in the airing of the segment on the baby's death.[16]

Others who have studied this particular broadcast have viewed it as a positive example of the willingness of CBS News to stand up to governmental pressure even during a period of unbridled criticism, while also gaining support from the FCC.[17] Interestingly, Robert Mac-Neil, in his book *The People Machine*, reviewed the effects of this broadcast on hunger and the controversy it raised, then quoted from a personal interview with Herbert Mitgang, who said that an attitude of "take it easy" on political figures was, for the most part, implicit at the network during this period. There was an awareness in lower management that you could not attack politicians and candidates, he said, "especially those heading toward the presidency."[18] Although critical in this case, the FCC was equally unwilling to interfere in a journalistic enterprise even when an error had obviously occurred and take direct action against the network.

NOTES

1. Jack Gould, "TV: The Farm Problem," *New York Times*, January 27, 1955, p. 49.

2. "Benson Charges 'Distortion,' " *New York Times*, January 27, 1955, p. 49.

3. William M. Blair, "Benson Hits Back at 'Frantic' Foes," *New York Times*, February 24, 1956, p. 15.

4. See Jack Gould, "TV: Cigarettes and Cancer: Murrow Gives First of Two Part Report," *New York Times*, June 1, 1956, p. 67; and "Art for Katonoh Irks Legion Aide," *New York Times*, July 16, 1955, p. 34.

5. Jack Gould, "TV: 'See It Now' Returns," *New York Times*, October 27, 1955, p. 67.

6. "CBS Crime Report," *New York Times*, December 1, 1961, p. 67. See also, for information on background of corruption coverage: "Boston Globe Hails Series in the Times," *New York Times*, November 5, 1961, p. 73.

7. Jack Gould, " 'Newts' for Networks," *New York Times*, August 12, 1962, p. X13.

8. David Lowe, "Where Angels Fear to Tread," *New York Times*, August 1, 1965, II, p. 13. Also see Fred W. Friendly, "TV Can Open America's Eyes," *TV Guide*, December 10, 1960, p. 10; and Friendly's account of the "Harvest of Shame" broadcast in *Due to Circumstances Beyond Our Control* (New York: Vintage Books, 1968), pp. 120–126.

9. See "Stanton Defends Recent Criticism That U.S. Image Damaged by Showing Programs Abroad," *New York Times*, March 4, 1962, p. 67.

10. Gould, " 'Newts' for Networks," p. X13.

11. See Robert Lewis Shayon, "What's Wrong with Documentaries," *Saturday Review*, January 23, 1965, p. 55. Also, Harry J. Skornia, *Television and the News* (Palo Alto: Pacific Books, 1968), p. 16.

12. In Re Complaints Covering CBS Program "Hunger in America" 20 FCC 2d 143, October 15, 1969.

13. "Hunger Pains," *Newsweek*, June 10, 1968, p. 100.

14. Ibid.

15. 20 FCC 2d 143, 144, October 15, 1969.

16. 20 FCC 2d 143, 147, October 15, 1969.

17. See Ernest F. Martin, Jr., "The 'Hunger in America' Controversy," *Journal of Broadcasting* 16(2) (Spring 1972): 185–194.

18. Robert MacNeil, *The People Machine* (New York: Harper and Row, 1968), p. 88.

Chapter 7

YOUTH MOVEMENT

In an effort to document the sixties student movement, CBS profiled one
scenario acknowledging developments on the Berkeley campus of the
University of California, a traditional hotbed of student involvement,
protest, and occasional unrest. The Free Speech movement and debates
on that campus led, at one point, to the resignation of the administration
of the school. Filmmaker Arthur Barron was advised to investigate
events at the university, and he did so with an eye toward focusing his
camera on individuals, particularly student representatives of the class
of 1965, examining their individual goals for the future and their possible role in public demonstrations that had taken place there. After an
initial assessment, Barron proposed a more content-specific approach
to this theme of student concerns and interests. The eventual methodology went beyond generalized attempts to address the activity and
values of average students on the campus, focusing instead on "activ-
ists," part of the new, more radical student movement that was getting
a great deal of surface attention by the press, but very little in the way
of explanation or understanding.[1]

Barron was ideally suited for this on-campus assignment because at
one time he had been an academic himself, completing a Ph.D. in
Russian studies from Columbia University and working for the Research Institute of America as a writer in charge of opinion research. He
also began his work in broadcasting as a writer and researcher, with
documentary assignments including "The U-2 Affair" for the "NBC
White Paper" series, which was recognized with a national Emmy

Award in 1961. He graduated to producing films for WNEW and made "Johnny" on the subject of mental illness, "China and the Bomb," which looked at the nuclear capacity of the People's Republic of China, and another documentary tracing the American labor movement entitled "The Rise of Labor." He also gained recognition for a short film on the use of folk music in the civil rights movement focusing specifically on the songs of Bob Dylan.[2]

Before joining the CBS network, Barron also produced films on medical issues such as the fight to treat tuberculosis. In yet another film he contrasted the childhood experiences of Hubert Humphrey and James Baldwin. He made "The Burden and the Glory of John F. Kennedy" at a time when documentary development was widely recognized at the network as becoming a source of great pride, with the full attention and support of news president Fred W. Friendly, who of course was highly thought of himself for his work as a documentarian.

When the Berkeley film started out, it was clearly an attempt to look at the goals and ambitions of a specific group of students, viewed as representatives of their peer group on campus. Barron investigated their individual backgrounds and decided, in spite of a predisposition toward simplifying their position vis-à-vis the established political order, that the viewer would be given some reasons why the students represented a positive element in the American political and social milieu, an alternative view at a critical juncture in American history.[3]

In Barron's beginning notes for the program, which are reprinted in the production text by Alan Rosenthal, *Writing, Directing, and Producing Documentaries*, the filmmaker stated some of his objectives and his general approach as personal and individualistic, not reportage but a highly subjective, somewhat autobiographical presentation. The objective was to show the viewer the world of the students, to convey the mood and environment of the campus setting at that time and from that perspective, rather than reporting surface details.[4] In doing that, he attempted to introduce a world of ideas as well, in which conscientious but iconoclastic young people explored themselves and American political performance and ideals of the era.[5]

Barron expressed the desire to keep narration to a minimum, concentrating instead on the students themselves, arguing for a less-traditional, nonnetwork cinema verité style of filmmaking rather than the television news norm, usually high in interpretation by reporters. The goal was to use the network spokesperson for this story, Harry Reasoner, as a guide to the world of the students, offering an overview and summation of their beliefs, attitudes, and values. An examination of causes of concern by the students and their lack of acceptance of the established order of things became the goal. Once the filmmaking began, the use of individual student experience was used as symbolic of the times.

In one instance, a serious student, a young woman, was shown in a mixture of emotions toward her California academic base and the more iconoclastic lifestyle in vogue at the time, offering both positive and negative views on the dominant culture and values of that liberal area of the country and the era. In wider-reaching terms, the student provided a commentary on the system of higher education she encountered. In a second segment, two students, a male and female who were living together, also reflected on a wide range of areas including the so-called generation gap and personal responsibility and morality, which, they felt, were at odds with views they personally accepted. In the last segment, the camera followed a young student teacher and focused specifically on his politics, illuminating the views of a segment of his generation as a mirror of American society.

This approach and the level of objectivity as set out and defined by network executives, as seen earlier, were sometimes at odds with the orientation of film producers such as Arthur Barron. Although network bigwigs sometimes hoped for a neat package, with tight conclusions presented in balanced, guarded, but journalistically sound format, some of these filmmakers opted for more creative treatment in which viewer interpretations were required. Other times the message was clear because it was orchestrated as in a Hollywood production. In this regard, the language of film employed by documentary filmmakers often coincided with the lexicon of popular motion pictures. In an interview with Barron for his book *Documentary Explorations*, G. Roy Levin asked the filmmaker about "casting" in his films, that is, what kind of selection process took place in nonfiction television documentaries during his tenure at CBS? Barron discussed the challenges of an intuitive process, often relying on instinct and experience in the field as a guide. In another instance, Barron used the theatrical term "acts" in describing his method of dividing up content, as in "The Berkeley Rebels," where the camera focused on individual students in a specific context before moving to another perspective represented by another student; he was therefore selecting students to represent a point of view.

Also in the Levin interview, Barron discussed the frequent institutional obstacles he faced in lining up subjects for films such as this particular youth-oriented telecast, from which network executives insisted that certain scenes be removed, including one filmed at a college fraternity house. In that particular setting, students downed mounds of spaghetti, a scene Barron described as both "unbelievable" and "decadent." Referring to Fred Friendly's account of the broadcast in *Due to Circumstances Beyond Our Control*, Barron discussed how and why that sequence had been cut from the film. Although this filmmaker set out to produce point-of-view films, documents that attempted to move people dramatically on an emotional level in a certain direction, it is clear again that the network hierarchy had something else in mind.

CONFLICT OVER CONTENT

CBS management sought a balanced, more educationally defensible position, which is precisely the area in which Barron experienced difficulty with CBS News and some critics from the campus community. At one point CBS camera crews were picketed by conservative students on campus, for example, once they received some initial feedback on the selection of scenes in the documentary. Under increasing pressure, Barron was asked initially by the network to cut staged sequences, which he did. One influential critic, UC-Berkeley president Clark Kerr, then interceded in the case of "The Berkeley Rebels" and effected considerable additional change in the final product by contacting senior officials in New York. Barron pointed out later that Clark Kerr was a friend of Frank Stanton and that the filmmaker felt pressure brought to bear to the extent that certain segments including both the spaghetti-laden fraternity house scene and an attempt at artistic expression involving examination of use of televised lectures on campus were ordered out of the program.

Host Harry Reasoner was given copy to read over introductory segments and other key video portions of the program, such as one in which student opinion on protest was presented as foundation ideas taken from the American Revolution. Barron was also asked to remove a segment in which motorcycles had been placed at various locations on campus, another one in which a student emerged from a bubble bath, and one involving a dog who appeared to talk on camera. These were all viewed as inappropriate by CBS management, but in Barron's view the effect of these alterations was to change the tone of the project and to some extent to trivialize the views of the students appearing in the film. This was especially unusual and perhaps unfair, he noted, because the students were under considerable pressure during the filming, and their lives had even been altered to some extent by their participation in the documentary as it had evolved. For example, one of the students, a young woman, reportedly experienced some reaction from her family and was disinvited from appearing as a flower girl in a relative's wedding as a result of appearing in the film.

This issue of influence of personal lives and privacy would emerge dramatically a decade later when the Public Broadcasting Service and documentary producer/filmmaker Craig Gilbert attempted to offer an insider's view of a bona fide American family, the William C. Louds of Santa Barbara, California. Filmmakers lived with the Louds for nearly seven months and recorded the breakup of the marriage, leading critics to wonder to what extent the cameras influenced behaviors and the outcome.[6]

Arthur Barron has also commented on other instances in which people in his films were removed from their jobs or simply did not have their contracts renewed as a result of having appeared in a documentary. Of course, in the opinion of many broadcasters, it is the "real people" aspect of the documentary film that distinguishes it from the Hollywood-style fiction film. For this reason, Barron praised other television documentary filmmakers who caused social change through their work, especially noting Martin Carr, for his "Hunger in America," and Jay McMullen, director of "Biography of a Bookie Joint." Barron also made it clear that these documentaries had a strong political message, even when the CBS network attempted to minimize overt attempts to proselytize in favor of presenting a more balanced picture of important issues of the day.

In the instance of "The Berkeley Rebels," as both William S. Paley and Frank Stanton opposed the orientation of its initial version, the changes were made; and Fred Friendly, who at first opposed them, admitted later that they were probably correct in taking a strong stand against the cinema techniques and point of view of this program, which reflected an unusual level of license that the filmmaker had initially been given. Friendly later commented that this case was unusual in that the only stern reprimand he ever received from William S. Paley was over this particular broadcast, which he felt was somewhat unjustified at that time and rather unusual, given his track record. He was uncertain as to whether the program merited this sort of special attention and what amounted to severe post-production editing by CBS senior management. He was also surprised when Paley reminded him of the "sacred trust" he assumed as head of CBS News. Some outside critics such as Todd Gitlin viewed the interference with the broadcast as an example of the influence of a class elite, in this case intervention by a well-connected ally, a high-ranking university administrator.

Interestingly, shortly afterwards, Bill Leonard himself faced a similar conflict concerning content in a subsequent Barron documentary, one which purported to examine the views of high school seniors in an upper-crust Midwestern suburb. The position on this broadcast was upheld years later when, as Friendly's successor, Leonard defended the decision in the case, pointing to the need for credibility in producing news and public affairs programming.[7]

This documentary, entitled "Sixteen in Webster Groves," examined the attitudes and behavior of middle-American teens by focusing on a conservative suburb of St. Louis, Missouri. It looked specifically at sixteen-year-old students enrolled in the local public high school. According to Arthur Barron, the topic was selected because CBS considered the status of American teenagers topical and newsworthy. Because he had done "The Berkeley Rebels," Barron was considered the resident youth expert and was given the topic of teenage attitudes and lifestyles and left to develop a concept for the program, with the admonition to strive for accuracy.[8] He would attempt to identify places in which a high level of education and affluence had been achieved, to determine the effects of that success on the overall quality of life. As a means of providing some scientific base and to help avoid the kind of criticism he received from the earlier Berkeley program, he commissioned a study of sixteen-year-olds in a single community, Webster Groves, Missouri, which was identified as suburban and upper-middle class, what correspondent Charles Kuralt later described in the program as "a town of 30,000 people which happens to be statistically fairly representative of such communities in America today."[9]

Barron approached the Webster Groves school board with the idea that he would present an affirmative picture of the life of real American teenagers, as opposed to the popular images of American youth of the sixties as either empty-headed or delinquent. It would be based on an objective scientific study. With permission to begin filming granted, Barron proceeded with the creation of a thirty-six-page questionnaire administered to the sixteen-year-olds at Webster Groves High School with results shared with polling experts from the University of Chicago National Opinion Research Center.

Barron and his colleagues were reportedly shocked by the questionnaire results, which showed students as narrow-minded and prejudiced by-products of their middle-class environment, with limited dreams and visions beyond the overriding ambition of maintaining an affluent lifestyle. With the information on the Webster Groves teenagers in hand, the CBS film crew, headed by Walter Dombrow, arrived in town in the fall of 1965. In an effort to get familiar with the community, interviews were conducted with parents, teachers, and students in almost every kind of environment, at school, in social settings, and in individual homes with families from the community.

ORIENTATION OF FILM

Barron recalled later that he was trying to achieve what he called an "intensification of reality" in the broadcast, which would present in both visual and emotional terms the results of the survey he had conducted at the school. For this reason, he admitted to selecting representative students to symbolize certain findings from the survey data. For example, the quarterback of the Webster Groves High School football team was filmed in an interview the day before the school's homecoming day game and was used as a symbol of teenage ambition. Some female students were filmed applying makeup and grooming themselves in preparation for the senior prom. The students were also classed by their social standing as representative of the social stratification going on in the high school.

A group of parents were photographed in a living room setting and at the dinner table being interviewed by Charles Kuralt on the attitudes of their sons and daughters and asked pointed questions about their knowledge of world affairs, attitudes on personal relationships, and civil rights. The parents were mostly in agreement that at sixteen years of age, high school students were not equipped to handle the important questions facing the nation and the world of the sixties. They agreed with Kuralt that their kids should want to be involved in the major issues of the day including the struggle for civil rights, but this admission came later on, after the initial broadcast.

The first Webster Groves documentary aired nationally on the evening of February 25, 1966, and resulted in a considerable amount of protest by many of the people in the community including participants in the broadcast itself. The producer, Arthur Barron, was accused of betraying a trust, and specific charges of distortion and exaggeration were sent to the Federal Communications Commission, CBS News, and the network affiliate in the Webster Groves coverage area, KMOX-TV, now KMOV, St. Louis.[10] A prevailing attitude was that the theme of the report that "the main goal of 77 percent of the 16 year olds was 'a good paying job, money and success' " was representative of only some of the members of this community of sixteen-year-olds.[11]

Because of the level of interest expressed from the outside before this particular telecast and because of what had preceded it in "The Berkeley Rebels" broadcast, Arthur Barron was asked by CBS if he would like to go back to Webster Groves on the evening of the broadcast and film the community response, then spend the rest of the day or so tracking down people in the community for their reaction in public places. Barron told CBS president Fred Friendly that he thought that would be a bad idea and "an atrocious film." The idea was filed for a day, then Barron was ordered by CBS to return to Missouri and make another film about the reaction to the first documentary on the grounds that it would provide what Friendly called "a unique opportunity for CBS to contribute to understanding and insight into the communication process."[12] Barron said the second film was motivated by a decision to let some angry residents of Webster Groves vent their frustrations, but if that was the intent, it did not work.

The follow-up broadcast opened with a review of the previous documentary and had Kuralt introducing himself as the reporter from the CBS studio control room in New York, just as Edward R. Murrow had done on previous occasions, including the McCarthy telecast. It went on the air exactly seven weeks after the original broadcast aired and was described as being about the kind of life sixteen-year-olds lead and the things they believe.[13] Kuralt went on to say that the current broadcast would pick up where the other one left off and that it would give viewers a unique opportunity to provide feedback on a broadcast by letting people discuss their feelings and perceptions after viewing a report about themselves and their community. He pointed out that it seemed as if the broadcast was all they were talking about in Webster Groves that day. For that reason, for the first time in television history, CBS would offer viewers a response and amplify the voices of those appearing in the first broadcast, for the nation to view and evaluate for themselves.

The second broadcast consisted of a wide variety of views on the documentary carefully balanced to represent both the pro and con sides of the issues and the format and style of the documentary itself. Interestingly, as expected, many of the views were directed at the way the CBS News team edited the film. Accusations would later be made that the film editing misrepresented sequences and that the use of music also distorted and exaggerated the intent of some segments. Kuralt presented the facts of how the broadcast came into being including a rundown of the selection process and the questionnaire used to form the basis of the film. He outlined the filming agenda and explained how thoroughly the twenty-eight hours of film shot on location in the community represented a variety of viewpoints and camera angles over a thirty-two-day period. He explained how a rapport had developed between the camera crew and the students and how, on one occasion, when it took nine hours to set up lights, microphones, cable, and cameras for filming in their homes, the parents were unfailingly good natured and hospitable.[14]

After charges concerning the CBS unit's predisposition toward the students were offered, Kuralt said they had expected to find youthful rebellion and some degree of dissatisfaction with the status quo but they had found the opposite.[15] He also made reference to reviewers who asked why this viewpoint was so objectionable. He said it was not necessarily a negative factor, but it was surprising to find in teenagers. He quoted a University of Chicago sociologist who, after studying results of the survey, said the original program should have been titled "Forty in Webster Groves."

Kuralt then introduced a segment from the original broadcast, interviewing the parents of some of the students about their expectations of success for their sons and daughters since, as Kuralt reported, the vast majority of the teens said their parents had high expectations for them, with the understanding that they would do well in college as a means to achieve success and financial security. On the other hand, another overwhelming percentage of the students said that they had trouble coping with the pressures of these expectations, excellence in their schoolwork, and, for example, the daily routine of taking tests.

This was followed by a segment on the relationship between the pressures placed on the teenagers and the level of achievement they are able to reach with the social and academic demands of high school in middle-class suburban America. Kuralt quoted himself from the first broadcast as having pointed out that teenagers in the community were labeled according to their leadership ability, personality, and financial standing and that some of the intellectual achievers and minorities in the school felt left out as a result of this system of labeling, in which members of the social set were known as "socies."

The program focused on some of those students who did not qualify as "socies," based on their academic standing, as being part of either an intellectual elite or a minority or the 15 percent on the other end of the academic spectrum who were not planning to go to college. Kuralt mentioned minorities as on the list of those students outside the social swing of things and followed up with a segment in which parents expressed strong disapproval for individual activity on the part of teenagers who would express their views by taking part in a civil rights demonstration.

The parents' view was one of expressed conformity, holding that high school students need not be burdened with major national or world problems. Kuralt reviewed the earlier text in which he commented on the insulation of the community and the emphasis on status and conformity. He admitted that there were some differing views based on experiences students had had outside the confines of Webster Groves and concluded his review of the first program by summarizing the attitudes of the sixteen-year-olds as they had been presented. He noted that the students were under pressure from parents to do well in school to fulfill expectations and insure an affluent lifestyle. But he also added that the teenagers also felt that other aspects of their lives could be more fulfilling.

Kuralt began his review of the aftermath of the broadcast and its effects by describing the scene in Webster Groves the evening it was first shown on national television. He mentioned how the Webster Groves Board of Education brought in television sets to watch as a group. The junior high school dance in town was interrupted for an hour so no thirteen-year-old would miss his older brother or sister on television. He summed up the emotional response by noting that some viewers laughed out loud during the broadcast while some cried. Before going to a commercial break, he added that some viewers also became quite angry with the program and the network.

STUDENT RESPONSE

The segment that followed was filmed in the living room of one teenager's home. Five students who had been featured in the first broadcast were questioned by Kuralt as the program progressed. They included the quarterback of the football team, the daughter of one of the most vocal parents to appear in the first program, a student government leader, a cheerleader, and a student described as both a budding social critic and a bit of a rebel. He had been featured in the first broadcast in stark contrast to conformist views expressed by most of the other students and parents. He talked about how all of the residents of this affluent community shared the same values and beliefs, dressed the same, drove the same kind of cars, and interacted with other members of their families and even house pets in the same ways.

The camera recorded the students' reaction to the program as it was broadcast, with Kuralt periodically asking a question or commenting on their reaction to the program. The students were shown responding somewhat defensively to segments focusing on conformity and social standing. The same was true of their response to some comments made by parents in the program. The students reacted emotionally to a patriotic theme from a school presentation and were seen laughing hysterically at a sequence in which young children from the area were sternly ordered by a dance instructor to throw their chewing gum out the window. At this point, Kuralt asked the students of their reaction so far. The response was predictable. Parents were indicted by the teens for not giving them enough credit in making adult-like decisions based on their concerns and experiences.

Was it a true picture of Webster Groves? The verdict seemed to indicate that there was a significant lack of understanding between the generations. Beyond that, the broadcast elicited an incredible outpouring of emotion on both sides. Kuralt introduced a series of over a dozen tape-recorded audio segments from phone calls to the local CBS affiliate station, KMOX-TV. The callers were fairly evenly divided in their views of the fairness of the broadcast, but the sequence included one Webster

Groves teenager who said the account was thoroughly unrepresentative and untrue.

Correspondent Kuralt reported that the telephone at the local station had rung well beyond midnight, then concluded with a segment of "man on the street" interviews that had been filmed the next day in the Webster Groves business district, at area stores, and back on the high school campus or in front of the school. Comments on the program were disjointed but ranged from "terrible" to "it is a nice city, and they just emphasized the point." During the questioning of sources outside the high school, one of the students confused the question and started stressing the difficulty of a test he had just taken. This segment undoubtedly had the effect of reinforcing the pressure on students to achieve high grades, as it had been represented in the original broadcast. Other people said it showed bias and even accused the network of playing politics with an overemphasis on achievement and test scores.

Also in this segment, Kuralt tried to draw out some of the students standing in front of the school on the issue of race relations and opportunities for minorities at Webster Groves High. The opinion of parents, as it was expressed in the film, was disparaged by students and reference was made to the Vietnam conflict, for example, and the fact that some of the students would probably be called to fight in that military effort, emphasizing their need to be aware of the world around them and their own responsibility for personal decision-making.

Finally, some adults were quoted as being in support of the broadcast, calling it both candid and frank. Another parent balanced the difficulty of achieving a well-rounded representation of facts with a negative assessment of the broadcaster's need to present an interesting, engaging program. The parent commended CBS for capturing some very real truths about life as a teenager but also noted that it is probably necessary to stress certain points in this type of endeavor for "dramatic effect." The concern expressed here was that, in the representation of certain truths, these not be viewed as the whole truth as it applied to material things and the young people of that community. He acknowledged that Webster Groves teens were tied up in materialism but that it was not the singular, overriding element of their existence. They also, he said, exhibited some genuine idealism and self-sacrifice, which were not represented adequately in the documentary.

Charles Kuralt went on to acknowledge a number of letters the network received regarding the broadcast—a total of 498. Of that number, 366 generally approved of the broadcast, he said, and 132 disapproved. The reporter went on to add that generally things balanced out in response to the film in that two letter writers suggested that he get a raise while two others offered the view that he should be fired.

The hometown media response in Webster Groves, Missouri, provided similar mixed reviews. Kuralt was pleased by the reaction of the *St. Louis Globe-Democrat*'s Pete Rahn and disappointed in Clarissa Start of the *Post-Dispatch*, a Webster Groves resident, who wrote a rather scathing attack on the broadcast, then sent a thousand copies to friends at newspapers throughout the country.

Kuralt also reserved the most extended part of this section of the follow-up broadcast to a rebroadcast of an excerpt from a popular St. Louis–based program, which had aired over the ABC affiliate, KTVI-TV. In it, program host Charlotte Peters, a popular broadcast figure in the community who had worked previously at the NBC affiliate station in town, castigated the CBS network as being ratings hungry and the program itself as "fuel for sick minds and part of the Communist conspiracy to export dissension to other countries."[16] She asked, in essence, why a television network would want to reinforce negative stereotypes of the American system by ridiculing the lifestyles and values of its citizens and their young people.

Also appearing on that local program were both the radio-television critic of the *St. Louis Globe-Democrat* and the chief law enforcement officer of Webster Groves, who agreed that the students came across in an unfavorable light in the documentary. In postmortems conducted after the second broadcast, critics continued to focus on certain segments of the program that they charged had distorted the image of teenagers and adults of that community. In particular, criticism focused on an opening shot of students looking sad, which was symbolic of the tone of much of the film, given the pressure the students were under from their parents. Critics charged, however, that this segment had been filmed at a funeral but never identified as such. This charge was hotly denied.

In another segment, a student athlete appears to be responding to a question about how he coped with the stress of getting good grades. *St. Louis Post-Dispatch* feature writer Clarissa Start stated that in the initial interview, the student was responding to a question of how he was coping with pressure related to the big homecoming football game, which was scheduled to take place the next day. In a very detailed analysis, which appeared in a book published in conjunction with the nation's Bicentennial, Start also maintained that while the typical reaction to a column on a controversial issue in the *Post-Dispatch* might produce as many as twenty or thirty letters, the column she published on this broadcast resulted in over a thousand letters, of which all but a handful were in total agreement with her position that the network and filmmaker had overstepped their bounds.[17]

One of the students at Webster Groves High School at that time, now also a writer for the *St. Louis Post-Dispatch*, Patricia Corrigan, conducted a poll of students after the broadcast and found them to be almost universally upset with the outcome of the film, unwilling to admit that what was portrayed on CBS was representative of their classmates. Corrigan focused on one particular staged sequence in which students at a school dance were compared to their parents dancing at an exclusive local club.[18] In the original broadcast, Kuralt used the sound of the music to emphasize that even as adults, Webster Groves residents follow a familiar beat, implying conformity. This theme was also used to contrast some high school students in a metal shop class, clearly out of step with the majority of academically advanced students at the school, who appeared to be receiving inferior treatment at the school.

Corrigan also questioned the program's representation of the high school as racist, noting that minority students were represented in the school government association and as club officers, another fact either overlooked or ignored by the broadcast.[19] In an assessment from the West Coast, *San Francisco Chronicle* critic Terence O'Flaherty summed up his views on the program by beginning with the opening segment stressing student unhappiness and cynically suggesting that discontent was assumed in the approach used by CBS.[20]

AFTERMATH

Film historian Lewis Jacobs placed the broadcast alongside a cinema verité classic independent film by Frederick Wiseman on the same subject, completed about the same time. Wiseman's well-known *High School* also exposed the pressures and attempts by the older generation to form the new in the context of secondary school education.[21] In his book *The People Machine*, PBS coanchor Robert MacNeil termed the CBS broadcasts "exceedingly interesting and original ... imaginatively filmed and utterly absorbing"[22] but also pointed out that the first program received only a 14.5 percent share of viewers while the follow-up telecast attracted just 14.1 percent, considered small for prime-time fare, he pointed out, but still representing an audience of many millions.

Subsequently, some of the participants have admitted to being taken up by the moment in the preparation of the film and their view of it. One featured student, twenty years later, admitted that the documentary was more truthful than high school students wanted to admit at the time because it conveyed an insulated, superficial world that, this source confided, was a fairly accurate representation at sixteen years of age. Others feel that Barron and his on-camera spokesperson misrepresented the approach he suggested he would use and the overall picture of the community. A local broadcaster, Nancy St. James, also a Webster Groves resident, who with her family was also featured in the film said much later that Barron had expressed a desire for his own children to be raised in a place like Webster Groves, giving residents an overall positive feeling about his observations and approach to the community.[23]

The conservative editorial voice of the *St. Louis Globe-Democrat* took another tack and labeled the tone of the film ignorant condescension in its posturing in an era "that will lead historians to dismiss the '60s as a time of intellectual rubbish, a brief interlude where children held the stage and flaunted their childishness."[24] Another observer, Ted Peppel, a resident of the community at that time, suggested that the viewpoint of the film was clear after the first few minutes and that the network overshot the mark, adding: "I think they tried too hard but that's the way CBS operated. I really believe it was on the threshold of this kind of TV journalism."[25] In a book addressing documentaries from the sixties, Charles Hammond called the film a "theme" documentary because of Barron's stated goals.[26]

It is interesting to note that two years before the Webster Groves broadcast was prepared Arthur Barron publicly decried documentaries that made no effort to present a particular point of view. At a forum sponsored by the New York chapter of the National Academy of Television Arts and Sciences, Barron said he could not understand why anyone would approach the content of a social issue in a documentary format without coming at it from a distinctive point of view in the same way that a writer expresses a direction and viewpoint. If one did not use a definite perspective, he added, the documentry would be regarded as bland, predictable, and somewhat aimless.

Whatever else it achieved, "Sixteen in Webster Groves" certainly could not be characterized as bland or aimless even within the context of CBS documentaries, and the telecast today occupies a unique position in the history of public affairs programming. In this instance, CBS took a strong stand on teen values of the era, not to mention Midwestern community standards, but hedged a bet on traditional documentary standards by offering a follow-up broadcast to present alternative views and to gauge reaction and perhaps assuage guilt arising from the initial broadcast. It offered controversy and a point of view but forestalled a great deal of additional criticism by preparing and programming a response in conjunction with the telecast of the first documentary.

In light of the broadcast and all that has transpired since that time it is interesting to note that in the fall of 1992 Dan Rather visited Webster Groves to test preelection political attitudes in that community. While he was making his exit from a voter's home in the area, a resident, William Willcockson, asked him if he remembered that documentary about teenagers from nearly twenty-five years ago, characterizing it as unfair, with much taken out of context. Rather replied that he indeed remembered the program but quipped, "The statute of limitations must have run out."[27] A quarter century after the program aired, "Sixteen in Webster Groves" is remembered and still stirs strong emotions among those from that small bedroom community.

NOTES

1. Lewis Jacobs, ed., *The Documentary Tradition* (New York: W. W. Norton, 1979).

2. Alan Rosenthal, *The New Documentary in Action* (Berkeley, CA: University of California Press, 1971).

3. Todd Gitlin, *The Whole World Is Watching* (Berkeley, CA: University of California Press, 1980), pp. 64–65.

4. Alan Rosenthal, ed., *New Challenges for Documentary* (Berkeley, CA: University of California Press, 1988).

5. For comment on the free speech movement and activities at UC–Berkeley during this period see, for example, Patricia Mar, "Plea for Academic Freedom," *San Francisco Examiner*, March 1, 1965, p. 1; "History of Free Speech Crisis behind UC Resignation," *San Francisco Examiner*, March 10, 1965, p. 19; James Benet, "UC Crisis: Kerr Quits," *San Francisco Chronicle*, March 19, 1965, p. 1; and Carolyn Anspacher and Don Weguro, "Big UC Vote for Kerr," *San Francisco Chronicle*, March 13, 1965, p. 1.

6. See Michael D. Murray, "A Real-Life Family in Prime Time," in Jennings Bryant, ed., *Television and the American Family* (Hillsdale, NJ: Lawrence Erlbaum, 1990), pp. 185–192.

7. Rosenthal, *The New Documentary in Action*, pp. 135–136.

8. For additional background on Barron's style see Stephen Mamber, "Cinema Verité and Social Concerns," *Film Comment* 9(6) (November-December 1973): 11–12. See also Lawrence Laurent, "TV Review," *Washington Post*, April 11, 1968, for a review of Barron's methods.

9. "Webster Groves Revisited," CBS Television broadcast, August 8, 1966.

10. See "TV Program on Teenagers Stirs Anger and Soul Searching," *St. Louis Post-Dispatch*, February 26, 1966, p. 3A.

11. "Webster Groves Upset by TV Show," *St. Louis Globe-Democrat*, February 26, 1966, p. 1; and "Webster OKs Commercial Development," *St. Louis Globe-Democrat*, March 4, 1966, p. 45.

12. Rosenthal, *The New Documentary in Action*, p. 139.

13. "Webster Groves Revisited," CBS Television broadcast, April 8, 1966.

14. Ibid. and personal interview with Patricia Corrigan, March 7, 1989.

15. Ironically, Kuralt became known for his sensitivity to local interest in his CBS reporting assignments. Kuralt later narrated "But What If the Dream Comes True?" a film about suburban life, and hosted the "On the Road" series for CBS. See, for example, "Kuralt's Greatest Hits," *St. Louis Post-Dispatch*, October 14, 1988, p. 9F; and Charles Kuralt, Joe Creason Lecture, School of Journalism, University of Kentucky, Lexington, Kentucky, April 28, 1989.

16. Quoted in "Webster Youths Like '16' TV Show," *St. Louis Globe-Democrat*, March 8, 1966, p. 7A.

17. Clarissa Start, *Webster Groves* (Webster Groves, MO: City of Webster Groves, 1975), p. 231.

18. Patricia Corrigan, "Webster Groves: Are Teens Still Clad in Diapers?" *St. Louis Globe-Democrat*, March 4, 1966, p. 1B. Also, see Patricia Corrigan, "Webster Once More in Spotlight," *St. Louis Globe-Democrat*, April 12, 1966, p. 10D; Harry Levins, "Film Still Drives 'Em Crazy After All These Years," *St. Louis Post-Dispatch*, March 6, 1989, p. 2D; personal interview with Patricia Corrigan, March 7, 1989; and Patricia Corrigan, "Class of '67: Image Still Rankles," *St. Louis Post-Dispatch*, July 6, 1992, p. 3D.

19. Quoted in Clarissa Start, "Sixteen in—Where?" *Webster Groves* (Webster Groves, MO: City of Webster Groves, 1975), p. 237.

20. See Peter Hernon, "Class of '66 Remembers," *St. Louis Post-Dispatch*, July 7, 1986, p. 1A.

21. KMOX Radio, December 10, 1991, Charles Brennan, moderator.

22. Robert MacNeil, *The People Machine: The Influence of Television on American Politics* (New York: Harper and Row, 1968), p. 82.

23. KMOX Radio, December 10, 1991, Charles Brennan, moderator.

24. "Webster Groves High Revisited," *St. Louis Globe-Democrat*, July 8, 1986, p. 8A. See also Lewis Jacobs, *The Documentary Tradition* (New York: W. W. Norton, 1979), p. 372.

25. KMOX Radio, December 10, 1991, Charles Brennan, moderator.

26. Charles Montgomery Hammond, Jr., *The Image Decade: Television Documentary, 1965–1975* (New York: Hastings House, 1981); and A. William Bluem, *Documentary in American Journalism* (New York: Hastings House, 1969), p. 261.

27. "CBS Reports: Dan Rather Visits Voters in Webster Groves," *St. Louis Post-Dispatch*, September 19, 1992, p. 3A.

Chapter 8

MILITARY MATTERS

Firepower was the order of the day. The program opened with a display of weaponry exhibited for an armed forces celebration at Fort Jackson, South Carolina. The starting segment concluded with a massive firing of weapons in rapid succession, described by CBS correspondent Roger Mudd as "the mad minute." Mudd added wryly that it would be "hard to argue" with that description, thus establishing a critical tone for the telecast. He zeroed in specifically on how the military promotes itself in public display, as in this case of conducting a firepower exercise for the benefit of select taxpayers. So began "The Selling of the Pentagon," with Mudd emphasizing the estimated versus actual costs of that exhibition of ordnance.[1] He also commented on the other possible deleterious effects of demonstrating the weapons of war for children and, in some cases, the use of physical force and firearms, which was also captured on camera.

The CBS producer for this broadcast, Peter Davis, was an experienced documentarian. He sharpened his skills in the early sixties at both NBC and ABC before joining CBS News in the documentary production area. He worked on some outstanding projects and had a well-deserved reputation when he reached CBS. In addition to "The Battle of East St. Louis" and "Hunger in America," Davis would go on to make another controversial independent documentary on the Vietnam War effort that was unique in that it was exhibited as a feature-length film for theater screening. Entitled "Hearts and Minds," it won praise in some quarters while others felt it was somewhat heavy-handed, as when it addressed the concept of devalued human life among Vietnamese, as it was characterized by military sources in the film.

In some respects the feature film picked up where "The Selling of the Pentagon" left off. The CBS program showed, for example, American children mimicking Green Berets in various combat poses after having witnessed a demonstration of hand-to-hand combat techniques. Also reported in depth in the film was a detailed study of special military excursions conducted for business, civic, and education leaders, identified on the tour and in the program as "major taxpayers." They described their experiences visiting military bases, meeting the soldiers and high-ranking officers as part of the itinerary, and even testing the equipment by firing off rounds from various weapons.

These special guests of the military were shown posing with equipment and senior-level officials described in the program as "four star chaperons." They were also photographed and interviewed in front of various military exhibits and pieces of hardware, and they commented on how much they enjoyed getting their hands on the genuine article when it came to various upgraded weapons. In one segment, in reaction to a reporter's question as to what summary message might be derived from the tour, the sources insisted that a key ingredient of the experience was the ability to assess the high quality of American servicemen. They added that they felt there would be less "carping" at the military if all of the American people could be exposed to this type of presentation and the backbone of the organization, the soldier in the field. Also noted was a comment by one of the participants on the tour denying that he had been "brainwashed," a term military critics used, by unlimited access to personnel and equipment. The costs were presented by CBS as being grossly underestimated.

A summary on how the military orchestrated these tours and firepower demonstrations in the field as a preparation for conflict was reviewed as well, but Roger Mudd concluded this introductory segment by noting that these represented artificial circumstances, or, as he put it, "War . . . is not fought in front of a grandstand." Mudd detailed military public relations efforts of the era through open public displays as they were presented in shopping malls, including one sequence in which the manager of a mall in St. Paul, Minnesota, explained how an exhibit was placed at that locale as a follow-up to a request by a local military recruiter.

Air shows featured stunt flying by the Air Force Thunderbirds, who were characterized at the exhibits as having been battle tested in Vietnam. These references to air performance in the field in Vietnam led Mudd to question whether citizens were viewing an exhibition or an elaborate commercial for air power. On the same theme, segments from speeches by senior military spokespersons seemed to comment on policy issues forbidden by Congress. This would become a major bone of contention after the initial broadcast. One of the speakers, for example, appeared to imply that victory in Vietnam was being deterred by protest efforts at home.

Mudd also questioned the form and extent of military self-promotion through use of the established broadcast media and film. He compared the budgets of the three major commercial television networks to that of the military information branch, with special emphasis on a major defense department film series, *The Big Picture*. This series dramatically dwarfed other film projects with its $900,000 budget. The correspondent wondered out loud about the appropriateness of a $6.5 million overall military film budget and the continued use of outdated films being shown to civilian audiences. These films, he said, presented Cold War messages in direct opposition to government policy prohibitions on their use. He also detailed the relationship between Hollywood and the military including activity by major movie and television stars, such as Robert Stack and John Wayne, who were shown endorsing messages in support of the Vietnam War effort.

Mudd discussed how prominent actors contributed pro-Vietnam views and how sympathetic filmmakers were allowed field support in their artistic efforts using Hollywood sources. An extended sequence from a Jack Webb production, *Red Nightmare*, described in the documentary as the Pentagon's most ambitious film, was integrated into the program along with Mudd's commentary on its content, a drama detailing Communist takeover strategies. Mudd also questioned use of broadcast journalists in some films including some of the best-known journalists from CBS News. He said that, for patriotic reasons, broadcasters such as Edward R. Murrow, Lowell Thomas, and John Daly had contributed to early military propaganda efforts and that more recently the Defense Department had received the assistance of Walter Cronkite and Chet Huntley. Mudd asserted in the interest of objective journalism that some of these sources later disagreed with the policy of supporting some messages they had recorded much earlier.

Excerpts from the film *The Eagle's Talon*, narrated by Walter Cronkite and dealing with America's reaction to international communism, were integrated into another film, *Road to the Wall*. This effort, which contained a feature on the implications of the Berlin Wall, noted that it was an example of a trend that narrator James Cagney said might grow further unless addressed by democratic means. Mudd examined the content of these films, which, as he pointed out, always seemed to contain a map that appeared to be bleeding, a symbolic representation of the growth of international communism. He added that, in spite of guidelines prohibiting use of these outdated programs with obsolete messages, the films, which often stressed confrontation over negotiation, were still in wide use, being shown to community and church groups throughout the nation in contrast to nationally stated objectives.

RESPECTED ADVERSARY

Included in the overview of military press relations were comments on specific press coverage of the Pentagon. This segment concluded that the vastness and pervasiveness of the military public relations operations meant that more reporters cover the pennant race than the arms race. It featured comments by a *Washington Post* military specialist, George Wilson, who credited the military for doing a good job of propagandizing the war because of the overwhelming number of military press spokespersons. He also lamented the lack of attention the military received from the mainstream press because of the limited interest shown by senior editors. He somberly added that the development of armaments seldom received press scrutiny, often because of their complexity. Wilson also expressed concern that the lack of coverage could eventually lead to other military problems, on a par with early warnings by Dwight Eisenhower concerning the growth of the military-industrial complex.

Contained in that segment, as well, were excerpts from press briefings in which Deputy Assistant Secretary of Defense Jerry Friedheim, dubbed "a respected adversary," is shown responding to press inquiries with very limited information. Of course, Mudd added, Friedheim wouldn't have his job long if he revealed everything he knew about those military stories in the news sought out by the press. Meanwhile, the Pentagon was described as controlling information emanating from the U.S. Army's Hometown Press Center in Kansas City. Once again, Mudd questioned the scope of this activity through use of personnel at that location, second-guessing the appropriateness of disseminating military information, especially what is known as the "hometown press release," at the taxpayer's expense. He also detailed efforts by the military public relations arm to put a positive spin on network television coverage of Vietnam. In this segment, Air Force Major Jack Tolbert, a former public information officer; Assistant Secretary of Defense Daniel Henkin; and a former air force photographer, Thomas DeMiter, discuss their personal experiences with network stories covered in the field in Vietnam.

Tolbert and DeMiter described successful efforts to maximize the view that the American military was on target and doing well in Vietnam. They explained how the military information arm frequently controlled images and views of the war effort, including one incident in which U.S. soldiers were presented as playing mostly a combat support role. This story depicted the South Vietnamese doing the bulk of the fighting, a story that misrepresented the facts. The Daniel Henkin interview centered on the staging of events, with the secretary pointing out that the CBS taped discussion itself was staged, in the sense that it was being taped in a studio. Mudd pointed out that the executive producer, Perry Wolff, had wanted to tape in Henkin's office but that the secretary had objected, reinforcing the view that any staging taking place was at the behest of military sources.

Interestingly, the Henkin interview, which was also later criticized for rearrangement of responses, was taped by the military as required by the Department of Defense. As a result, Henkin was later able to demonstrate that CBS had taken his words out of context as he had charged; in doing so, the documentary unit violated CBS News and Public Affairs Operating Standards, which set out guidelines relative to editing and attribution of answers to questions during taped interviews.[2] CBS strongly denied charges by writer Martin Mayer that the effort was intentionally designed to make Henkin look bad, but again, in response to later charges, it did admit to a violation of its own internal policies regarding the editing of the Henkin interview.

Another interview segment with Thomas DeMiter focused on network coverage of prisoner treatment in which humane opportunities for recreational and sporting activity were stressed while network photographers were on the scene. But the spokesman said there was limited access to activities when network cameras were not in evidence. In fact, the prisoners had never been allowed to play soccer before, he said. Tolbert also told of the specific network crew's attention to how the air war was being fought, with the military being able to control the coverage, which was, of course, quite positive. Pushed by Mudd to identify which television network had been taken in by this approach, Tolbert responded reluctantly by saying that it was indeed CBS.

Of course, the so-called "Five O'Clock Follies," when military officers presented their daily press briefings, were also profiled. These were often viewed as an effort to sugarcoat and even misrepresent military actions and statistics on troop strength and mortality, as well as using certain terms to obfuscate military realities, to downplay negative aspects of the conflict. In the conclusion to the program, Mudd cited a presidential order for the curtailment of military press relations activity, an obvious effort to bring what he termed a runaway bureaucracy under control.

He followed up with the note that an imposing listing of additional military promotional activities was planned for the immediate future, and he detailed the location and nature of the upcoming exhibits. The message was clear that, in spite of good-faith efforts to the contrary, the information arm of the military was clearly out of control, misrepresenting and perpetuating confrontational messages and images from the Cold War era in stark contrast to peacemaking efforts under way at that time in national political policy circles. To those with military interests at heart, the message of "The Selling of the Pentagon" presented an unfair attack on the armed forces, one which further undermined efforts to achieve a favorable outcome in Vietnam. This message would further underscore disunity and dissension at home, along with other televised events often shown on the evening news and CBS.

TELEVISION WAR

Vietnam was, of course, television's first major war, although the Korean conflict gained some coverage by Edward R. Murrow and others. But the Vietnam conflict, as many critics and historians have discussed, was often televised in living color, and the bloodshed and brutality of war were brought into American living rooms for the first time. This coverage created an unusual and largely unanticipated response. Some of the major media events of the era related specifically to conflict reported by CBS News. Morley Safer's report from Cam Ne village, which documented American Marines setting fire to that hamlet, and Walter Cronkite's later indictment of the war, an effort that, according to some sources, helped to change public opinion, both underscored television's emerging influence on public policy. This was reinforced when Fred Friendly resigned from his post as head of the network news division over failure to cover Vietnam hearings in Congress.

Friendly, who always emphasized the television documentary's potential to transmit what he termed the "little picture," was critical of his organization's failure to provide important coverage in spite of expanded resources and an expressed commitment to telling the Vietnam story from the outset. When CBS stretched its newscast to a half hour on September 2, 1963, only a small part of a Walter Cronkite interview with John F. Kennedy was devoted to the subject of Vietnam. By the time Cronkite relayed his view that it looked like a "bunch of thugs" manhandling associates on the floor of the 1968 Democratic convention, President Kennedy had been assassinated and Saigon could lay claim to being the CBS network's second-largest news bureau. By that time, the "Five O'Clock Follies" press briefings in Vietnam had become something of a dreaded press convention. Combat photographers shooting "bloody" or providing combat footage, preferably from the

An early photo of Fred W. Friendly. He started at CBS as producer of "Hear It Now" on radio with Edward R. Murrow, then graduated to television with "See It Now" and "CBS Reports," eventually becoming CBS News president. When he left the network he became the Edward R. Murrow Professor at Columbia University and host of a popular public affairs series on public television. Used with the permission of CBS Inc.

perspective of the lowest-level soldier or "grunt," was often a network goal, even with the knowledge that military sources disliked that kind of microperspective on the war effort.

In military terms, the conflict always looked better from the level of company headquarters than from a foxhole or firelight, because close attention to combat could result in footage of war casualties, which hurt morale at home. Army Chief of Staff General William C. Westmoreland objected to broadcast coverage of dead and wounded soldiers initially on privacy grounds, and the Defense Department formally complained on occasion to the networks about such coverage. At one point a ban on filming in the field was discussed by Pentagon sources. CBS executive William Small, while sympathetic, he said, to the concerns of individual soldiers, made it clear that the broadcast coverage would continue. He also noted that although network sources felt that the war was unpleasant and ugly, it had to be reported as is and not sanitized for home viewing.

A credibility or press-relations gap began to develop long before the flap over "The Selling of the Pentagon," which often focused on the accuracy of military reporting methods and records, especially reports to the press corps on war casualties, a subject CBS would later address in detail. This topic and network handling of it would carry ramifications over decades, questions about the veracity of military briefings as well as attempts to influence public opinion on the conduct of the war. The military made the expected effort to avoid criticism whenever possible, at times demanding that individual soldiers work through information officers in commenting on the war.

When Morley Safer reported on the burning of Cam Ne village by U.S. Marines in August 1965, describing the incident as an example of the frustration of Vietnam "in miniature," the Department of Defense responded in public by ordering troops to make every effort to minimize civilian casualties. Privately, questions were being asked about the accuracy of Safer's report, his patriotism, and even his personal integrity. CBS president Fred Friendly verified the facts of the story while the assistant secretary of defense for public affairs at the time, Arthur Sylvester, provided Friendly with the Marine Corps review of the incident and a description of Safer as a Canadian citizen who perhaps was not too interested in or aware of the significance of the conflict.

It was noted too that Secretary Sylvester, although he expressed faith in CBS News, adopted a critical stance toward Safer that stayed with him for the course of the war, perhaps, it has been suggested, fueled by the five journalism awards the correspondent received for his reporting on that story. National sentiment on the Southeast Asian conflict was mixed but, in some quarters, growing more strident. Battle lines at home had developed over American involvement. In another documentary, "Vietnam: Hawks and Doves," Charles Collingwood presented an overview of the conflict and offered opposing views by Senators George McGovern and Gale McGee.

That broadcast, which aired March 8, 1965, has been credited for legitimizing dissent on the issue of American involvement and providing an alternative view on official Vietnam policy, but from within the government. Nearly four months later, CBS News presented another video documentary, "Vietnam Dialogue: Mr. Bundy and the Professors," in which McGeorge Bundy presented the administration view from his outpost as President Lyndon Johnson's assistant for security affairs, while then Columbia University professor Zbigniew Brezinski led the opposing side. This was followed by a series of four "Vietnam Perspective" documentaries, which included Bill Moyers serving as LBJ's press secretary.

The first three programs examined State Department and Pentagon perspectives on the war, and the last examined a day in the life of American soldiers in the field. This series continued while a bombing embargo resulted in additional debate at home. When bombing resumed, CBS relied on Senator J. William Fulbright, chairman of the Senate Foreign Relations Committee, for views in opposition to escalation of the war, with specific reference to the Gulf of Tonkin Resolution, calling into question the justification for U.S. involvement in the war.

Spiro T. Agnew, vice president under Richard Nixon, presented a diatribe against network news in November 1969, and this special administration attention undoubtedly affected media decision-making; but it is difficult to speculate on a relationship or influence associated with this particular broadcast even though a number of prominent broadcasters responded to them. Actually, it was a series of Senate speeches by Senator J. William Fulbright in 1969 and his book, *The Pentagon Propaganda Machine*, published the next year, that created a foundation for the "Selling of the Pentagon" broadcast. According to author Garth Jowett, CBS News president Richard Salant also made suggestions about a program on public relations spending by the government. Concerns expressed by Senator Fulbright created additional anxiety and the desire to get more information.[3] Fred Friendly had resigned specifically over his insistence on covering live the Senate hearings on Vietnam featuring Professor George Kennan, former ambassador to the Soviet Union. Coverage was rejected by upper management, and Friendly left to protest the decision.

Many newspapers sided with his action while CBS continued to press the involvement question, including the Gulf of Tonkin Resolution, which gave the Johnson administration approval to proceed in building up the war.[4] Marvin Kalb of CBS let it be known that "drafts" of the resolution existed before the incident had taken place, while many Americans took to the streets to protest in a prelude to the Tet Offensive of 1968 in which two thousand American soldiers lost their lives. That is when Walter Cronkite left for Southeast Asia and returned with a report critical of American involvement that was later said to have affected both public perception and even perhaps government policy, in that Lyndon Johnson reportedly commented to associates on Cronkite's perspective and national influence.

TROUBLE AT HOME

The 1968 Democratic national convention in Chicago was symbolic of the social disharmony of the nation. Anti-Vietnam Democrats had opposed Lyndon Johnson and succeeded in having him removed from the presidential race. His vice president, Hubert Humphrey, failed to rally popular support. The violence outside the convention hall in Chicago affected both protesters and journalists covering the story, some of whom were hurt in the conflict between police and demonstrators. CBS photographer Del Hall was hit from behind while filming protest activity, and Mike Wallace was assaulted just off the convention floor. Wallace was even arrested briefly, then released with an apology. The formal study of the convention and conflict, *The Walker Report*,[5] supported the fact that the event was a police riot in which reporters and protesters came under attack. These are just a few of the circumstances contributing to the CBS analysis of military information efforts with political implications.

War coverage became a preoccupation with the military. On the same day in 1969 when President Nixon was giving a televised presidential address defending his actions in Vietnam, CBS correspondent Don Webster was reporting on a war atrocity, the murder of a North Vietnamese prisoner by the South Vietnamese soldiers with American military advisors close by. The integrity of this CBS report was attacked by Clark Mollenhoff, a special counsel to President Nixon, who conducted an investigation of that story while refusing to identify who ordered the study. This was followed by efforts to discredit the veracity of the story. About six months later, Walter Cronkite reviewed with viewers of the evening news how this CBS report had been targeted for investigation by the White House, with correspondent Don Webster providing details.[6]

The text of that report had been provided to the Pentagon without outtakes, which had also been requested. The CBS anchor insisted that the original report was important for what it revealed about the conduct of the war, but he also stressed how follow-up activity reflected poorly on the Nixon administration and its relations with the press. In his book *Living Room War*, television critic Michael Arlen credited CBS for letting Morley Safer tell the Vietnam story from his own personal point of view.[7] Safer, whose credibility was again questioned, had opened the CBS Saigon bureau in 1965 and become identified with other major stories from the field, which attracted attention in both political and military circles and became the source of controversy. The approach of one special, "Morley Safer's Vietnam," was credited for taking conventional approaches to reporting military operations but adding strong touches of irony.

The traditional approach of following General William Westmoreland on visits and talks with soldiers, or what we would once have termed frontline troops, was in sharp contrast to Safer's own field interviews, in which GIs appeared less than enthusiastic with the war and their role in it. Arlen, admitting that his positive evaluation of this Safer program may have reflected his own prejudice against the war, also credited the networks for their willingness to allow divergent views in their news programming. Later on, Morley Safer himself spoke out against subsequent efforts to revise the role the press played in Vietnam. For example, at a 1983 conference at the University of Southern California, he identified a not-so-subtle movement to "rewrite history and assign the blame to the messengers of that war."[8]

John Laurence, who won an Emmy Award for his "The World of Charlie Company" documentary and covered the Vietnam conflict as correspondent for CBS News from 1965 to 1971, agreed with Safer's postwar assessment. Laurence said that after the Southeast Asian conflict ended, the press corps was viewed as a scapegoat for failed public policy because of the overall quality and consistency of its coverage. For its part, CBS became noted for "The Selling of the Pentagon," in the sense that it raised public awareness and debate.

In his analysis of the controversy involving "The Selling of the Pentagon," writer F. Leslie Smith divides the public debate over the broadcast into three phases, with the first phase lasting over a month and a half. This centered on an attack on the broadcast by F. Edward Hebert, of the U.S. House of Representatives, also chairman of the House Armed Services Committee.[9] Hebert reported that although he had not seen the documentary he had read a review of the broadcast in the *New York Times*. He charged that the program gave a false impression and hurt the military. Hebert's comments preempted second-guessing by two military spokespersons who appeared in the broadcast and claimed that they had been misrepresented, with their statements distorted and taken out of context.

A Marine colonel, John A. MacNeil, who was shown in the program giving a speech sponsored by the Caterpillar Tractor Company in Peoria, Illinois, claimed that the identification of the film excerpt of his talk implied that he was offering a personal opinion, anticipating actions in the event the American military pulled out. He clarified that at that point in his speech he was quoting another source, Laotian premier Souvanna Phouma. But his edited remarks in the broadcast documentary made it appear as if he were violating military policy. The assistant secretary of defense for public affairs offered another dissenting view from the standpoint of a participant, objecting to the way his interview had been edited, he said, to distort his intent.

Both F. Edward Hebert and another representative, Harley O. Staggers, chairman of the House Committee on Interstate and Foreign Commerce, filed objections formally with the Federal Communications Commission, using both Henkin and MacNeil's charges in their complaints. House committee chairman Staggers ordered his staff to begin a preliminary investigation of the broadcast to include the collection of materials related to program production. This was a prelude to a subpoena of all CBS material related to the broadcast and additional reports on payment to any individual participants appearing in the program. Frank Stanton responded for the network with an offer to provide only transcripts and a copy of the film itself, as it was broadcast.

CBS vice president and general counsel Robert V. Evans questioned the relevancy of further requested subpoenaed material for any "legitimate legislative purpose" beyond script and film, the material CBS voluntarily provided. At this point the network was threatened with a citation for contempt of Congress, which could have resulted in federal court action and ultimately a decision by the Supreme Court. But it did not get that far. Confusing the matter further was a request for some information already available for public scrutiny and additional requests from other networks, viewed by many as merely a symbolic gesture, addressing the issue of CBS's willingness to cooperate. After an appearance before the Senate committee by CBS deputy general counsel John D. Appel, the network provided some additional material but refused to offer "outtakes" from the program. Those would establish the legitimacy of editing questions but also raise a number of First Amendment issues regarding the freedom of the press, a fact which was not lost on major elements of the print media, who rallied to support CBS News.[10]

A second subpoena spelled out the request for outtakes, which was interpreted by some as something of a face-saving measure for CBS. The new subpoena also demanded Frank Stanton's appearance before the committee, which he made, resulting in the recommendation that both he and CBS be cited for contempt for staunch refusal to turn over the subpoenaed material. The immediate conflict was resolved when the House of Representatives voted against recommitment of a motion against CBS for their action in the controversy. On the other hand, those involved in the dispute continued to debate the merits of the case revolving around both the methods of producing such a documentary broadcast and organized efforts to discredit it.[11]

MORE COVERAGE

Fred Friendly once presented the steps often taken by those who feel uncomfortable with a documentary, using "The Selling of the Pentagon" as his basis of examination.[12] Other writers cited the tradition Murrow and Friendly established in their analysis and criticism of the program concerning the matter of manipulation versus straight reporting. In his commentary, Friendly added that the ranking member of the House committee that studied the program, William L. Springer, called the Murrow legacy into question, saying that by definition it did not live up to the term "documentary" and thus violated the trust of viewers.

The issue of trust and veracity was subsequently raised by other CBS efforts dealing with the military, not the least of which was "The Uncounted Enemy: A Vietnam Deception," broadcast January 23, 1982, which resulted in a lawsuit against the network by General William C. Westmoreland and an internal investigation into CBS methods by veteran producer Burton Benjamin, who cited a number of errors of judgment and policy violations in the production of that documentary.[13] The program itself featured correspondent Mike Wallace. Wallace, along with producer George Crile, presented the view that Vietnam commanders "cooked the books" with respect to intelligence estimates of enemy numbers during the conflict in Southeast Asia. This documentary was unusual in a number of respects, but perhaps the strangest aspect is the fact that CBS News itself commissioned that internal investigation, which clearly demonstrated major flaws and violations of company procedure.

Through the support of the Gannett Center for Media Studies, now the Freedom Forum, veteran CBS producer Burton Benjamin was able to chronicle and publish the results of that study of the broadcast in a book entitled *Fair Play: CBS, General Westmoreland and How a Television Documentary Went Wrong*. Benjamin interviewed all those involved in the production process and examined the program itself, concluding that many of the codified rules of CBS News standards and practices set up by CBS News head Richard Salant, a lawyer by training, were among the first victims of that telecast. Ironically, legal representatives of General William C. Westmoreland, whose credibility was attacked in the program, were able to use those CBS standards of conduct to demonstrate that violations of those ground rules had occurred.

Just as important from the standpoint of public understanding, Benjamin explained the process of decision-making involved in a network effort of this magnitude and the specific instances in which mistakes had taken place with the apparent oversight of management. For example, he was able to tell of the series of screenings the program received from the executive producers up the line, from the "soft" news vice president in charge of documentaries to the news president himself.

Benjamin also explained how his investigation was necessitated not by General Westmoreland's legal challenge, as when the study first started that suit had not yet been initiated, but out of a decision to see if the program had violated CBS News standards as outlined in a *TV Guide* article, "Anatomy of a Smear," written by Don Kowet and Sally Bedell. This appeared four months after the telecast, the longest article ever published in that magazine. The magazine piece demonstrated the authors' access to uncut interview segment transcripts and other internal documents showing violations in terms of balanced reporting, misrepresentation of facts, and instances in which material was taken out of context. It also indicated that screening and rehearsal of participants for the program had taken place with favored treatment and coaching given to some subjects and with obvious hostility toward others.

The internal investigation by Benjamin reviewed these charges as well as the performance of its chief correspondent, Mike Wallace, who was interviewed for the study along with senior executives, including the executive vice president of the news division at that time, Ed Joyce. Joyce said that a regular review of network news standards should have been mandatory for all correspondents and producers at the network. Joyce went on, of course, to write a very critical review of his tenure at the network, but also later credited Benjamin on his work and dedication to CBS News.

General Westmoreland abandoned his lawsuit against CBS one week before it was to go to the jury although no apology was ever made by the network. CBS did issue a statement saying that it did not believe Westmoreland was unpatriotic or disloyal in performing his duties "as he saw them." In the conclusion of his published study, Benjamin quoted author Stanley Karnouw's epitaph for the broadcast from his book *Vietnam: A History* as being most revealing, labeling it something of a no-win situation and adding, "CBS did a lousy program, and Westmoreland never understood what the war was about."[14]

In the case of both "The Selling of the Pentagon" and "The Uncounted Enemy," military personnel expressed anger and outrage. These concerns would manifest themselves again and again in the aftermath of the war because of the continuing debate over military goals and objectives versus the nature of press coverage, including attention at home during and after the conflict. Of course, this conflict extended beyond television news documentaries.

As far as Vietnam coverage was concerned, a segment of "60 Minutes" also involving Mike Wallace and producer Barry Lando had raised additional questions about objectivity with regard to alleged military behavior during the war that were also litigated, and at great length.[15] Former Army Lieutenant Colonel Anthony Herbert charged that the segment about the war was false and damaged his reputation. The program producer refused to answer questions concerning his disposition toward the story and the veracity of source material.

Another of the "60 Minutes" segments, "What Really Happened in the Tonkin Gulf?" (1971), involving the justification for America's activity in Southeast Asia at the Gulf of Tonkin, is frequently cited by network officials, including "60 Minutes" executive producer Don Hewitt, as being the best report among hundreds that series has produced, while admitting it had very little impact because of poor viewership in 1971. Hewitt is quick to add that if the segment had been shown years later, when "60 Minutes" was attracting ten times as many viewers, it would have had quite an effect on the public and politics because it pointed the finger at Lyndon Johnson. It suggested that LBJ was responsible for bombing North Vietnam and had used the Tonkin Gulf event as the invitation to do so.[16]

In the aftermath of that controversy, it is also interesting to note the reaction by some in government and the network itself. As stated earlier, CBS admitted that it had deviated from its own policy of insuring objectivity in the "Selling of the Pentagon" broadcast and some others, most notably "The Uncounted Enemy." Of course, military personnel expressed concern over the outcome in every case. This concern would manifest itself again and again in the aftermath of the war because of the continuing debate over military goals and objectives versus the level of support and nature of press coverage at home.[17] Filmmaker Peter Davis received considerable negative feedback with his follow-up, independent film "Hearts and Minds" but went on to produce in 1976 the public television series "Home Town," examining life in small-town America for WNET, New York. At about the same time, CBS was also looking at elements of American life at home, including the justice system; usually the evaluation was made in an urban context.

CBS "60 Minutes" executive producer Don Hewitt accepts the Goldsmith Award for Investigative Reporting at Harvard University in 1992. He used the occasion to discuss the best of his program, including a segment on Vietnam and the Gulf of Tonkin. Courtesy of Martha Stewart, Harvard University, and Don Hewitt.

NOTES

1. See transcripts of "CBS Reports: The Selling of the Pentagon," CBS News, February 23, 1971; "The Selling of the Pentagon: A Postscript," CBS News, March 23, 1971; and "Perspective: The Selling of the Pentagon," CBS News, April 18, 1971.

2. Hearings: Subpoenaed Material Re Certain TV News Documentary Programs, 92nd Congress, Second Session, 1970, Serial No. 9216; Proceedings against Frank Stanton and Columbia Broadcasting System, Inc., House Report 92–349.

3. For an analysis of adopted arguments, see J. William Fulbright, *The Pentagon Propaganda Machine* (New York: Liveright, 1970); and, to test the application of that book, see Jimmie N. Rogers and Theodore Clevenger, Jr., " 'The Selling of the Pentagon': Was CBS the Fulbright Propaganda Machine?" *Quarterly Journal of Speech* (October 1971): 266–273; and Garth S. Jowett, " 'The Selling of the Pentagon': Television Confronts the First Amendment," in *American History/American Television*, John E. O'Connor, ed. (New York: Frederick Ungar, 1983).

4. This would later gain the attention of "60 Minutes."

5. See William Small, *To Kill a Messenger: TV News and the Real World* (New York: Hastings House, 1970), pp. 210–213.

6. "The CBS Evening News with Walter Cronkite," CBS News broadcast, November 3, 1989. The follow-up report aired as part of "The CBS Evening News with Walter Cronkite," CBS News broadcast, May 21, 1970.

7. Michael J. Arlen, *Living Room War* (New York: Viking Press, 1969), pp. 61–65.

8. "Vietnam Reconsidered: Lessons from a War," University of Southern California, Los Angeles, California, February 1, 1983. Quoted in Perry Deane Young, "From Saigon to Salvador: Revisionism Reconsidered," *The Quill* (May 1983): 7.

9. For a review of the controversy and political implications, see "CBS and Congress: The Selling of the Pentagon Papers," *Educational Broadcasting Review* (Winter 1971–72); F. Leslie Smith, "CBS Reports: The Selling of the Pentagon," in *Mass News: Practices, Controversies and Alternatives*, David J. Leroy and Christopher H. Sterling, eds. (Englewood Cliffs, NJ: Prentice-Hall, 1973); and F. Leslie Smith, " 'Selling of the Pentagon' and the First Amendment," *Journalism History* (Spring 1975): 2–5, 14. For an industry account, see Rufus Crater's "Perspective on the News: What the Shooting Was All About," *Broadcasting*, July 19, 1971, pp. 20–22.

10. See "They're Standing in Line behind CBS," *Broadcasting*, April 19, 1971, pp. 19–20, " 'Selling of Pentagon' Wins Special Peabody," *Broadcasting*, April 19, 1971, p. 21; and "ASNE Condemns Subpoena of CBS," *Broadcasting*, April 19, 1971, p. 21. Later, see "Staggers Contempt Move Assailed," *Broadcasting*, July 12, 1971, pp. 42–43; and "Staggers Headed Off at Pass," *Broadcasting*, July 19, 1971, pp. 17–19.

11. For a discussion of the distinction in types of documentaries see Hal Himmelstein, "Television News and the Television Documentary," in *Television Myth and the American Mind* (New York: Praeger, 1984), pp. 197–231, reprinted in Horace Newcomb, *Television: The Critical View* (New York: Oxford University Press, 1987), pp. 255–291.

12. See "Unmasking the Pentagon," *Newsweek*, March 8, 1971; "Face Off on the First Amendment," *Broadcasting*, April 26, 1971, p. 36; Fred W. Friendly, "The Unselling of the 'Selling of the Pentagon,' " *Harper's*, June 1971; and Reed Irvine, "The Selling of the Selling of the Pentagon," *National Review*, August 10, 1971. Robert Sherrill, "The Happy Ending (Maybe) of 'The Selling of the Pentagon,' " *New York Times Magazine*, May 16, 1971; and Bill Leonard's account, *In the Storm of the Eye: A Lifetime at CBS* (New York: G. P. Putnam's Sons, 1987), pp. 222–224.

13. Burton Benjamin, *Fair Play: CBS, General Westmoreland, and How a Television Documentary Went Wrong* (New York: Harper and Row, 1988).

14. See also "Westmoreland Takes on CBS," *Newsweek*, October 22, 1984, pp. 60–64; and "Judge Wants to Pick the Mind and Notes of Wallace, Lando in Libel Suit against CBS's '60 Minutes,' " *Broadcasting*, January 24, 1977, p. 57.

15. See *Herbert v. Lando*, 441 U.S. 153, 99 S. Ct. 1653 (1079). For a very preliminary piece on the conflict, which predates extended litigation on the story, see Barry Lando's account of the CBS development of the story, from the standpoint of the segment producer, in "The Herbert Affair," in the second edition of *Reading in Mass Communication: Concepts and Issues in the Mass Media*, Michael C. Emery and Ted Curtis Smythe, eds. (Dubuque, IA: William C. Brown, 1974), pp. 154–167. For a more comprehensive treatment of the series, see Axel Madsen, *60 Minutes: The Power and the Politics of America's Most Popular TV News Show* (New York: Dodd, Mead and Company, 1984), pp. 100–103.

16. See "What Really Happened at the Gulf of Tonkin?" "60 Minutes," CBS broadcast, March 16, 1971; and Don Hewitt, *Minute by Minute . . .* (New York: Random House, 1985), pp. 47–49.

17. See Jonathan Friendly, "CBS Producer Defends Program on Vietnam," *New York Times*, July 17, 1982, p. 44; John Corry, "Weighing the Facts in Westmoreland vs. CBS," *New York Times*, September 4, 1983, p. B19; William A. Henry III, "Autopsy on a CBS 'Expose,' " *Time*, July 26, 1982, p. 40; and Daniel C. Hallin, *The "Uncensored War": The Media and Vietnam* (Berkeley: University of California Press, 1986).

Chapter 9

URBAN QUESTIONS

Shortly after the assassination of Dr. Martin Luther King, Jr., and on the heels of a number of violent racial demonstrations and riots in 1968, CBS decided to broadcast "Of Black America," a series of three documentaries about the black experience in America. Written by Andy Rooney and produced by Jay McMullen, with Bill Cosby serving as host, Part One of the series examined how African American history was presented in the United States. The title, "Black History: Lost, Stolen or Strayed?" set the parameters of the problem, offering the story of an untold, or at least underreported, aspect of American life and culture.[1] Cosby, in very evenhanded and low-key fashion, conveyed a sense of outrage while relating the depiction of African Americans in an educational context, using both historic and more contemporary pop culture sources.

The program began and ended in classroom settings. The opening focused attention on what appeared to be a fairly representative classroom of young black students singing songs under a teacher's watchful eye. When they ended a song, Bill Cosby discussed the class itself and the knowledge and perspective the students were acquiring, as well as some information being left out, a number of significant contributions made by African Americans. Cosby mentioned specifically how a number of black inventors, discoverers, soldiers, and even cowboys had been left out of the history books.

Cosby talked about Norbert Rillieux, who invented a vacuum pan that revolutionized sugar refining; Jan Ernst Matelgier, whose invention made the mass production of shoes possible; and Jean Baptiste duSable, founder of Chicago. The contributions of the first man to reach the North Pole, the navigator to Admiral Peary, Mathew Henson, and the first to successfully perform open-heart surgery, Daniel Hale Williams, were also discussed. More disturbing were distortions and prejudicial statements involving African Americans within the ranks of respected historical texts used in the classroom and the failure of the educational establishment to communicate the relationship between African American art and culture.

Cosby pointed out that there were blacks who made history but did not get into the history textbooks. Textbook oversights included instances in which white artists and inventors had borrowed generously, without attribution, from their African American counterparts. Cosby gave a number of specific and fairly obvious examples of how this worked, then began a segment on the relationship between America's historical position with respect to slavery and its current implications, including one portion of the telecast in which a psychotherapist discussed the effects of obvious omissions on black children. He examined their artwork, for example, and concluded that much of it communicated a diminished sense of self-esteem and self-worth, attributed to years of being subjected to a deformed sense of history that excluded the contributions of African Americans.

Next, in what turned out to be the most controversial part of the program, because it was criticized by some African American performers, the documentary examined how the mass media, particularly film, radio, and television had contributed to African American stereotyping. Cosby pointed out that, historically, most feature films had been written, produced, and directed by white men and that even the film classics had distorted the historical role of blacks, especially the African American male.[2] *Uncle Tom's Cabin*, for example, although dealing with the subject of an African American man, relied primarily on white actors to play all key roles. Cosby said, tongue in cheek, that the film had been remade five times and by the last version "Mickey Rooney could have played the central character." Similar, but even more disturbing, were the characterizations of D. W. Griffith in *Birth of a Nation*, a silent film that, Cosby added, looks a little bit silly out of context but nonetheless conveyed a strong, very negative image of African Americans while glorifying the activity of the Ku Klux Klan.

Cosby went so far as to indict individual African American performers for appearing in films demeaning blacks as well as white actors who went along with these negative stereotypes, which were widely consumed in theaters before the introduction of television. He identified three African American men, Bert Williams, Bill "Bojangles" Robinson, and Stepin Fetchit, as being key examples of the problem. Cosby explained how African American men were usually depicted as being lazy and shiftless in film, and also frequently afraid of dangerous situations in which their white counterparts or female African American characters exhibited bravery, strength, and independence. Making matters worse, the premier white performer of the day, child-star Shirley Temple, appeared in many of these films in which she always projected a strong, positive image, a sharp contrast to the adult African American costars she was sometimes shown protecting or overseeing. Cosby summed it up this way: "She was good to them and they were good to her, sort of like a master and pet relationship."

The host also alluded to the limited acting parts available to African American performers and the nature of the jobs they held in films: almost always as a secondary character and sometimes a downright demeaning role, usually a railway porter, bartender, chauffeur, maid, or nanny. Cosby pointed out that few white moviegoers ever asked themselves the question, Who was watching African American children while the mammy took care of white kids? Seeing some of the preeminent actors of that day such as Bill "Bojangles" Robinson dance into a motion picture through the servants entrance or kowtow to a little girl, even if it was very likeable Shirley Temple, could, as Cosby said, "make some black people sick to their stomach." Also sickening were portrayals adopting the British film treatment with a "noble savage" theme in which the African American character was sacrificed in the film, often shown fighting to the death in the final scene while saving a white heroine from certain death.

After condemning feature-film treatment of African Americans, Cosby examined the forerunners of television news, the film newsreels, and found them equally lacking, full of mistreatment of blacks and carrying a distorted image in which African American men were often subjected to ridicule and sometimes made the brunt of cruel humiliation. He added that even when African American actors were employed in feature films or starring roles as in *The Green Pastures*, a very highly regarded motion picture of the 1930s, the same African American stereotypes dominated the screen, treatment that extended to radio, and later television, with the advent and popularity of "Amos and Andy." Even when this extremely popular show evolved from radio to TV and African American actors were hired to portray the central characters, they were seen as being shiftless and slow, lazy and having special difficulty in handling money and in interpersonal relations with members of the opposite sex, usually portrayed as dominating their men.

With the introduction of a film segment from Stanley Kramer's feature film *Guess Who's Coming to Dinner?* Cosby asked whether a new

African American stereotype was being introduced on the screen, as the protagonist in that film, played by Sydney Poitier, and the supporting players Katharine Hepburn and Spencer Tracy were almost too good to be true when it came to an appreciation for racial harmony and justice. In spite of this, the film was credited for taking some steps in the right direction and presenting a more sophisticated and multidimensional image of the African American male.

BLACKS AND WHITE CULTURE

The next segment of the documentary dealt with the challenges African American people must face in establishing and maintaining an identity in a white-dominated culture. In attempts to look white in appearance, African Americans were viewed as demeaning themselves somewhat in many contexts, the outcome of trying to fit into a popular-culture image of affluence created by white-dominated commercial advertising. In an extended concluding segment, the camera eaves-dropped on an African American preschool, the Freedom Library Day School in Philadelphia, Pennsylvania, where youngsters were being prepared to take a stand against outside influences and pressures to conform.

Students were provided with what their teacher John Churchville called "emotional armor" to anticipate treatment they were likely to encounter as they got older. Churchville, who founded the school with his own money, insisted that the children emphasize the need, for example, to be identified as an Afro-American rather than an American Negro. Bill Cosby concluded this segment and the show by protesting that the treatment these children were receiving, although appearing similar to brainwashing, could be better understood within the context this program had provided, a history of misunderstanding, mistreatment, and misrepresentation.

The concluding segment, with preschool children being badgered for answers by the African American educator, became one source of criticism for the show. Also, not surprisingly, individual performers who were mentioned in the program responded almost immediately to the portrayal presented in the documentary. Stepin Fetchit, Lincoln Perry in real life, for example, called the description of his Hollywood career in the documentary a "hate creating" caricature, which did nothing to acknowledge the role he played in breaking down racial barriers in Hollywood.[3] In fact, his legal representatives threatened action against the network even before the program was aired, alleging unapproved and inappropriate use of his name and picture by the series and the network for prebroadcast promotional purposes. He maintained that the image he presented in film and the role he played in Hollywood development formed a positive step in helping African Americans understand how to use the media to their advantage.

Perry also pointed out that he was responsible for many historic "firsts" in America, both on and off screen, and that he paved the way for other African American performers. He added that his career was curtailed considerably when he insisted that he would not play demeaning parts in film at the close of the 1930s. He also said that more contemporary films, particularly *Guess Who's Coming to Dinner?*, which was profiled in the documentary, actually, in his judgment, had a negative effect on the civil rights movement because it emphasized a single African American character and did nothing to enhance the status of blacks on overall issues such as intermarriage, thus enhancing the aims of white supremacy and African American stereotyping.

After the documentary was telecast, former child actress Shirley Temple, whose films were identified in the documentary as presenting a negative image of African Americans, responded by pointing out that most of the films under examination in which she appeared were based on books and not merely concocted by Hollywood, pointing to the idea that in many instances the image created in the film was a representation of historical fact. In addition, she said she regarded African American actors from her films of that era as among her best friends and that she could never recall any instances of discrimination in the films. She also said that performers working in her films had always reflected the highest levels of professionalism and clarified the point that films discussed in the documentary were reflections of the times in which they were produced, which were quite different in many aspects of American life.

In reporting on the aftermath and response to the broadcast, the CBS network established that the segment of the "Of Black America" series aired on 165 out of 200 affiliate stations, or five more than usually carry the network's news hour during that time period.[4] The network said further that all southern affiliates elected to air the documentary and estimated that overall, close to 22 million viewers had seen all or part of the program. The network also reported receiving over 400 telephone calls the evening of the telecast in response to the program, with most callers registering their approval for the documentary. The next day, fifty more calls and additional telegrams were received, and a number of letters were also registered.

The program's executive producer, Perry Wolff, reported that, of the calls eventually received by the network, close to 250 praised the documentary while nearly 150 respondents condemned it. The Xerox Corporation, which sponsored the program and aired it without commercial interruption, reported receiving forty telephone calls expressing "varying degrees of enthusiasm." It was also mentioned in press coverage that CBS News policy had prohibited anyone from the sponsoring organization from prescreening the program.[5]

Some press accounts also noted that seven black CBS staffers were involved in various aspects of the program's production. Two African American reporters, Hal Walker and George Foster, worked on the telecast. Individual stations were also surveyed for response on this documentary. The CBS affiliate in Atlanta, WAGA-TV, received close to 170 calls with an unusually high level of dissatisfaction registered, nearly 150 callers being critical of the program. Another southern affiliate, at the location of historical civil rights action, Birmingham, Alabama, mentioned that a number of calls had been received at the station, all temperate and well-reasoned, although no official count of callers had been made.

In the aftermath of the broadcast, CBS used the response it had received to promote viewership of its news programming and a rebroadcast of Part One of the "Of Black America" series. A full-page display ad in the *New York Times* on July 23, 1968, said the program addressed "perhaps the single most important issue of our time," the role of the African American in our society. It went on to say that what had happened on the night of July 2 in reaction to that program "happens in some measure every Tuesday on the 'CBS News Hour,' the only regularly scheduled hour of information on network television."[6] The program, which was being rebroadcast that evening, was also praised in the ad through quoted published reviews of the show from major newspaper outlets including the *Los Angeles Times, Chicago Tribune,* and *Boston Record American.*

OTHER ENDEAVORS

The second part of the series, "The Black Soldier," offered a narrative on minority involvement in America's military efforts from revolutionary times to Vietnam. The number of African Americans distinguishing themselves during the wide range of military conflicts was emphasized, prior to President Truman's official integration of troops in 1948. The fact that many African American soldiers died valiantly, although at times their services seemed unwanted, made an especially valid and important point, unlike the series segment that followed. *New York Times* critic Jack Gould castigated CBS News for Part Three of the series, entitled "Body and Soul," which focused on black athletes and entertainers. He said that program host Harry Reasoner failed to focus on the really critical elements of African Americans in sports, including the hypocrisy in the ways they are treated on and off the playing field.[7]

The second part of the third program, which offered interviews with black entertainers including singer Ray Charles, was taken to task for utilizing a highly conventional approach, adding no new information. Although Charles discussed briefly the fact that most blacks were unimpressed with minority performers who catered to white audiences, this and related topics were left largely unexplored in the documentary. Gould condemned the program overall, calling it an "inexpensive breather" that skimmed the surface, totally lacking in novelty and impact.

The remaining part of the series explored the attitudes of African American youngsters toward their heritage and included a trip some teenagers took to Africa. Beyond that, the series examined the feelings of African American leaders toward a growing movement of young blacks toward an independent cultural identity. The final program used a survey to check out race-related issues such as those reviewed earlier by the Kerner Commission, showing an alarming presence of white racism and television failure to communicate the sense of hopelessness engendered by living in the ghetto. The survey also asked both black and white respondents to identify African American leaders, some militant, and the extent to which they identified with their goals. Only conservative leaders Ralph Abernathy and Roy Wilkins received impressive levels of support.

To test the accuracy of the opinion survey, CBS News added program producer Perry Wolff's name to the list and, although a small percentage claimed to be familiar with him, no one offered support for his views. The broadcast concluded by offering some degree of solace in that, in spite of some signs of racism by many respondents, most Americans, both black and white, took a middle road on racial questions.[8] In addition, the vast majority of respondents said that they would not participate in demonstrations if they thought it would lead to violence. The concern was expressed, finally, that some radical elements of society were making it appear as if their views were widely accepted rather than being the exception to the rule.

Former CBS News chief William Small, in his book *Television News and the Real World*, labeled this program "inspired" and said it was "as candid a presentation as commercial television had yet seen."[9] Both Perry Wolff and Andy Rooney won Emmy Awards for their work on the program, and a film copy was made available by CBS for use by school libraries.

In his work *Blacks and White TV: African Americans in Television since 1948*, J. Fred MacDonald[10] used the program to illustrate how the late

1960s was a watershed period for acknowledging black achievements, in an age of urban rebellion. Interestingly, however, CBS was also committed to taking on partisan groups in the Murrow-Friendly tradition and within a decade was stirring up public reaction with an attack on the hunting industry.

FIRING FOR EFFECT

Even before it hit the airwaves, "The Guns of Autumn" had generated enough emotional heat to fuel a firestorm of controversy. The documentary, narrated by Dan Rather, had Irv Drasnin at the production controls. CBS News executive Bill Leonard made the assignment in an effort to uncover the motivation behind this recreation of close to 20 million Americans: "Most people don't realize what is really taking place, or why, or even what the rules are; we've tried to find out."[11] Drasnin claimed that he had started the project with no predisposition toward hunting, and his approach was to sit back and let the hunters tell their story. His selection of hunters became an element of the controversy, as did the locations and types of hunt: buffalo in Arizona, big bear in Michigan, and waterfowl in Pennsylvania. Some of the hunts took place in confined quarters where hunters were almost guaranteed a successful outing.

The program's context was considered low-key, but a prebroadcast screening to CBS affiliates, including a representative of the National Rifle Association, resulted in a call for removal of commercial sponsorship. Some advertisers did pull out before airtime. In fact, the only paying commercial spots came early in the program and endorsed two Block Drug products. Anticipating public reaction, CBS announced a follow-up program, "Echoes of 'The Guns of Autumn,' " to be broadcast three weeks after the original. As in some earlier programs, this proved to be a wise strategy on the part of CBS News in the sense that it showed that the ledger was being balanced in terms of fairness. Some sources, while sympathetic to the message, felt the network was somewhat heavy-handed in its approach, especially with respect to the visual aspects of the program.

New York Times critic John O'Connor pointed out that while the documentary raised disturbing questions, some of the graphic and somewhat shocking close-ups of animal "kills" were irrelevant and represented what that writer called the "Bambi Syndrome," or the anthropomorphic conceptualization of animals. The emphasis on hunting within "preserves," areas in which animals were limited to confined quarters with little chance of escape, undoubtedly left an indelible mark on the estimated 21.5 million viewers who tuned in the program, unaccustomed to seeing the killing of animals carried out on television.

John Carmody of the *Washington Post* called it the biggest flap CBS News had endured since the Murrow-McCarthy broadcast. Carmody also discussed how the debate over the approach of the documentary began long before the original broadcast, when CBS first announced its intention to examine hunting three months earlier. *TV Guide* quoted Bill Leonard as having said, "It's 50 percent from the animals' point of view."[12] This statement and preprogram publicity resulted in five thousand letters to the network before anyone had even prescreened the program, long before the broadcast. When the program was aired, the network was lambasted for production techniques including the clever awakening of nature's quiet new day and its gentle wildlife punctuated by the echoes of gunfire with the sounds of scurrying, frightened animals in the background.

A segment in which hunters are shown partying and acting silly was also target for criticism. But perhaps more consistent with some earlier analysis of CBS documentaries was the view that the content might have been treated more effectively, if less dramatically from a visual point of view, by simply targeting the fact that hunting had become a $2 billion-a-year industry. An approach showing that technology had evolved to the point at which what was once a man-versus-beast endeavor had been reduced to the mass execution of animals via the opportunity to pay for an almost-certain "kill" might have been more effective. In other words, what some view as an American ritual and celebration of hunting skill had, according to the documentary, sunk to new depths, thus inviting careful investigation and discussion.

The evening of the broadcast the CBS switchboard lit up both in New York and at affiliate stations throughout the country. Incoming letters were received in great numbers, and Harry Reasoner, then at a competitor network, ABC-TV, even received a letter of protest. Eight hundred protest letters were received by the Federal Communications Commission. The then chief of the FCC's public information office, Samuel M. Sharkey, Jr., announced an official investigation to determine whether the Fairness Doctrine was violated, but added the Commission's intent to wait for the follow-up broadcast, which CBS said would permit alternative views to be aired, including those of the executive vice president of the National Rifle Association.

Another voice of concern, Representative William L. Dickenson, a Republican from Alabama, issued a news release entitled "CBS Shoots from the Hip," in which he characterized the broadcast as repugnant and incredibly biased against millions of American sportsmen across the United States, many of whom, he said, were angered by the documentary, adding: "To me, this program was just another classic example of how the networks use the publicly owned airwaves to propagate their own narrow, often distorted, views of reality under the guise of 'news specials.' "[13] He concluded his comments by challenging CBS to offer opposing views before a final decision in this matter could be reached.

Years later, Bill Leonard maintained that not a single word of Dan Rather's narration in "Guns of Autumn" was critical of hunters or hunting. He also pointed out that he had maintained an unusual amount of involvement in this particular project to insure the content would stand up to the scrutiny he anticipated. The fact that the program's producer, Irv Drasnin, had never been involved in any project as controversial as "Hunger in America" or "The Selling of the Pentagon" concerned Leonard; and he has said that he kept a careful eye on production aspects, especially with respect to network guidelines on staging, an area that had crept into the debates on those previous CBS documentaries.

The follow-up broadcast, "Echoes of the 'Guns of Autumn,' " seemed to satisfy some critics. Excerpts from many of the protest letters CBS had received were read as part of the second documentary. The narrator of that program, Charles Collingwood, also introduced segments from a film entitled *A Question of Hunting*, distributed by the National Shooting Sports Foundation, which helped to balance the message of the first program. Viewing these segments, one might ask how political representatives from prohunting states who work on behalf of passionate people dedicated to this cause, those who Leonard insisted wore "cultural blinders," would ever be willing to consider opposing views on the issue of hunting. For his part, Leonard dismissed the many letters he received in response to the program on grounds that it represented organizational vested interests and big business.

In spite of this, three charges of rigging content were made and three lawsuits grew out of this film. Two of these were dismissed, with the third finding CBS News guilty of invading the privacy of a duck hunter. He was awarded one dollar in compensatory damages. In discussing the broadcast today, Leonard offers the view that major lobbying efforts, by opposing such broadcasts, have often led to greater recognition and a longer shelf life for some of the major public affairs programming efforts.[14] Ironically, he charges, many of the less controversial but sound programming efforts such as documentaries focusing on health and the legal system and those of major historical significance have received much less attention and are all but forgotten. Is it possible to achieve popular recognition in a field so heavily reliant on self-promotion and controversy? For an answer to that question, one might start at the top of the profession and examine the thoughts, ideas, and experience of one man, Walter Cronkite.

NOTES

1. "Of Black America," "Black History: Lost, Stolen or Strayed?" CBS News, July 2, 1968.

2. For additional comparisons, see J. Fred MacDonald, *Blacks and White TV: African Americans in Television since 1948* (Chicago: Nelson-Hall, 1992); and George T. Norford, *The Black Rule in Radio and Television*, in Mabel M. Smythe, ed., *The Black American Reference Book* (Englewood Cliffs, NJ: Prentice-Hall, 1976).

3. "Stepin Fetchit Calls His Film Image Progressive," *New York Times*, July 24, 1968, p. L83.

4. George Gent, "Show on Negroes Arouses Viewers," *New York Times*, July 4, 1968, p. L41.

5. George Gent, "TV: Common Struggle?" *New York Times*, July 17, 1968, p. L87.

6. Display ad for "Of Black America" rebroadcast, *New York Times*, July 23, 1968, p. L78.

7. George Gent, "The Black Soldier," *New York Times*, July 10, 1968, p. L79.

8. Jack Gould, "Body, Soul and CBS," *New York Times*, July 31, 1968, p. 83.

9. William Small, *To Kill a Messenger: TV News and the Real World* (New York: Hastings House, 1970), pp. 50–55.

10. MacDonald, *Blacks and White TV,* pp. 147–148.

11. John J. O'Connor, " 'The Guns of Autumn' Hunting the Hunters," *New York Times*, September 14, 1975, p. D25.

12. John Carmody, " 'Guns of Autumn': A Recoil, A Response," *Washington Post*, September 27, 1975, p. C1.

13. "Wait for 'Echoes of the Guns,' " *Washington Post*, September 15, 1975, p. B9.

14. Bill Leonard, *In the Storm of the Eye: A Lifetime at CBS* (New York: G. P. Putnam's Sons, 1987). See also Michael D. Murray, "The End of an Era at CBS: A Conversation with Bill Leonard," *American Journalism* 8(1) (Winter 1991): 48–61, and Appendix B.

Chapter 10

MOST TRUSTED

Walter Cronkite is frequently cited as a role model for broadcast journalists, sometimes taking precedence even over Edward R. Murrow, especially among younger reporters. Of course, much of that has to do with longevity and the wide variety of assignments he held, not to mention his association with key contemporary stories as CBS anchor and spokesperson: reporting the Kennedy assassination, taking a position on Vietnam, and applauding American accomplishments in space. It is somewhat ironic that a younger generation of reporters would target "Uncle Walter" as an object of admiration, since Cronkite often derided broadcast news for the use of young people without newspaper experience.

In spite of his willingness to critique colleagues, he achieved the status of "most trusted" by the public and most highly thought of by those in his field. "60 Minutes" correspondent Ed Bradley, for example, pointed out in an interview that of those he most admired and emulated: "If I had a role model as a journalist it would be Cronkite. The first time that I ever had a sense that would be fun, was watching Cronkite do those old documentaries."[1] Bradley went on to cite a particular news documentary in which President Dwight Eisenhower reminisced with Cronkite about World War II, while driving down the beach at Normandy, discussing how the invasion took place.

Many years later, when Bradley, who started his career as a Philadelphia school teacher, reached the network, he was able to talk to Cronkite about production aspects of that broadcast because, while viewing it, the astute young correspondent noted a segment at the start of the program in which Eisenhower was driving the jeep with Cronkite on board as a passenger. He observed that the vehicle was sputtering along as Ike tried to shift into second gear. Bradley said he could remember reading in an Eisenhower biography later on that when he left the White House, the general had to take driving lessons because it had been so long since he had driven a car himself, since well before the war, that he did not remember how to drive. He appeared at first in the jeep, trying to chauffeur Cronkite around Normandy Beach in one early segment of the program, then in the next shot the CBS anchor was driving. Bradley said that he enjoyed that observation, which a lot of people had obviously missed, later clarified by Cronkite.

It is the activity of the anchor/reporter that is often most remembered and most highly regarded. Bradley also said he admired Cronkite for his efforts to get inside a story by studying in depth and making every effort to convey the experience of participants. "I remember Walter reporting on the early space program," Bradley said. "He got inside a space suit and he was doing these flips simulating weightlessness rigged up in springs and chains and I thought, that looks like fun. That's the first time I thought I might like to do that," Bradley added.[2] Thus, another broadcast journalist joins the ranks impressed by a hands-on commitment to a story, even if his mentor mostly savors thought over action in assignments he completed for CBS News.

In a 1967 address, Cronkite pointed out that one of the key aspects of bravery and ingenuity to which a newsperson should be dedicated is the courage to report the easy cliche. In this talk, entitled "The Journalist at Thermopylae,"[3] he focused not as one might expect on the Greek pass where the Spartans stood, but on a gap in credibility, rampant cynicism, distortion, and disbelief accompanying political reporting during the era of the sixties, an era in which the so-called liberal press was targeted for criticism by major political figures such as Vice President Spiro Agnew. Cronkite quoted Yale University president Kingman Brewster's words on the occasion of the *Hartford Courant*'s 200th anniversary, during which he compared the newspaper and academic traditions of free and open inquiry, "the courage to speak our minds."

Ironically, at that time, it was not freedom of speech or of the press that was at issue but the believability of the press and challenges to the veracity of news reports led by a variety of enemies in many disguises. Cronkite identified some enemies as being unable or unwilling to tolerate dissent, what he termed present-day "know-nothings." Without being specific, Cronkite admonished one prominent candidate for the 1964 election who attacked the press for reporting what he said and the military establishment for its systematic efforts to obscure information on Vietnam. He used Pulitzer Prize–winning reporter Malcolm Browne and *New York Times* military correspondent Hanson Baldwin as sources who discussed the military movement toward public relations and away from the public's right to know.

While reviewing statements made from various sources regarding the training military information officers receive, Cronkite acknowledged a natural inclination toward the information gap in Vietnam by virtue of its perceived status as a guerrilla war. According to Cronkite, the army resorted to use of a "body count" as a measure of success, in lieu of the more traditional territorial conquests, meaning troop advancements and the capture of enemy turf. Owning up to press errors in Vietnam, including the tendency to isolate events and take them out of context, Cronkite cited a failure to share accurate information and obscure events on the part of the military as being partly responsible for errors reported by the press. He used the Pentagon's admission that American air bases in Vietnam were almost double that of previous reports, as an example of why problems persisted.

Similarly, he cited Harrison Salisbury's *New York Times* reports on bombed civilian centers as the reason why military authorities ultimately admitted that civilians had sustained injury and death. In light of these misrepresentations, Cronkite pointed out that the public had lost faith in the military capacity to report accurately on its activity in Southeast Asia, misstatement and secrecy being the norm and an increasing cynicism and dissatisfaction being the result.

At the other extreme, among those involved in the exchange of information process, he disparaged political players who adopted the policy of "news management," of bending the truth to their own ends, in an attempt to achieve a favorable image. This challenges the fact, he said, that there generally are no half-measures in efforts to control the press. Attempts to limit the press preclude independent thought and democratic decision-making on the part of the public, he added. Again, Vietnam examples were cited. Misleading figures of troop strength and levels of commitment on the part of the Johnson administration were offered as evidence that all of the facts were not being provided to the public. Calling it a "misleading by silence," Cronkite indicted the Pentagon for its failure to report truthfully during this conflict.

Tracing this problem to the 1964 presidential campaign, Cronkite viewed Lyndon Johnson's failure to provide a position statement as depriving the public of a chance to cast a policy vote. Student demonstrations served the purpose of showing that dissent and opposition views existed in spite of administration claims to the contrary. According to Cronkite, a vigorous campaign with wide public debate might have preempted this dissent by forcing national politicians to come to grips with opposing points of view. He again cited the Johnson administration's gap in confidence and its tendency to function as if it represented a consensus, without a foundation or the desired public mandate. Of course, newspersons of some vintage, as acknowledged by Cronkite, come to realize that if their reports are accepted by political figures it is based not on their ability to report the truth, but on their commitment to causes consistent with those of the politicians.

In this particular address, America's "most trusted" newsman also talked about the benefits accruing to those politicians wise enough to take full advantage of the free accession to information by reporters. He gave historic examples of press restraint that led to misunderstanding, mistrust, and an erosion of confidence in the integrity of government. Good, enterprising reporters help to preserve public confidence in government policy, he noted, and he clarified his view that this principle went beyond Vietnam and applied as well to social programs.

Using an article from the *Columbia Journalism Review* as an example, Cronkite discussed efforts to report on the activity of the Office of Economic Opportunity, a war-on-poverty agency, and the challenges and intimidation that accompanied their efforts. This work was widely cited by the agency in spite of obvious abuses, which should have, according to Cronkite, been viewed as affronts to the public's right to know. Similarly, John F. Kennedy's attempt to secretly orchestrate news coverage in the wake of the Bay of Pigs crisis proved a natural disaster and again demonstrated the error of masking policy from the public.

Offering his perspective on the "one voice" concept in which all government information was filtered from a single source with a unified and indisputable message, Cronkite defused its effectiveness by pointing out that, even in its most benign use, a single source does not translate to a free flow of information in a democracy, particularly when a crisis is at hand. Kennedy's edict of silence during the Cuban Bay of Pigs crisis was effective initially from a government point of view, according to the CBS spokesperson, only because the challenge was of short duration. Extended efforts to manipulate information and deny facts to the American press to prevent dissemination to the public resulted in foolhardy actions with often fatal results, as the Vietnam lesson clearly demonstrated.

To fail in its efforts to inform the public of governmental abuses abroad is to violate a sacred trust, according to Cronkite, particularly since foreign governments could be better informed of American policy in certain areas than its own citizens. This would be an intolerable circumstance and one Cronkite found to be unacceptable. Full public disclosure, even if held temporarily, should be the ideal in a candid, open democracy. Cronkite's advocacy spoke to efforts to strip away the decision-making powers of not only government but also other established institutions: labor, universities, and the press itself, the so-called intellectual leadership of the country. In accepting this challenge he also spoke against sensational news coverage that might provide quick profit, but debase the content and the messenger.

REQUIREMENTS OF THE FIELD

He also addressed the requirements of good reporting on that occasion. While recognizing the need to press deadline demands, he rejected unnecessary pressure that might result in distortion as opposed to good editorial judgment. Likewise, he emphasized the need for newspeople to remain outside the inner circle of the establishment, to maintain a level of objectivity in order to avoid conformity, and on occasion perhaps inviting social ostracism in a vigilant search for factual information. Nearly one year after Vice President Spiro Agnew's attack on broadcast news, in November 1970, Cronkite went further in setting down his thoughts on performance in the field in a speech before Sigma Delta Chi/the Society of Professional Journalists, "The Believability of Broadcasting."[4]

His talk to the preeminent professional journalists' organization centered on the inevitable imbalance between the views of elected officials toward the media and their predisposition toward the belief that they are frequently treated unfairly by the press. In a somewhat defensive posture, he began by lambasting those who would disparage and dissect television news coverage. Then, taking a few steps back, he invited scrutiny by responsible critics and serious students of television news while wondering aloud about those within the industry intimidated by political partisans attacking the press with a distinctive ax to grind. The message was clear: Do not be buffaloed.

Dismissing the moral, political, social, and economic effects of reporting, Cronkite urged his colleagues to get on with the business of doing their jobs as journalists, minimizing the consequences of their actions and ignoring what he called the "apoplectic apostles of alliteration," a clear comic reference to Spiro Agnew's use of language in challenging the veracity and objectivity of news sources. Cronkite admitted the faults and omissions of broadcast news professionals and offered the view that they faced many challenges, not the least of which were those imposed by time restrictions of the medium, using a half-hour news broadcast, equivalent of two thirds of a newspaper page, as his most telling example.

The need to write for the ear, a heavy reliance on stories with video accompaniment, the transient nature of the medium, all of these detract from accuracy and effectiveness in a broad context, he said on that occasion. On the other hand, he spoke of television's great asset, the ability to take viewers directly to the scene of major breaking events and to provide live coverage of continuing, developing stories and in doing so to face challenges unlike those of the print reporter. These demands often cause the decision-making and editorial processes to multiply to the extent that it is difficult to gather all facts and report from the location of a breaking story as if speaking directly to the audience rather than using the proverbial rewrite operative at the newspaper. In spite of this, a high quotient for accuracy was achieved, especially in light of the competitive demands of the profession.

In this talk, delivered before a group of mostly print journalists, Cronkite went on to define related jobs in the field such as the role of the television director working within the context of a live broadcast report. Again, comparing this assignment to a newspaper counterpart, a photo editor, he discussed how the television program director is called upon to make split-second decisions on picture selection. This is, in effect, a totally new craft in journalism, he said, relying greatly on sophisticated but often heavy and obtrusive electronic equipment. The result, as Cronkite acknowledged, is that the presence of both equipment and staff can alter the event itself, although he also recognized the inherent benefits associated with performance taking place under wide public scrutiny.

Using political conventions as an example, he discussed how television's presence has forced the political parties to reform their sessions and decision-making, thus enhancing democratic dialogue and further opening up the process to public view. In reviewing coverage of demonstrators, a particularly hot issue during that period, Cronkite concluded that the tendency was to repel the networks rather than enlist support, as some had charged at the time. Admitting that diligence by broadcast reporters could arouse the ire of those comfortable with the status quo by forcing them to face up to unpleasant facts, he also emphasized the need of professional journalists to own up to their responsibility to give citizens a complete picture of events, thus avoiding a form of self-censorship.

He used potential self-imposed barriers in this address to show how reporting could be distorted, ignored, or tailored to avoid conflict and maximize profit. An emphasis on good news should not, in Cronkite's view, become a euphemism for avoiding bad news. To make an overt effort to include only upbeat, "happy" stories at the expense of significant material of a less genial nature accepts the notion that perhaps evil, if ignored, will disappear from view, a strategy he identified as a propaganda tool utilized in totalitarian environments.

To accept the burden of criticism for coverage of negative aspects of society, Cronkite said, broadcast managers face a professionally schizoid, contradictory position, as their job is to win friends and build audiences for most of the broadcast day, then to switch gears and take the heat for instances in which news stories and journalistic judgment may counter the popular, public grain of sentiment. Similarly, journalists themselves face the challenging task of helping managers stay on course with respect to keeping major overall news coverage editorially balanced in presentation to instill and retain confidence in the American press. On this occasion, he asked broadcast management to retain a stiff backbone to resist challenges to a free and responsible press.

The significance of a strong stand could not be underestimated in light of the diminishing role of American newspapers, Cronkite asserted, and he lamented this irreplaceable loss and the need to serve as monitor over potentially intimidating and constraining threats. He also once again cautioned of a press dominated by majority views, without the vitality dissent provides. He argued against press restrictions applied to broadcasters and called for the need to stand together and use the power of professional organizations against forces within the industry that would detract from the integrity and mission of a free press. The need for introspection and the invitation to offer opportunities for outsiders to evaluate performance were other obvious themes, which professional newspeople must accept as part of their role.

Broadcasters can anticipate and expect unhappiness among political partisans, even when playing a secondary role in covering the really big story. The Watergate burglary and cover-up, which evolved of course from Bob Woodward and Carl Bernstein's initial local coverage for the *Washington Post*, got a tremendous boost in national attention when CBS producer Stanhope Gould joined with correspondents Dan Rather and Daniel Schorr to offer evening news viewers extended broadcast reports on the story, the first, a full fourteen minutes in length, which aired October 27, 1972.

The second segment, which became the subject of extended debate at CBS between network chief William S. Paley and then news president Richard Salant, was edited down to eight minutes. Dan Rather was viewed as being vulnerable to charges of holding an anti-Nixon bias through this period, but once the Watergate story caught hold, he contributed in one additional way to the understanding of that story, publishing *The Palace Guard* and helping to clarify the influence of Charles Colson, H. R. Haldeman, and John Ehrlichman in the Nixon White House.

INSIDE CBS NEWS

In the aftermath of this period of considerable scrutiny and criticism and in an effort to remain accessible in the eyes of the public, CBS put its money where its mouth was and initiated a series of programs allowing network executives an opportunity to visit communities and answer the questions of local representatives concerned about news coverage. On one such occasion a team of key CBS staffers, led by Cronkite, descended on Louisville, Kentucky. "60 Minutes" correspondent Morley Safer also joined with members of the network's top management team, consisting of news president Richard Salant, "60 Minutes" executive Robert Chandler, and former WHAS (CBS affiliate in Louisville, Kentucky) news director William Small, who originally suggested the establishment of the "Inside CBS News" series.[5]

Small had pitched the idea to then CBS News president Richard Salant on the basis of a local program developed at that same CBS affiliate in Louisville, WHAS-TV, the origination point for this national broadcast. The network would arrange for a live audience of community leaders and a cross-section of people from the city in which a well-known affiliate was located offering the opportunity to meet with top news officials, on-air talent, and producers. The CBS people would field their questions and the station would carry the program of 90 to 120 minutes, then edit to one hour. The network would then carry the broadcast nationally, as well as offering transcripts and the complete original to anyone wishing to have a copy. This worked well and meetings were taped in a cross-section of American cities such as Charlotte, North Carolina, and Minneapolis, Minnesota.

At this particular meeting, the CBS managers and staff answered close to twenty questions from community representatives. The questions ranged from story selection and extent of viewer feedback to personnel matters.[6] Some of the questions were driven by broad issues of that day and concerns in that particular area of the country such as press coverage of the issue of busing. Others addressed broader areas, which some representatives felt received far less attention by the network than their importance warranted. A question regarding the sensitive issue of forced busing, for example, charged CBS News with using biased spokespersons on the positive pro-busing side of the issue while ignoring the anti-busing experts. William Small clarified the position of the network, by pointing out that busing not only represented "the law of the land" but arguing, in addition, that most representatives of the other side of the issue would disagree with the assessment of the questioner that their pro-busing side had received more favorable treatment in CBS News reports.

Walter Cronkite led the contingent of network news leaders for "Inside CBS News," a public affairs series which allowed local observers (author Michael Murray among them) to question network news coverage. This segment was taped in Louisville, KY, and aired nationally in 1978.

Another questioner asked why the network was "left-leaning" in its coverage of international issues such as the Panama Canal Treaty. The CBS broadcasters aggressively responded by taking strong exception to that characterization of network coverage, pointing out that on that issue and some of the other most controversial areas of the day, such as abortion, almost mathematical impartiality was rendered. Broad public issues such as network coverage of space exploration and national political events were lumped together with trade issues such as equity and employment for women and minorities in the broadcast industry.

In a couple of instances Walter Cronkite was compelled to outline the process used to address particular issues related to coverage of other hot issues such as the women's movement. At two different points in the telecast Cronkite listed major issues competing with breaking events for network attention on a daily basis. He even went so far as to try to explain the decision-making process, which, as he stated it, begins with principles learned in Journalism 1, that is, to determine which issues have the greatest effect on the greatest number of people. He also offered his observations on political coverage, including attempts by CBS to provide background information on how the newsgathering organizations were being used by political spokespersons to get a certain type of message over the airwaves. "60 Minutes" executive Robert Chandler added examples of CBS correspondents presenting the public with inside information on how political conventions were scripted for television.

Even though this meeting took place nearly a decade after the violence of the 1960s, the issue of television coverage of the civil rights movement and the role of confrontation and violence in gaining media attention were raised.[7] Panelists, including Cronkite, admitted that the network had given a great deal of attention to this problem internally. He mentioned, for example, the extreme difficulty of covering terrorist actions without suffering the criticism that the coverage was encouraging others to engage in similar criminal behavior. Questions critical of the coverage of issues such as alcohol and substance abuse as well as the rights of the disabled were fielded by the staff, who often admitted the great challenge they faced daily of offering fair and unbiased attention to important issues by virtue of the large number of alternatives and limited time.

In response to a question regarding hiring of minorities and women in the CBS management ranks, Richard Salant offered a rundown on network personnel, admitting that minorities and women were underrepresented at the company, with a total percentage of 38 percent female employees and with fifty or sixty minority people in the management ranks. He added that two of ten CBS vice presidents were women and discussed how minorities and women were advancing in on-air positions at a steady rate. He talked specifically about the work of Ed Bradley and Lesley Stahl, both of whom went on to "60 Minutes" assignments, in creating a major force for change in the reporting ranks in the future.

Salant also mentioned that previous "Inside CBS News" programs had offered minority representation and said it was unfortunate that their personnel were not in attendance for this program. For many years, Marya McLaughlin was the lone female CBS correspondent. Among the second wave of female hires at the network in 1971 were Connie Chung, Michele Clark, Sylvia Chase, and, of course, Lesley Stahl. In the Washington bureau of CBS at one time, six out of twenty-nine on-air people were female. A decade later, the overall number of women had increased to about twenty out of nearly one hundred on-air correspondents.

During that period of growth, Martha Teichner was credited for her reports from Beirut, and some of the new breed of female journalists such as Diane Sawyer, Meredith Viera, and Betsy Aaron were also making their mark. In another part of the "Inside CBS" broadcast, Salant responded to a question on the physically handicapped in America by stating that the individual's question was an illustration of why the "Inside CBS News" series was so valuable to the network and not just the public. It provided an opportunity to get into areas that may have traditionally been neglected.

Earlier in the program, both Morley Safer and Robert Chandler discussed the attention segments of their "60 Minutes" series had provided in important areas such as in support for the handicapped, citing a specific story on a major Washington policymaker who had been disabled in the Vietnam War. Safer was quizzed on why some sources for that program did not physically assault the staff while being aggressively pursued for a story. Safer responded at first by joking that that was the reason for portable microphones, so that reporters could run unencumbered on those occasions when they had to make a fast getaway.

In a more serious vein, Safer described sources who often sought to clear themselves in the face of serious charges, feeling confident that they could make their case before the American people. He also speculated that as they may have stated their intentions to less critical audiences in the course of conducting the business that got them into trouble, they felt confident in facing CBS cameras. Of course, that kind of attitude presents a target of opportunity for "60 Minutes." The on-camera conflict and confrontation, the allegorical drama with a perceived bad guy caught in the act, creates the kind of great television that "60 Minutes" executive producer Don Hewitt has often described as the adventures of five news reporters, news "personalities" really, with whom his audience has come to identify.[8]

It is often the story-telling dimension of "60 Minutes" that has caused concern among members of management, along with the physical demands and travel required by the reporting crew. Robert Chandler pointed out, "I suppose the thing I worry about most is balance, in the sense of the kinds of stories we do. There's a fine line to be drawn somewhere in terms of the numbers of uses of hidden cameras and microphones, the use of surprise confrontation, in the expose stories we do. If we cross over that line, we risk becoming a parody of ourselves."[9] Chandler added that the other obvious drawback is the heavy workload assumed by the staff and that by spring the entire group is in a state of physical and occasionally mental exhaustion and in need of some sort of renewal. This is particularly true of the correspondents, who have to relay the essence of the story segments to the viewer, an especially difficult task in political stories.

In spite of many challenges, CBS News succeeded in offering some interesting and at times unorthodox viewing including in 1974 "The Trouble with Rock," an investigation of its sister company, CBS Records. This report included allegations of kickbacks to radio disc jockeys in exchange for broadcast time and also looked at the influence of rock music on American culture, including a review of the payola scandal from the 1950s. Correspondent David Culhane reviewed the rock scene and discussed alleged mob influence and accusations of drug trafficking. The fact that the documentary addressed the operations of part of the CBS family created a stir among some members of the press, who viewed this program as a historical first for a commercial enterprise.

In the late 1970s, the network experimented with "Your Turn: . . . Letters to CBS News," a monthly program hosted by Sharon Lovejoy and designed to offer insight into feedback it received from viewers about news and documentary coverage. Each letter featured on the show included a profile of its source, explaining that person's background and motivation for voicing a complaint. Often, viewers voiced conflicting concerns, which demonstrated the difficulty networks faced in trying to address controversy from differing perspectives. One segment of the November 1, 1979, program dealt with a report on poll results by Bruce Morton reflecting independent presidential candidate John Anderson's popularity with affluent voters, a claim viewers took to task. In another segment of that same program, correspondent Robert Pierpoint refers to benefits that might accrue to incumbent president Jimmy Carter as a by-product of visiting Mount St. Helens right after its eruption. This interpretation was challenged by viewers Jean and Charles Debowski, who claimed the report was a thinly veiled editorial statement on Carter's motives. Objecting to coverage of a CBS Special Report on violence in a Miami ghetto, a research biologist questioned the need to focus on so-called black leaders such as Andrew Young for reaction to these events. The letter writer expressed the view that the leaders selected for network interviews often lacked perspective on events. Another viewer called into question Dan Rather's interview with three CBS reporters who covered the violence in light of the fact that the correspondents, Bruce Hall, Steve Kroft, and Ed Rabel, were all white males with limited perspective on ghetto life.

Professional writer Robert Rosenthal complained about the selection of sources who commented on the performance of Henry Kissinger in office in a segment of "60 Minutes." Rosenthal maintained that the spokespersons for the story on Kissinger, including William Simon and George Ball, represented the same point of view. An alternative source, Dr. Charles Clay, a professor at California State University–Pomona, praised the balance in that report, although he did see the need for Kissinger to explain some of his activity to the public. Also, interestingly, while black leader Vernon Jordan was recuperating in a hospital bed, viewers complained to CBS about network coverage that seemed to violate his privacy. Others expressed an interest in the behind-the-scenes activity of public figures and press performance related to coverage of important stories.

"Your Turn" host Sharon Lovejoy had previously received credit for her work on the CBS program "Magazine," which examined media performance on a regular basis. In one program, "Scared Straight: Hope or Hype," she investigated claims reported in a highly acclaimed documentary produced by Golden West Broadcasters, which had been seen over 130 independent television stations and distributed free of charge to some major market stations. The documentary applauded a juvenile awareness program in New Jersey that advocated teen contacts with hardened criminals as a means of getting them out of a life of crime. In this CBS follow-up, experts challenged the central claim of the program, that juvenile behavior could be altered through fear tactics, as depicted in the documentary.

Lovejoy reviewed the wide acclaim "Scared Straight" received, including both Emmy and Oscar awards as well as the attention of many state legislatures, before presenting the alternative views of critics who characterized the three-hour intimidation sessions shown in the film as mere scare tactics, with a short retention rate for juvenile delinquents. She interviewed some juveniles who compared the visit to prison to a Coney Island spook house, quickly forgotten after exiting the ride. She also offered some insights about the apparent misrepresentation of some of the teens appearing in the film who had been introduced to viewers as hard-core offenders, not an entirely accurate characterization and one that cast further doubt on the film's conclusions.

In 1987, Robert Chandler, who had retired from a twenty-two-year career at CBS just two years earlier, including a stint as senior vice president for administration, offered his views on the CBS financial picture by noting that the CBS News budget rose from $78 million in 1978 to nearly $300 million a decade later. More important, perhaps, were efforts to make CBS more competitive during that era. Chandler, who began his career as a writer and authored a book based on the 1970 CBS broadcast of "The National Environment Test," once explained to *Broadcasting* magazine that growth at the network included expanding the "CBS Morning News" to two hours and offering an early-edition newscast in an attempt to compete with the other networks on weekday mornings.

Chandler also pointed to creation of "Nightwatch," an overnight news venture, and the presentation of expensive summer series including "Universe" with Walter Cronkite, Bill Moyers's "Our Times," and Charles Kuralt's prime-time "On the Road" as being ambitious but often expensive additions to the schedule at a time of increased competition. Chandler also pointed to inflation, efforts by Cable News Network (CNN), the demands of breaking international stories that caught some news organizations off guard, and talent wars initiated by ABC in the previous decade.

Concerns over liberties taken in the public arena are by no means limited, of course, to CBS broadcasters. In an address at the Joan Shorenstein Barone Center on the Press, Politics and Public Policy at Harvard University on November 15, 1990, Walter Cronkite went out of his way to discuss how political manipulation occurs as part of a campaign, along with practices that distort the political process. He noted that this manipulation was first widely exposed to public scrutiny by Theodore H. White in his first *The Making of the President*.[10] The former anchorman relayed the effect of White's book on journalists, who suddenly switched their course and began pursuing coverage of campaign techniques over substance in their reporting. According to Cronkite, they only recently, in the decade of the nineties, have begun to get back on track to some extent, emphasizing the substance of issues as opposed to campaign tactics and candidates' personal lives.

Although Teddy White noted how the press corps had gotten off track years ago, the consensus among observers of the current decade is that the emphasis in political reporting was understood to be needed back on the steak, rather than the sizzle. Cronkite attributed part of public apathy to this preoccupation with political manipulation and an education system not fulfilling democratic ideals and opportunities. In this speech, he also traced the development of television in politics and noted changes in the public interest as early as 1956. For example, when he was accompanying candidate Estes Kefauver on a bus campaign through Florida, the candidate requested that the network correspondent step off the bus last, to avoid attracting crowds to himself rather than the political candidate.

This was long before Walter Cronkite acquired the anchor chair and reached the peak of his popularity as a television performer who achieved the status of the "most trusted" person in America. He also noted another example from personal experience, in which he was confronted by Lyndon Johnson, who insisted that his own prepared questions be used in cross-examination on a network news discussion program. Interestingly, some concessions had to be made as far as the direction of the questioning in order to insure Johnson's participation and get the program on the air.

Cronkite discussed the irony of a study just completed at Harvard by Kiky Adatto, which showed that the average block of uninterrupted speech by a presidential candidate on a network newscast was an oratorical burst of 9.8 seconds. This development of what Cronkite referred to as headline reporting is due to efforts to satisfy the short attention span of what Cronkite termed the "hyperkinetic, speeded up world" in which we live. Twisted values resulting from a process in which no candidate was given as much as one minute of uninterrupted time in an evening newscast during the 1988 presidential campaign obviously resulted in a seriously limited discussion of issues.

Adding another challenging element to the process of gaining and keeping attention, the "photo opportunity" phenomenon which makes looking good in a visually appropriate setting at least as important as saying something meaningful on an evening news telecast, was also acknowledged to play an even greater distracting role in the public mind. This phenomenon was illustrated with well-known examples, including a note of thanks Lesley Stahl received from Republican spokespersons after a report verbally critical of the Reagan administration but containing great video images. In light of this, Cronkite labeled contemporary political campaign overreliance on television news coverage an unconscionable fraud, limiting serious debate. He admonished candidates' use of sound bites and twenty- or thirty-second commercials and said that they should be charged with sabotaging the electoral process in light of their contributions to creating what amounted to purely political theater.

Beyond the issue of agenda-setting for entertainment values, he identified journalists' economic well-being as another area in which the public was being ill-served. He mentioned, for instance, that some broadcasters now represent an elitist class that has little in common with those it purports to serve. Television anchorpeople, in particular, have tremendous economic and political power and can even confer a degree of importance or distort coverage by choosing to address issues, thus defining news events.

Along with anecdotes regarding major political figures, including both John and Robert Kennedy, with whom he exchanged words over various aspects of network coverage, Cronkite identified and condemned the problem of compression of time as being the single greatest ingredient with respect to distortion of broadcast news coverage. When newspaper sources are strapped for basic information, he said, much of the detail and context gets edited out. He concluded this address by calling for an increased role on the part of new players in the political issues information arena, especially CNN and C-SPAN, with more of an opportunity to develop stories in depth, similar to that of newspapers. He also asked for reform in analysis of issues, perhaps hoping that this could lead back to longer public affairs programming on a par with what CBS has already begun to add to its commercial programming fare.

NOTES

1. Ed Bradley, "Later with Bob Costas," NBC-TV broadcast, October 3, 1991.
2. Ibid.
3. Walter Cronkite, "The Journalist at Thermopylae," keynote address at Johns Hopkins University, February 9, 1967.
4. See Mike Moore, "Cronkite Basted; Society Lambasted," *The Quill* (December 1985): 37; and later Walter Cronkite, keynote address, Conference of College Broadcasters, Brown University, reprinted in *College Broadcaster* (February 1989): 19–20.
5. William Small, former senior vice president, CBS News, letter to the author, June 23, 1992.
6. "Inside CBS News," CBS Television broadcast, April 15, 1978.
7. William A. Henry III, "Don Hewitt: Man of the Hour," *Washington Journalism Review* (May 1986): 26.
8. Ed Bliss, "What Makes Don Hewitt Tick?" *RTNDA Communicator* (September 1987): 32.
9. Robert Chandler, former vice president and director of public affairs, CBS News, letter to the author, April 20, 1978. For commentary on the physical demands of the program, see Arthur Ungar, "300 Minutes with Mike Wallace at Sixty-Seven . . . ," *Television Quarterly* 22(1) (1986): 7–25.
10. Walter Cronkite, "First Annual Theodore H. White Lecture," Joan Shorenstein Barone Center, John F. Kennedy School, Harvard University, November 15, 1990.

Chapter 11

PASTOR OF PUBLIC AFFAIRS

Accepting the burden of being compared to Edward R. Murrow or Walter Cronkite means taking on the really tough topics of our times. Bill Moyers, who has been identified as the contemporary broadcaster most like Murrow, with some similarity to Cronkite, addressed one of the most difficult stories of modern American society in the "CBS Reports" program "The Vanishing Family" on January 25, 1986.[1] He looked at the challenges to American family life and focused specifically on the problem of black teenage pregnancy, a topic many agree that few white men could examine without being accused of racism and discrimination.

The report was introduced by Moyers from a ghetto location in Newark, New Jersey. This is a locale which Moyers said was usually not viewed on television, unless some violent news video was being shown, perhaps scenes from the aftermath of a murder or a mugging, he added, certainly not a discussion on the status of the family. From that point of departure, he presented the view that, for the majority of white children in America, "family" still meant a mother and a father; but he suggested that was not the case for youth in the black inner city, where practically no black mother gets married and black children overall have the highest pregnancy rate in the industrialized world.

Indeed, the phenomenon of children begetting children had reached epidemic proportions, he said, which is ironic at a time when educational opportunity and institutional efforts to assist black women were purported to be at an all-time high. In addressing the issue of what some observers might regard as blatant racism in the selection of this topic and backup research for the report, Moyers indicated that the question went far beyond race and poverty and that the objective of this documentary was not to be judgmental about individual choices, but rather to explore why this phenomenon was taking place in a developed country at that particular time. In summing up his introductory remarks, Moyers added that this report would seek answers regarding what happens in an environment in which "mothers are children, fathers don't count, and the street is the strongest school."[2]

After introducing the subject to the viewer, he interviewed a black teenager with her infant and discussed the delicate subject of her pregnancy and its effects on her education. He then talked to the baby's father, a high school dropout, and inquired about the public welfare aspects of the pregnancy, asking if a level of government support perhaps encouraged the behavior that had become dominant in the ghetto with respect to multiple children in a one-parent home. The mother responded by pointing out that government support was not her motivation in having the baby and that the child she bore out of wedlock provided companionship, "someone to live for, someone to love, and someone to love me back."

Moyers offered the view that both the mother and grandmother of this teenager had been single mothers themselves, who also had children at an early age. He added that the father of the infant was also descended from a single mother. This was followed by a segment in which the teenage parents of the child were shown arguing with one another. Moyers explained that after the abortion of their second child, the two broke off relations. Asked what she thought the odds would be that her infant daughter would follow the same life path, the young mother said she would take extra precautions to discuss openly with her daughter the challenges of single parenthood, the importance of consultation, personal responsibility, and protection in sexual relations.

A second personal profile or case study in the program examined the life of a twenty-three-year-old unmarried mother of two, who, like nearly half of all black children in America, Moyers said, had children "being raised in poverty." This sequence opened with a shot of the young mother using food stamps to pay for groceries, a subsidized life, as Moyers put it, but that's not what she wanted or intended, he added. Unlike the first subject of the broadcast, this more mature young woman had graduated from high school, attended a business school, and was making some financial progress to lift herself out of ghetto poverty before the birth of her first child. When the child was born, she left her job to care for the baby on a full-time basis. Bills started to pile up. Two additional children were born. The twenty-six-year-old father, who was described as having a police record, was interviewed by Moyers and profiled in some depth. He had dropped out of school at the age of sixteen and spent two years in the Job Corps. Unemployed for the last three years, he said he would get married eventually when he could afford to have a big wedding, with all the trimmings.

Moyers also questioned the young father regarding the level of support he provided for his children. It was at this point that he clarified the fact that he had fathered six children by four different women. Moyers asked: "How did it feel to have those?" "Women?" the young man responded. "No," Moyers said, showing some slight disgust, "the kids?" The subject said he compared it to creating works of art. Moyers tried to gain some insight into his attitude on childbirth, and the young father said that having babies demonstrated what you have done in life. The interviewee added: "They might grow up to be doctors or actors, and you can say 'that's my boy' or 'that's my girl.' " This segment and subject became a major element of criticism for those who sought to disparage the documentary later on, although most of the attention and disdain was reserved for this clearly irrepressible young father.

Moyers went on to clarify that the children of this father were supported financially by the government welfare system, then he went on to describe how that process of payment works and what effect it has on the recipients. On the first day of each month, appropriately labeled "mothers day" by some recipients, a line formed outside of the mailroom of the housing project in which the young mothers reside. One of the young welfare recipients admitted frankly that, if it had not been for welfare payments, she might not have had a second or third child. She added that she disliked the established government system of support and felt that it produced a degree of laziness in welfare mothers. Asked why the father did not help out financially in raising the children, she said that he tried on occasion to help out but had limited income. On returning to the single father for answers, he insisted that the government should support the children and that a lack of institutional payment would result in chaos.

HEART OF THE MATTER

In an especially revealing segment, Moyers asked additional questions regarding the need for government assistance: "What I'm not doing, the government does," the young father responded. Moyers probed further: "What would happen if the government didn't?" He responded, "It would be a disaster, because you can't give something that you don't have." Moyers, in what was an especially telling moment in acknowledging public concern, asked, "People watching this out there are thinking, why didn't he think about that before he brought six kids into the world?" The response was "Well, the mother had a choice. She could have had an abortion or she could have the child. She decided she wanted to have the child."

The next part of the program focused, to a great extent, on health care opportunities and limitations. These are limited to young children because they are tied to finances and thus viewed as a low priority, especially given strained economic times. Moyers also added information on the educational aspects of the situation, pointing out that the children of welfare mothers are generally poor students who tend to be sick more often and are more likely to drop out of school, just as their mothers and fathers did. Asked why a young mother puts up with a father who cannot support children, one young mother said that she was motivated by a sense of loneliness and the need for love and companionship.

Moyers began the next segment of the program by mentioning a classic examination of the black experience in America entitled *The Visible Man*, by George Gilder. Then he pointed out the accuracy in that book title, because black men, according to government unemployment and crime records, had become very prominent and visible as a national statistic. He presented the view that black males are under pressure in American society to live a life of crime almost from birth, with few avenues to escape ghetto life. Some of the horror stories of life in the ghetto included a story of how one young man punched nails through the end of a baseball bat, then went out seeking retribution from others who had insulted him.

Moyers also interviewed young black men who were aspiring musicians, the "Educated Three," using their street experience, often crime-related, as the basis for their music. They performed songs that described the problems Moyers addressed, including murder in the streets, which often happened, as they pointed out in a song, in the blink of an eye. He then spoke to the mother of one of the young musicians and discussed her personal situation and family history. She was in a very demanding and psychologically strained environment. She was thirty years old and had never been married, the mother of four children by three different men. She offered the opinion that the toughest element of her life in being a single parent was her age and that her youth and lack of maturity had been the key factors in entering this cycle of poverty and government support.

The young woman was just fourteen when she became pregnant with her first child. The father was only fifteen years old. Three additional unplanned children came shortly afterwards. Although she had some limited income at that time, working as a nurse's aide, it was not enough to support herself and the children. She said her part-time employment and lack of support from the fathers made child-care opportunities difficult if not impossible without welfare assistance. Asked why the fathers failed to take responsibility for their kids, she said that she did not expect or welcome assistance from the fathers, because to do so would create the expectation of their being able to spend additional time with her, an idea she rejected out of hand. Asked what her children meant to her, she responded with: "They're my friends. . . . If you don't have a husband, your children are always there. So you don't have to be alone." Sadly, an understanding of the conditions leading to poverty was clearly conveyed through this interview, along with the details of daily existence and the fight for survival in the ghetto.

It was conveyed that the subject's own family had emigrated from rural North Carolina and that she and her children, including her oldest son who was viewed as a borderline case with respect to future prospects, took an annual trek homeward in conjunction with a family reunion. She discussed how her children, born in Newark, were having a different type of childhood experience, one she regretted by comparison to her own background, especially in light of the lack of family and community support in raising her kids. Factored into that experience was the role of the church as part of an extended support system, which was also discussed in detail on the visit to the families' rural home territory.

It was explained that the church was once viewed as something of a sanctuary and helped to establish and reinforce a strong family bond. Also important was the commonality of experience, or what Moyers termed "family memory," which developed common ties with their personal history and an extended web of kinship in the area in which they grew up, an area the New Jersey–born oldest son viewed as dull. Younger family members had trouble identifying the values of parents as important, something viewed as particularly troublesome to Moyers because of a lack of positive role models in the urban setting.

In a concluding segment, another young father of one of the oldest children was also profiled. He recounted a violent personal history, a broken family from the inner city, a life of crime, including murder, and a lack of male role models. He described the continuing tug of war between a violent street life and the knowledge of what he might yet become, given different circumstances, with the proper support and positive opportunities. His views were reinforced by local youth workers who observed his behavior and speculated on his prospects for success. Moyers pointed out that you will not find the prime-time family of Bill Cosby in the ghetto in Newark, but he observed pockets of hope, or what some people in that environment referred to as "damage control."

A black police detective and the operator of a community center, both of whom assumed leadership positions in the area and who worked with local youths, explained their personal challenges. Being products of the ghetto themselves, they preached self-control, self-reliance, and self-esteem for these young people who, they said, find themselves in an almost impossible situation. The detective made the observation that a cycle of government support had undercut family values in the ghetto and that some individuals were now "married" to the welfare system. The social worker said, "We're destroying ourselves." Moyers commented that government assistance, while offered with good intentions, may have helped to create a problem, with the backbone of the family now coming out of a government office, thus producing a cycle of dependency.

The wife of one of the key sources, a community center administrator, Carolyn Wallace, assured Moyers that his documentary and attempt to address the issue of greater social responsibility and commitment to values was worthwhile, to which Moyers responded, "But they won't listen to me." She said, "It doesn't make any difference. You've got to say it anyway. . . . If you say it in your corner and I say it in my corner, and everybody's saying it, it's going to be like a drumbeat, and sooner or later, it will sound." This eloquent concluding comment was picked up by many members of the press in responding to the program's positive message of hope, idealism, and commitment to bring back values in the face of despair.

FOLLOW-UP

The feedback on the broadcast was immediate, direct, and mostly very praiseworthy. A CBS discussion program followed the original broadcast, which Bill Moyers also moderated, including Harvard's Glenn Loury, who called the dilemma the "moral quandary of the black community," of how to convey the message of the erosion of underclass values while providing the proper emphasis on the overwhelming nature of the problem. Dr. Eleanor Holmes Norton of Georgetown University reinforced the importance of the issue because, she said, it undercuts the entire country. Jesse Jackson added that the mass media were now having a greater impact on some youth of the country than the traditional pillars of society, home and school, and other panelists acknowledged the role of popular music and film in forming cultural norms.

Washington Post television critic Tom Shales wasted no time pointing out that this documentary was "as essential as news programs get," and the reason "why Edward R. Murrow put CBS News on the map in the first place."[3] David Broder, columnist for the *Post*, contrasted this network program with the then newly published book by Senator Daniel Patrick Moynihan, *Family and Nation*, a follow-up on his earlier studies on the topic of the black family and urban ills. Broder insisted that since both well-known social investigators decided to focus on the same problem, "a growing culture of poverty," at the same time, it might be worthwhile to listen to their message.[4] He reinforced the view that, starting in about 1954 and with the beginnings of civil rights opportunities, many black Americans were leaving behind isolated neighbors with limited prospects. He added that coincidentally, social mores also began to change about the same time.

Broder reviewed the results of the study Moynihan presented earlier in 1965,[5] anticipating a crisis in race relations, resulting when a group starts to accept poverty as a natural condition. Another syndicated columnist, Richard Cohen, also appearing in the *Washington Post*, compared Moyers's attempt to raise this issue to Walter Cronkite's 1968 dramatic statement regarding American involvement in Vietnam. The fact that Moyers was press secretary to Lyndon Johnson and viewed by some as a voice of Great Society liberalism made the message more effective; he added that government efforts to help the poor had somehow gotten off track. Like Cronkite, sometimes identified as a voice of the cautious center, Moyers had identified public policy gone bad, policy he helped to create.

Measures that Moyers had supported as a political functionary resulted in, or at least contributed to, a tragic situation he was now attempting to address as a broadcast journalist; thus, in Cohen's words, alluding again to Walter Cronkite: "In a video age, it takes an anchorman to sound retreat."[6] He commended Moyers for the service he had provided with this documentary program, showing the American public the truth of what scholars had been writing about for some time.

Another columnist, Jeffrey Hart, said that this documentary offered something different in that many of the people interviewed for the program demonstrated a keen intelligence and awareness of various aspects of their personal plight, so that this was not in what he called the usual liberal mode of "victimology."[7] Hart labeled Moyers a hero of journalism for stating in dramatic form a message known from textbooks, surveys, and private conversations, something Senator Moynihan was vilified for delivering years before, with publication of his first book on the subject at a time when Moyers was press aide to Lyndon Johnson. William Rusher, in a column entitled "Power of the Press:

Listening to Liberals," offered the view that attention by many elements of the press to this particular broadcast was due to Moyers's status as a reformed liberal on the issues involved, a sad commentary on the unwillingness of the press to accept a conservative opinion on a complex social problem.[8]

Much of the press attention was focused on that single father from the broadcast, the one who had fathered six illegitimate children by different mothers and had no employment or desire to provide support. Jeffrey Hart pointed out, tongue in cheek, that the subject's job was, for all intents and purposes, making babies, a federally subsidized "Aid to Families with Dependent Children" position, for which he was obviously eminently qualified. Although most critics dealt with this subject less generously, the fact that this young man was willing to go on camera and express his views so candidly was offered as further evidence that the problem had grown almost beyond belief.

In a January 30 column in the *Washington Post*, Dorothy Gilliam described this one individual as the dream of a fiction writer looking for a character to live up to all the negative stereotypes of the black male. He not only qualified as a bona fide baby maker but also communicated fecund joys with an unrealistic bravado and narcissism, which had created an enormous backlash. She commented on the fact that he snickered and even laughed out loud when describing his personal charms and sexual conquests, admitting that he was attractive to women. In spite of this, Gilliam pointed out that, although unaware, he too was being victimized by both the perverse values of his culture and the historical racism he inherited in his name in the ghetto.[9]

Meanwhile, William Rasberry said the documentary viewed as a whole might be a godsend for teachers and principals searching for material for sex education classes. He said it sounded an alarm that society's institutions needed to get to work to rebuild a collapsed value system in which the government usurped the father's breadwinning role in the family. *Newsweek* said that Moyers's portrait could have been the most important documentary in recent memory. On the other hand, the magazine condemned the CBS network for assigning the program to a dead time slot, saying they also skimped on promotion for this important documentary. But the magazine credited Moyers for facing up to the failure of American society to address the pathology of poverty and pointing out that the destruction of black America is no longer due just to racism or failed government policy.[10]

New York Times television critic John Corry said, on the eve of the broadcast, that television journalism might well come of age with this documentary, or at least "as close to maturity as we are likely to get." He discussed the historical background of the issue of the deterioration of the black family, including the Moynihan Report from the 1960s that had been attacked by many leaders, including Martin Luther King, Jr., on the grounds that it might be used to justify an attack on blacks as being innately weak. This response, in Corry's view, unfortunately made the subject of the report virtually dead as a viable topic for journalistic, academic, or political discussion at that time. Corry summed up the documentary message: "A matriarchal society in Urban America does not work. The absence of two parents encourages root-lessness. The question of white middle class values is irrelevant; the climate of poverty, dependency and despair that the rootlessness causes is not."[11] He identified this as the primary theme of the broadcast.

The secondary theme, that government-produced programs established to address the problem may be counterproductive, was also explored, along with a note that racial stereotypes were mostly absent from the program. The spokespersons were intelligent, attractive people, he said; they did not come across as parasites or losers of society, even though one had to conclude that they are victims of the system. He also credited by name the people who put the program together: producers Perry Wolff and Ruth Streeter and associate producers Kate Roth Knull and Lionel Phillips. He thought they had performed admirably. Corry concluded his *New York Times* column by saying that the thirty-minute panel discussion scheduled to follow the first airing of the program was probably a mistake, that the broadcast should speak for itself and was one of the best television reports in years.

BACKDRAFT

When this CBS program was rebroadcast two months later, Moyers offered the postscript that sometimes a documentary becomes an event and creates an impact that results in public dialogue, going far beyond what the producers intended or expected. He reported that thousands of letters were received by CBS after the program and that, unfortunately, one of the young mothers seen in the broadcast had died since the initial airing of the documentary. The network devoted an entire "Viewpoint" program to the reactions to the program and perceptions of the black community to its observations and conclusions, after the broadcast aired a second time. Among those voicing their opinions from the broadcast location of a leading black Baptist church in Washington, D.C., the alternative view was expressed that ulterior motives were being exploited in the program.

A member of the press corps, Dwayne Witten of Gannett News Service, said that the documentary created an image and perception that was unfair. It reinforced a prejudiced, negative view of black American family life, he said, one that is frequently presented in the American mass media, especially radio and television. Witten called into question the statistics presented in the program and the overall effect of a dominant negative image of "oversexed black men and promiscuous women," which he explained as incorrect and potentially damaging, and certainly not the key causes of the problems facing blacks.[12] American commentators and media critics had a field day dissecting the program and, to some extent, the host and his performance. Most credited Moyers for a careful and fair effort in which he asked simple questions and got direct answers.

Eric Mink, television critic for the *St. Louis Post-Dispatch*, offered the view that given the explosiveness of the content, the documentary was evenhanded and low-key, not alarmist in approach or execution. He added that Moyers was straightforward with his questioning, with supplemental production elements kept to a minimum and with a prominent focus on the faces of those being interviewed.[13] Some critics commented that at times it seemed as if Moyers might lose his temper, given responses by fathers whose comments were most flagrantly at odds with traditional morality or propriety. But the correspondent was credited with being able to project calm and compassion in the face of challenging circumstance and was almost universally applauded for this effort.

Michael Novak, writing in the February 28, 1986, issue of the *National Review*, said it was "one of the bravest TV documentaries ever made,"[14] also commending Moyers, calling him courageous for providing the background story behind gruesome and destructive statistics that others might move on. Moyers later admitted in a June 1990 interview in *American Film* that although this documentary was not intended to have an impact on Congress, it did contribute to political debate about the welfare system because, he said, commercial broadcasting's effect is almost universal and often instantaneous.[15] Most of the nation's press also credited him for including some positive role models, offering and reinforcing solutions to the problem, including the rebirth of traditional moral values once established and nurtured by the family through fidelity, personal commitment, and individual responsibility.[16]

The overall approach of this documentary, like so many others in the CBS tradition, was consistent with views Moyers had been expressing for over a decade regarding the potential of the television documentary form to take a strong stand. In an *American Film* article with Lawrence Bergreen in 1980, he admitted that his presentation of ideas had gotten closer to his subjects and that he had moved away from simply performing the role of narrator inside of an important story.[17] As this process has become more heavily laden with personal points of view it has become much less objective with respect to neutrality and distance from the story. This approach was repeated in reports he did for CBS on the merging of the right wing and the Moral Majority movement and on the status of gambling in Atlantic City, New Jersey. It has also been Moyers's mission since joining the Public Broadcasting Service (PBS) in 1986, letting his personal thoughts clearly show through in a series of popular interview programs with academic and literary types and in over a hundred programs produced by his own company for distribution to PBS stations.

NOTES

1. See Charles Kuralt's statement in Betty Houchin Winfield and Lois B. Defleur, *The Edward R. Murrow Heritage* (Ames, IA: Iowa State University, 1986), p. 34.

2. "CBS Reports": "The Vanishing Family," CBS Television broadcast, January 25, 1986.

3. Tom Shales, "The Black Family: A Tale of Pain," *Washington Post*, January 25, 1986, p. C1.

4. David S. Broder, "Drumbeat for the Family," *Washington Post*, January 26, 1986, p. B7.

5. Daniel Patrick Moynihan, *Family and Nation: The Godkin Lectures, Harvard University* (New York: Harcourt Brace Jovanovich, 1986).

6. Richard Cohen, " . . . And for Government Aid," *Washington Post*, January 26, 1986, p. B7.

7. Jeffrey Hart, "Moyers Said It Well in Series on Blacks," *St. Louis Post-Dispatch*, February 5, 1986, p. 3B.

8. William Rusher, "Power of the Press: Listening to Liberals," *St. Louis Post-Dispatch*, February 12, 1986, p. 3B.

9. Dorothy Gilliam, "The Crumbling Black Family," *Washington Post*, January 30, 1986, p. C3.

10. Jonathan Alter, "Bill Moyers Examines the Black Family," *Newsweek*, January 27, 1986, p. 58.

11. John Corry, " 'CBS Reports' Examines Black Families," *New York Times*, January 25, 1986, p. L49.

12. "Viewpoint": "The Vanishing Family," CBS Television broadcast, March 25, 1986.

13. Eric Mink, "Warning to Blacks and Whites," *St. Louis Post-Dispatch*, January 24, 1986, p. 9F.

14. Michael Novak, "The Content of Their Character," *National Review*, February 28, 1986, p. 47.

15. "Bill Moyers: In a Medium of Sounde-Bite Journalism, He Serves up Porterhouse," *American Film* (June 1990): 17–20.

16. See, for example, Jon Katz, "Brooding, Pious and Popular: Bill Moyers Is the Media's Pastor of Public Affairs," *St. Louis Post-Dispatch*, March 25, 1992, p. 78.

17. Lawrence Bergreen, "The Moyers Style," *American Film* (February 1980): 53.

Chapter 12

CARRYING ON

CBS News was conceived by Ed Klauber, nurtured by Paul White, and developed into a prestigious and widely respected entity in the field of journalism through the work of Edward R. Murrow. Staff standards that evolved over many years comprise a history that predates television news. The sixty-four-page work that makes up "CBS News Standards" describes all of the guidelines related to reporting, analysis, and commentary. Guidelines on interview and editing procedures, correction of errors, terrorist coverage, and the use of polls and surveys offer a comprehensive overview of potential trouble spots, attempting to assure that objectivity and accuracy will be the bulwark of network operations, although at times the rules have been transgressed.

In an address at Duke University in 1985, CBS chairman Thomas H. Wyman said that the "CBS News Standards" could also be read as the autobiography of the organization, reflecting the gritty, everyday, and often confusing circumstances in which broadcasts and issues evolve.[1] Wyman cited instances in which the network faced serious challenges, such as in the "CBS Reports" program "The Uncounted Enemy: A Vietnam Deception," a broadcast he cited as an effort to face up to the past instead of self-imposed prior restraint. When the network was accused of violating its own standards in the preparation of that program, Wyman noted that an internal investigation uncovered and publicly acknowledged its shortcomings.

On a similar theme, he discussed efforts by political parties to question the fairness of CBS reporting as it related to their self-interests. He offered the example of Senator Jesse Helms and his attempt at one point to influence network coverage by urging his partisans to engage in the purchase of CBS stock in order to "become Dan Rather's boss." Wyman also presented Orville Freeman's criticism of the "Hunger in America" controversy for special scrutiny on the balance sheet of fairness. Secretary of agriculture in the Johnson administration, Freeman expressed his dissatisfaction with CBS on a par with that of Charles Colson of the Nixon White House, evidence that both political parties have felt the effect of network attention and tried to do something about it.

Some would argue today that CBS has often been its own worst enemy in many instances because it carried the legacy of news leadership from an early age. Longtime network associate Ed Bliss, in response to a *New York Times Magazine* piece entitled "CBS News in Search of Itself," took time to clarify Edward R. Murrow's many contributions, as well as those of key correspondents William L. Shirer, Charles Collingwood, and Eric Sevareid. He also credited Murrow biographer Ann Sperber, along with Alexander Kendrick, for giving Murrow's legacy and legend a special meaning. As the conscience of CBS News, Bliss also speculated on how Murrow would have regarded major network staff cuts during the middle 1980s, acknowledging what he viewed as a preoccupation with profit. He added that Murrow would likely have denounced the cuts with the aside: "Profits, yes, but don't make it the apple of CBS' eye."[2] His thoughts were an admonition that perhaps a high price had been paid in both prestige and morale, which would be difficult to regain.

For years, television critics have lamented the decline of documentaries, claiming that they were becoming endangered species or pointing out that management support and interest had always been inconsistent, with network attention usually focused more on ratings than problem solving.[3] Recent experience shows that although they have fallen on challenging times, the classic documentaries of yesteryear are sometimes revisited in a contemporary context. That does not always mean that the problem areas they addressed have been resolved, but it does demonstrate a recognition and a desire to keep the concerns and tradition of concern alive. Eric Sevareid, for many years the best-known public commentator on CBS, addressed the issue of influence in news by corporate bigwigs. In a 1976 *Saturday Review* article, he pointed out that in the preceding sixteen years before news became a separate division at CBS its personnel had increased more than 100 percent and its budget mushroomed 600 percent. Sevareid estimated that the company probably spent more money in covering the news during that period than did any other organization in the world. He also attacked the view that since the days of Murrow and Friendly, CBS had become less aggressive in its efforts to address matters of controversy.[4]

Sevareid challenged critics to disprove the discussed conversations he had with network veterans who, he said, could not recall a single attempt by management to cancel a news report or documentary. He admitted that in his thirteen years of doing commentary over the air at CBS, consisting of over two thousand scripts, only three were killed and that different network executives were involved in each instance. He asked rhetorically whether that record could be matched by a newspaper commentator or editorialist. On other occasions, when not scrutinizing the work of fellow broadcasters, Sevareid questioned the broad-based criticism his network received from print counterparts, since "Broadcast journalism is the only business in the country I can think of that has its chief competitor as its chief critic."[5]

Taking it a step further, "60 Minutes" executive Don Hewitt asked broadcast news directors to take note of instances in which they are accused of "happy talk" by newspaper columnists, those who compete with and sometimes copy what they see on television, noting that the work of those critics usually appears in the same section of the newspaper as Ann Landers, Dear Abby, Jeanne Dixon, Andy Capp, and Beetle Bailey.[6] Entertainment values dominate many information arenas.

In some cases, the CBS tradition has been updated and mimicked by other broadcast sources and other networks. For example, the Public Broadcasting Service's "Frontline" series updated Edward R. Murrow's "Harvest of Shame" a generation after the original broadcast, as did NBC's Martin Carr in "Migrant" and Ed Bradley in a segment for "60 Minutes." They found that working and living conditions for migratory laborers and their families had not dramatically improved.

The thirty-year PBS update, entitled "New Harvest, Old Shame," showed that the only dramatic change was in workers' ethnic backgrounds, with Haitian and Guatemalan immigrants, some legal, some illegal, replacing the black Americans as the predominant workers in the fields. But the ramshackle living conditions, low life expectancy, and outrageously inadequate compensation remain a national disgrace. "Frontline" correspondent Dave Marash ended that newer migrant treatment with the same concluding caveat as his predecessor, except that he brought it up to date with "This happened in the United States in 1990," instead of Murrow's "1960."[7] The decades were different, the story was the same.

Just as in the original program, government officials, in this case the director of the United States Immigration and Naturalization Service, Gene McNary, are utilized to provide the government side of the dilemma, pointing out that federal laws restrict illegal immigrants from occupying jobs in the United States, a statement Florida officials were shown to dispute. In spite of the negative findings of this updated story, the fact that broadcasters are still targeting complicated, important, and now classic problem areas shows that Murrow's work was not in vain, as in this case, where his post-Thanksgiving program from three decades earlier was obviously studied as a prelude to reporting on poverty and exploitation, just as in other cases involving politics and social issues.

The theme of racial injustice has also been addressed again and again. All major networks have engaged in investigations showing how discrimination works to limit opportunities just as it always has, except now in a much more subtle fashion. In a contemporary segment from ABC-TV's "Prime Time Live," rebroadcast on Thanksgiving 1992, "60 Minutes" alumna Diane Sawyer, for example, presented the case of two young men, one black and the other white, both college educated, seeking to relocate, find employment, and get established in a major Midwestern city. Sawyer documented how the black man was discriminated against in matters concerning housing opportunities, employment, the purchase of major items including an automobile, and even shopping excursions.[8]

The methodology of this story was to show how both men met with different results given identical circumstances and credentials, except for the difference of race. Sawyer let both participants draw their own conclusions about their prospects for success, given the limitations they faced, in extended interviews with the subjects and with experts, a strategy Edward R. Murrow and his colleagues employed on many occasions. Sawyer herself has commented on the influence of Murrow on her own work, first in local journalism and then in politics, before joining the networks.

TALK ABOUT TOMORROW

In a speech entitled "The Challenge of Tomorrow," Sawyer admitted to carefully examining the classic CBS documentaries at the Museum of Broadcasting (recently changed to the Museum of Television and Radio) in New York. Interestingly, it was forethought and appreciation for his field that led her mentor, CBS founder William S. Paley, to establish broadcasting's first major program collection and that facility in November 1976. Sometimes referred to as "Paley's Comet," the Museum of Broadcasting started with over twenty thousand radio and television early entries, collected and stored for use by scholars and the public. A decade later, Paley announced that he had donated land next to the 21 Club in New York City for a seventeen-story building to house the collection.[9]

Earlier, the CBS network had balked at efforts to tape programs for outside use. Nashville insurance executive Paul Simpson discovered in early 1968 that the commercial networks kept no tapes of their evening news broadcasts. When he returned to Nashville, Simpson, a philanthropist and benefactor of Vanderbilt University, asked that institution if it would consider housing a television news archive for this purpose. CBS initially fought this activity, but taping of the three network newscasts began at Vanderbilt on August 5, 1968. Since its founding, the Television News Archive has become a major source of material for scholars and a wide variety of related projects. For example, video segments of the evening news were used by the State Department to update Tehran hostages on what they missed while in captivity. The archive also supplied actuality segments from political conventions for use in the popular motion picture "All the President's Men." An unorthodox modern art project gleaned from the collection consisted of 369 consecutive evening news sign-offs by Walter Cronkite.

In any case, Diane Sawyer admonished broadcast students to direct their attention to the classics, studying history instead of technique in an effort to relay important ideas in the tradition of the great correspondents and key stories. She said: "Edward R. Murrow and Fred Friendly had courage, but when I visited the museum this past week and watched the McCarthy broadcast again, I was struck as much by the care as by the courage, as much by the precision and the restraint as by the boldness of the stroke that the story would be told primarily through McCarthy's own words and pictures."[10] She also admonished aspiring broadcasters to seek a total education, advice she is obviously putting into practice herself, along with network colleagues, in the ever-growing number of public affairs programs.

Where the long-form, single-subject documentary has taken a few steps backward at the major networks, including CBS, it has frequently been supplanted by magazine programs, which are still able to make gains and attract bigger audiences with important public topics, albeit shorter stories. The storytelling dimension of "60 Minutes," now an American institution, is a throwback to the days and ways of Pulitzer and Hearst; and some writers are also quick to identify the visual aspect of "60 Minutes" stories as key to the program's success. Melodramatic confrontation strategies such as the "ambush" interview are much less likely to be used today than when the series made its debut on September 24, 1968. That introductory program featured Mike Wallace with Harry Reasoner and focused on an election year marked by violent protest, including the aftermath of the Democratic National Convention in Chicago. A segment entitled "Cops" was followed by very visual excerpts from the Saul Bass film *Why Man Creates*.

Sources have always tended to emphasize that the series lead hand, Don Hewitt, has been preoccupied with visual stories dating back even to his pretelevision, newspaper days at the *New York Herald Tribune*, his news service experience with the Associated Press in Memphis, and especially a job he landed with ACME News Pictures, the United Press photo division. The fact that he grew up in New Rochelle, as the song says, "Just Forty-Five Minutes from Broadway" and that his father actually worked in advertising for the Hearst Corporation are also factored into the equation. In addition, he has expressed an admiration for the print tradition of investigative reporting but also an affinity for the unusual newsmagazines of the *Life* and *Look* variety, which occupied American news values for years before television caught on.[11]

Hewitt is often described as someone with a great sense of news judgment who knows how to best use the specific talents of the staff, especially his reporters, but also someone with his finger on the pulse of middle-American interests. His experience extends as far back as directing the historic initial "See It Now" broadcast in which CBS showed viewers the east and west coasts of the country simultaneously, under the careful commentary of Edward R. Murrow. Hewitt also directed the first of the televised "Great Debates" with John Kennedy and Richard Nixon, the broadcast frequently credited with helping Kennedy make enormous gains with voters because of his visual appeal and relaxed demeanor. So Hewitt has always been in the thick of it, with a knack for covering a good story and being where the action is and with an ability to attract a staff who can do likewise.

For practical reasons all of the members of the "60 Minutes" crew are expected to be enterprising reporters with a nose for news and an awareness of visual appeal. Investigative stories are calculated by a reporter or program producer who happens upon something interesting, usually from another news source, something that also promises to be visually attractive. The fact that many stories have already been developed to some extent from alternative sources means that much of the initial digging has already been performed. This leaves the "60 Minutes" crew basically to audition story ideas, in many cases with the reporter who originated the story, who may be functioning as a willing advisor or consultant to CBS News.

IMAGE CONSCIOUS

Other stories come from viewers. The staff seeks out articulate, photogenic spokespersons and investigates the potential for a good visual presentation of facts or opinion. The overview Hewitt likes to present is that he coordinates a large staff of reporters, with only a small number appearing on camera. Newspaper critics sometimes like to point out that the reporter emphasis is something of a charade and that Hewitt has a knack for making American viewers believe that on-camera talent are doing the great bulk of the work in the story development.[12] There is a history of public misunderstanding of story development. The program structure of "60 Minutes" has changed from pocket documentaries and profiles at its start, with letters to the show and a "Point/Counterpoint" segment that featured Washington columnists James J. Kilpatrick and Nicholas Von Hoffman, with Shana Alexander eventually replacing Von Hoffman. This feature was later dropped from the program, in part because of what was viewed as a contrived, artificial format that some staff, including Morley Safer, disliked a great deal. Andy Rooney's segment was added to pick up the slack at the end of the program.

Author Axel Madsen describes the editing process for the "60 Minutes" program in three simple terms: story "hook" or dramatic premise, the "top spin" to maintain viewer interest and attention, and dramatic tension or "heat," often resulting in confrontation.[13] Madsen also prizes the series but offers the view that it has been one-sided, on occasion, in the interest of keeping the conclusions neat, clean, and uncomplicated. He notes that too much ambiguity and too many complicating qualifiers can damage story understanding and effectiveness and eliminate the visceral charge that Hewitt seeks.

Madsen also condemns interviewing devices that encourage sources to believe in a reporter's sense of agreement during discussions, and only later to learn that the interviewer's expression of approval has evolved to disdain in the editing process. In the 1970s, the practice of having CBS staff reporters conduct interviews, only to have the voice of Mike Wallace or Walter Cronkite later dubbed in to make it appear that he had talked to the source, was revealed. The taint of a possible deception created the need for a disclaimer on Wallace's "At Large" radio series for CBS News. Of course, the allegations of deception are denied by key correspondents, especially Mike Wallace, the program's best-known reporter, whose tenacious and confrontational interviews are often credited by some for the early success of "60 Minutes" in attracting viewers but who is also targeted by critics for his methods and persona. David Shaw, for example, accused Wallace of role playing a character in the "prime time soap opera saga that '60 Minutes' often is."[14]

On the occasion of the twentieth anniversary of "60 Minutes" in 1987, Don Hewitt reminded viewers of the program's legendary status by pointing out that it had topped "Bonanza" as the third longest running show in television's top-ten with 40 million viewers and an estimated

$1 billion in profits since its start. At one point, it was second only to "Dallas," the internationally famous prime-time CBS soap opera. Nearly three quarters of all mail to CBS News involves the program; and judging by the number of requests for transcripts of the series by American students, it has been estimated that close to 10 percent of the audience is made up of grade schoolers, highly unusual for a public affairs broadcast.

Many elements of the program have also contributed to the series' success. The hard-news, investigative stories have often resulted in legislation or policy change. "60 Minutes" frequently attacked unexplored territory such as racial discrimination in the armed forces. As segregation in the military had been outlawed since the Truman administration, little discussion focused on civil rights abuses in uniform. But black G.I.s had openly challenged this view, insisting that racial discrimination and injustice were still rampant in the military. Another Morley Safer piece on the legal sale of weapons purchased in South Carolina but sold illegally in New York City resulted in a restrictive handgun law, the first of its kind in that state. Dan Rather's story on the contamination of the James River cost Allied Chemical $13 million in fines.

On some international stories, the reporters paired off to cover both sides. For example, on the issue of violence in Northern Ireland, Mike Wallace handled the Protestant side of the dispute and Harry Reasoner saw to the Catholic views. Later, in Biafra, Wallace traveled to Lagos, Nigeria, and Reasoner covered the opposing side in their civil war, leading some pundits to speculate that perhaps, at some future date, the reporters might anticipate military action and seek out some soldiers to comment on how it felt to be on the verge of attack.

Personality profiles focusing on "colorful characters" such as entertainers Bette Davis and Jackie Gleason, Indiana basketball coach Bobby Knight, and Boston University president John Silber attracted a great deal of attention; but other features have focused on less obvious figures, such as an eccentric academic inventor not credited for his contributions to government research while at Harvard and a Chicago school administrator, Marva Collins, who was credited with a tremendous knack for turning ghetto children into college prodigies.

On a special edition of "60 Minutes," Lesley Stahl offered a profile of Camille Giraldi of Miami, Florida, whom Stahl introduced as one of the most amazing characters she had ever met. A doctor's wife, a nurse, and the mother of seventeen children, she and her pediatrician husband, Michael, had two biological children and fifteen others they had legally adopted. All of the adopted children had been gravely ill when they were taken out of the hospital for adoption. Most of the children had Down's Syndrome, low IQs, and severe medical problems requiring constant care and attention. Stahl chronicled how the Giraldis were assisted by volunteers from the community and childcare workers including four adults who were themselves categorized as retarded. In questioning Camille Giraldi, Stahl stated: "Nobody on this planet is doing what you are doing!" Giraldi responded by saying the children themselves provided her with motivation to see the kids do well when others had predicted lives of failure.

On the practical side, "60 Minutes" explored the cost of care by accompanying Camille on a trip through a supermarket. Viewers saw a wagon-train procession of grocery carts through the store, ending with a major expenditure of cash. Keeping the bill under $500 was a challenge, Camille stated, and when this trip was recorded at $450.21, she commented that she must have missed a couple of aisles in the store. Stahl clarified that the success of Michael Giraldi's medical practice, along with the formation of the Up with Down's Syndrome Foundation, allowed the family to meet these expenses. The logistical necessities of preparing the children on a daily basis for social acceptance, insisting that they be neat, clean, and well-behaved, were relayed in classes Camille conducts for other parents of children with Down's Syndrome. In an update of the story, Stahl reported that the Giraldis, although victims of Hurricane Andrew, had adopted six more babies.

Feature stories on pop culture phenomena such as Harry Reasoner's clarification of what Humphrey Bogart and Ingrid Bergman really said in *Casablanca* or the secretive life of film star Marlene Dietrich and regular commentary by Andy Rooney focusing on his mail or grocery items are also mentioned as important elements, over time, of program balance and viewer satisfaction.

In spite of its popularity, the program has sustained severe criticism and some legal challenges, including a case involving Vietnam combat veteran Colonel Anthony Herbert and charges that his military record had been misrepresented by a "60 Minutes" segment. Another maligned story involved false medical claims.[15] The network settled out of court with a physician who charged the program defamed him in a segment in which a woman claimed she had taken an excessive number of diet pills under her doctor's direction. Payment for interviews or "checkbook journalism" was also raised as an issue stemming from a taped segment with former Richard Nixon aide H. R. Haldeman. But as program staffers are quick to point out, that two-part interview was not conducted or aired by "60 Minutes," even though it preempted the series and the interviews were done by Mike Wallace. Just prior to that interview, however, "60 Minutes" did compensate G. Gordon Liddy for an interview as part of a January 5, 1975, segment entitled "The Man Who Wouldn't Talk . . . Talks."

Payment once again became an issue when it was disclosed that $10,000 had been paid to an informant who allegedly was to have led program representatives to the body of Jimmy Hoffa, former leader of the Teamsters Union. The money was paid in advance, but the body was not forthcoming. "60 Minutes" was held up to ridicule by some elements of the newspaper press for appearing to have been stung, in a fashion similar to those individuals it traditionally assisted under similar circumstances. Don Hewitt took the heat for this lapse in judgment, calling it "the biggest mistake in my life."[16] At the same time, Hewitt took critical swings at both the print media establishment and his own brethren in the broadcast business. He criticized newspaper people for their obsession with the salaries broadcasters earn, which he attributed to professional jealousy. On occasion, he used the show as a vehicle to examine the workings of his colleagues, especially at the local level. In one "60 Minutes" segment, he examined the phenomenon of tabloid television and a preoccupation with stories focusing on sex and violence.[17]

As one might expect, "60 Minutes" program segments were also singled out for criticism by international organizations and American industry. The greatest response came from the American Jewish Congress, and the most unusual method of providing critical feedback from a story was provided by a representative of the nuclear power industry. A sixteen-minute segment in 1975 entitled "Syria: Israel's Toughest Enemy" focused on Mike Wallace's coverage of Syrian Jews and resulted in a concerted attack on the series on grounds of distortion and inaccuracy by the Jewish community, resulting in a formal complaint to the National News Council, then in operation.[18]

Four years later, right after the excommunication by the Mormon Church of a dissident feminist, a "60 Minutes" segment in which Harry Reasoner profiled a fight between that church and a Utah fruit processor, Gary Baum, was offered, demonstrating incredible church influence in state government, extending to the Utah Department of Agriculture. Another much questioned and maligned segment of the program, also with Harry Reasoner as reporter, was broadcast in the late 1970s and investigated operations at the Clinton Power Plant of the Illinois Power Company, which "60 Minutes" charged with mismanagement and cost overruns.

POWERFUL RESPONSE

Illinois Power followed up on the report by producing its own version of the "60 Minutes" coverage of their story, entitled "60 Minutes, Our Reply," complete with video excerpts from a key interview the company had taped at the time to document. By sending over a thousand video-tapes of unedited segments of an executive interview to company shareholders in "60 Minutes" format but with an analysis of the methods employed by the original program allegedly to misrepresent and distort facts in the story, the company showed that there had been an uncharacteristic lack of care in production.[19] The theme of the story was that a nuclear power plant, then under construction in Clinton, Illinois, was a premier example of cost overruns, or as host Harry Reasoner described it, an excessive "China syndrome of cost."[20]

Illinois Power (IP) started its analysis of the program segment by pointing out that the initial interest in the story came at the request of an opponent to the company's plans and that, because of the program's popularity, the damage done to the company by the report could not be calculated. The host of the response, company public relations specialist Howard Rowe, also mentioned that the organization had been assured by "60 Minutes" segment producer Paul Loewenwarter, before the company agreed to cooperate, that the story would be balanced. In spite of that promise, Rowe revealed company plans to tape all of "60 Minutes" activities while on the premises; he added that this strategy had turned out to be a good idea, as the segment took liberties with facts on a number of occasions. In a very well-produced analytical piece, which included the original "60 Minutes" segment in its entirety but interspersed periodic comments and clarification, Rowe began by discussing how an interview with IP executive vice president William Gerstner, which lasted over an hour and a half, was edited down to two and a half minutes by CBS and failed to give the company's view.

A contention by "60 Minutes" that the Clinton facility outdistanced comparable plants in terms of cost overruns was never fully demonstrated, and direct comparisons were offered as evidence in the follow-up tape. The credibility of two IP company critics who appeared in the "60 Minutes" segment was also brought under fire in the follow-up with the IP spokesperson critical of the network's failure to identify the relation of the sources to their previous roles at the company. The fact, for example, that they were both former employees with limited tenure at the plant was never addressed. He also questioned the academic credentials of a source and quoted from hearing testimony indicating that qualifications had been overstated.

In another instance, the "60 Minutes" method of masking the visual and voice identity of a source known only as "Mr. X" was called into question as, Rowe said, the person was clearly identifiable to company personnel. He demonstrated how he came across in similar fashion, with voice and video altered to distort his identity and discussed the implication that the futile attempt at limiting identification on the part of "60 Minutes" could be viewed by some as reflecting a fear that perhaps the power company had some kind of goon squad available to seek retribution on those critics of the plant. He dismissed this as absurd, labeling the method bad theater.

The *Wall Street Journal* reported that the day after the original report, Illinois Power's Decatur utility stock fell a full point on the New York Stock Exchange in the company's busiest day of trading to that date.[21] Two months after the initial broadcast of the segment, "60 Minutes" issued two on-air corrections involving errors in interest payments on a rate hike cited in the original story, as well as a clarification that the Illinois Commerce Commission staff did not oppose the company rate hike, contradicting what CBS claimed in the original segment. Could that have been the low point of "60 Minutes" performance? Possibly, but it certainly is not unique with respect to attracting attention to the program. In fact, most of the major contributors to the series have come under fire at one time or other. Even Andy Rooney faced criticism and temporary furlough from the show when he was called to task for comments he allegedly made to a reporter for a small publication on the issue of minority treatment.

"60 Minutes" is frequently credited with helping television stand up to major commercial sponsors on the issue of editorial independence because of the program's tremendous popularity with viewers. A great deal of heat resulted in 1978 over a segment on sugar, with both General Foods and Kellogg furious that the story ignored some scientific evidence regarded as solid by some, but questioned by others including nutritionists. Those big sponsors of CBS programming (but not of "60 Minutes" itself) made it known at the network that they regarded the views expressed in the story as distorted. Similarly, government agencies such as the Environmental Protection Agency, Internal Revenue Service, Federal Drug Agency, and of course the Defense Department have been repeated targets of the program, as have the medical and educational establishments and individuals within those areas.

In addition to the imitation "60 Minutes" programs, a number of public affairs entries at CBS have recently staked out a worthwhile territory while taking on some formidable issues and adversaries in both extended format and even shorter evening news segments.

Of course, much of the burden is carried by the network's current lead hand. It is more than a symbolic gesture that Dan Rather anchors both "48 Hours" and the network's evening newscast. As an alumnus of the CBS News system, Rather worked himself up from the network's southern bureau, eventually even functioning as a "60 Minutes" correspondent. His reporting activity has touched virtually every major political issue of our day. He covered the civil rights movement from his starting base in Dallas and was even seen reporting from the South on the first evening of that expanded national half-hour newscast with Walter Cronkite. He conducted a key interview with Martin Luther King, Jr., on that occasion and even hosted a ninety-minute special report from Birmingham, Alabama, in 1962. CBS moved their southern bureau to New Orleans the next year, but Rather returned to Dallas in time to report on the Kennedy assassination for the network. He even attempted to purchase the Zapruder film documenting the shooting for CBS.

After being named head of the CBS London bureau, Rather traveled extensively and functioned in the foreign correspondent's role, eventually filling a three-month stint in Vietnam. With the support of General Lewis Walt, he was able to go beyond military press briefings and gain firsthand exposure to engagement in the field. When he returned to the states, he was made CBS White House correspondent and gained a number of conservative critics, Richard Nixon included, for his close coverage of the Republican administration leading up to Watergate.[22] He was then transferred to New York and, in the Murrow tradition, became anchor/correspondent for "CBS Reports," a job he held until late in 1979, when he was recruited by ABC-TV, the start of a protracted battle for his talents. CBS won the fight, with Bill Leonard handling the negotiations, and Rather assumed the anchor desk for the "CBS Evening News" when Walter Cronkite retired in 1980.[23]

In spite of the perceived limitations of anchoring, Rather has frequently demonstrated a desire to maintain an active role in political reporting as evidenced by a heated on-air exchange with George Bush on January 27, 1988. The vice president defended his performance relative to the Iran-Contra scandal by asking Rather if he felt his entire broadcasting career should be judged by an occasion in which he walked off the news set to protest programming of a sporting event that ran over into the news period. Rather subsequently retained his evening news anchor role and was also selected to host "48 Hours," which gives him a chance to address important areas on a daily basis and also keep in touch with the complexities of issues.

Many of the subjects selected for the network's best-known documentary efforts are now addressed by having a single unit deal with a specific aspect of a problem. For example, "48 Hours" and "Street Stories" not only have been able to address critical contemporary issues but have done so in a segmented format that helps them retain viewer interest by addressing key sub-areas of an overall problem, employing different reporters and staff. Press critic Edwin Diamond has termed the series the "antidocumentary" because of the tendency to concentrate resources on a story on a short-term basis rather than studying and filming over an extended period.

"48 HOURS"

The initial broadcast of the "48 Hours" series, "48 Hours on Crack Street," on September 2, 1986, dealt with the urban drug problem and produced the best ratings of any CBS News special of the 1980s. Nearly 15 million viewers tuned into this program with its emphasis on a critical issue. Another key installment in the medical area looked at the high cost of health care, insurance fraud, and unnecessary surgery with separate segments on each. Surgery performed by a few physicians who were shown in the broadcast to have moved their practice across state lines after they had been targeted for investigation showed unusual breaches of faith by a few doctors in two different segments. They also provided detailed background on effects on families in another segment of the program.

Often identified as being among the most politically powerful lobbying groups, physicians were targeted in one investigative "48 Hours" program entitled "Bad Medicine." Dan Rather began by introducing the topic and noting that a Harvard study concluded that medical malpractice contributes to the death of two hundred Americans each day. Rather asked how that could happen in a country claiming to have the best medical care in the world. He answered the question himself by presenting the results of a three-month CBS investigation showing a flawed peer-review system of understaffed state licensing boards by which physicians police their cohorts in the medical profession, with a pronounced reluctance to offer negative evaluation, resulting in very limited checks on their activity.

In the first segment of that particular program, entitled "There Oughta Be a Law," correspondent Bernard Goldberg told the story of a teenage boy who sought assistance through plastic surgery for a weight problem. A mother's emotional testimony supplemented by home movie video from childhood helped the viewer to understand the family situation and how the young man sought help from a local doctor. He was initially dropped off at the physician's office for what was supposed to be a simple plastic surgery procedure for removing fat tissue. Two hours later, upon the mother's return to pick up her son, she was informed that the young man's heart had stopped and he had been hospitalized. Shortly after that, the parents were told of their son's death and that, in fact, his heart stopped beating before surgery, while he was undergoing anesthesia.

After the burial of her son, the mother discovered that the doctor involved in the case had been accused of incompetence on other occasions and had twenty malpractice complaints against him, with six of those settled out of court. Another former patient, a young woman, was asked by CBS to describe what was supposed to be a routine breast reduction surgery with very poor results. At this point in the program correspondent Bernard Goldberg explained how the doctor under study, unknown to his patients, had had his license suspended for a year in 1987 in New York State because of "gross negligence." The doctor had merely moved his practice from New York to New Jersey to continue plastic surgery. It was also noted that he had not held any malpractice insurance since 1986.

In spite of a number of previous complaints and problems, the correspondent observed that the physician's practice appeared to be thriving, and "48 Hours" went undercover to demonstrate how these abuses occurred. A CBS staff member entered the clinic requesting a breast reduction operation. She was shown, using a hidden camera, being told by the doctor that he had performed this surgery hundreds of times, each one a success.

A representative of the National Center for Patients Rights then discussed the problem of doctors having the ability to move from state to state without any effort to track or report activity. The spokesperson characterized this prospect as "criminal." CBS correspondent Goldberg clarified that, in this instance, the spokesperson's language was inappropriate, as there were no legal restrictions in that area. The spokesperson added that there should be a law against doctors deemed too dangerous to practice in one state but allowed to move and start up in another locale.

A representative of the State Medical Examining Board in New Jersey was introduced as someone who had to deal with complaints against physicians and was asked specifically about the fact that some were operating without medical malpractice insurance. The CBS correspondent argued that as drivers of automobiles were required to have insurance, why not doctors?

This personal interview was followed by a brief exchange with the physician involved in this case in a parking lot and his refusal to comment on allegations concerning specific complaints. Asked about the "48 Hours" staffer who had been videotaped during an interview in his clinic office, he denied knowledge of any comments he had made previously. Goldberg ended this segment by noting that after becoming aware of the CBS News investigation, just days before the broadcast, the New Jersey Medical Board decided to charge the physician with negligence and incompetence, adding that he could lose his license. The segment ended as it had begun, with the emotional comments of the mother who had lost her son, accompanied by video of him as a boy.

The second segment of "Bad Medicine" focused on cardiac surgery involving another physician who had relocated from one state to another after a significant number of complaints had been lodged concerning his performance. It was accompanied by the mixed reviews of peers from his former place of employment. This segment also looked at the monitoring process or method of reviewing used to keep tabs on medical doctors and their credentials to practice. It came to similar conclusions, calling it a hit-or-miss system in which some physicians successfully avoid coming to grips with their lack of success by simply moving to another locale. Standing in front of the hospital employing the doctor examined in this segment, a "48 Hours" correspondent explained how the network had received no cooperation in the case, because of a claimed need to maintain confidentiality of peer review activity. This was followed by a statement from the spouse of a deceased patient whose case had ended with the doctor's resignation. An attempt to interview the physician in another parking lot was unsuccessful when he refused to comment; by then he was faced with both civil lawsuits and a criminal investigation.

The last segment of this edition of "48 Hours" offered a close look at one of the medical examiners who, by law in Texas, had no medical training and was appointed specifically to represent patient interests. That role and mission was presented while the individual being offered as an example explained the medical profession's powerful lobbying force, which, as she expressed it, could solve many problems in the field if determined to do so. The correspondent in this segment, Edie Magnus, also told of an intense physician-retraining process instituted at a Denver hospital. The description of that program, which helps to identify doctors in need of fine-tuning, was seen in this report through the eyes of an experienced doctor who admittedly lost touch while working abroad. She elected to sign on for additional exposure to new methods. The retraining program's director, Dr. Pat Moran, outlined the demands and need for regular opportunities for physicians to get back into an educational environment. He estimated that close to 20 percent of American doctors may be lacking in some area of their training.

The segment also profiled a highly successful trial attorney who specialized in representing clients targeted for improper diagnosis and medical care in major malpractice suits. This part of the story was told from the perspective of a high school football coach who lost his leg because of a misdiagnosis, with his legal case being presented as a critical part of the segment. Dan Rather concluded this program with an advisory to viewers to use hospital affiliation as an index in selecting a doctor, as a guard against malpractice.

STREET STORIES

In spite of the characterization of powerful political lobbying potential on the part of the medical profession, both in the public arena and acknowledged as part of the broadcast, CBS is clearly and consistently addressing critical problems head-on. This also includes episodes from "Street Stories," hosted by Ed Bradley, which have received a great deal of feedback from the public, industry, and government agencies. A segment of that program from September 10, 1992, entitled "Accident Prone," which was rebroadcast, showed how automobile seat belts sometimes failed. It drew an extraordinary response from government sources as well as the automotive industry.[24] Using the files of the industry itself, reporter Roberta Baskin demonstrated how center-button seat belts, standard features on most American cars, failed when subjected to severe jolts such as those experienced in multiple impact or rollover accidents.

Parents Virginia and James Boyle explained how they had viewed this "Street Stories" program and saw the segment that provided some clue as to why, just three weeks earlier, their seventeen-year-old daughter, Michelle, died when her automobile flipped over with her reportedly being thrown from the vehicle. Mr. Boyle, a former driving instructor, revisited the scene of the accident with the CBS reporter and described his sorrow, initial bewilderment, and eventual anger, given his family's obsession with auto safety and the growing understanding that indeed his daughter's death must have been due to a faulty seat belt, as described as a growing concern on the initial CBS airing of this story.

The original segment included denials by auto industry spokespeople who clarified their position on the unlatching of seat belts in accidents by placing an advertisement in the *New York Times*. Addressed as an "Open Letter to the Driving Public," it advised television viewers not to be misled by "Street Stories" about the reliability of seat belts. Correspondent Baskin discussed denials by the National Highway Safety Administration, when they were besieged with calls after the first broadcast, that the problem existed in the "real world" of automobile accidents. She also quoted from a letter she had received from industry sources saying that there was not a single instance in which crashes created the outcome described in the program. CBS followed with video of test crashes from industry sources, which indicated a problem. It also included taped segments of a sworn deposition by an auto engineer attesting to the fact that he had helped to screw seat-belt bottoms down in an effort to avoid having the belts jolt open in industry test crashes.

Speaking in the next segment from the United States Patent Office, Baskin explained how several seat-belt manufacturers acknowledged design flaws in some models in an effort to obtain new patents. Additional evidence in the form of letters of complaint from consumers was backed up by a statement from Joan Claybrook, who once headed the National Highway Traffic Safety Administration and who questioned how the government could have dismissed this question. She urged the start of a full-scale investigation. An automotive engineer was also identified in the show as someone who had been aware of this issue for over a decade and who issued a critical report as early as 1978, as head of the government's office of defects investigations.

At that time, he reportedly tested over two hundred seat belts, and fifty of those opened. Beyond that, among certain models, belts opened close to 50 percent of the time when struck from behind during the test. In spite of this, little attention was paid, according to one source, because safety-belt use was relatively low at that juncture, the point at which complaints first started to register at the relevant government agencies. Jerry Curry, a former agency administrator who resigned from his post, also noted the need for study based on the volume of complaints, which was steadily mounting. Concluding the segment, Roberta Baskin accompanied Jim Boyle, the father of the teenager killed in the accident described at the start of the program, to the location of the car in which his daughter was driving when the accident occurred. Together, they inspected the vehicle while discussing the response he had received from government sources saying that, upon review, their investigation revealed that his daughter's belt was in use when the accident occurred.

Mr. Boyle and reporter Baskin tested the seat belt manually first, then used a jolting blow to the mechanism to show how it opened upon impact, indicating that the belt could have opened in the accident. "Street Stories" host Ed Bradley concluded this segment by saying that both the Federal Transportation Office and the automakers refused to be interviewed for the broadcast, while also noting that more autos were now being manufactured with alternative, no-button seat-belt designs. He noted that government action would be required for a recall of autos with defective seat belts while urging viewers, in spite of the report, to continue to buckle up for safety on the road.

Ironically, a competing network series, "Dateline NBC," was taken to task that same season for reporting on explosions during a demonstration of side accident collision in General Motors trucks. GMC sued NBC for defamation when it was revealed that small incendiary devices had been added to the demonstration vehicle to insure an explosion, flames, and good video to accompany the story. As a follow-up to the lawsuit, in a highly unusual move, "Dateline NBC" program hosts Stone Phillips and Jane Pauley explained what happened, apologizing to GMC and the public on the air.

General Motors dropped the suit while a variety of sources castigated NBC for the violation of journalistic norms in this case. Charles Eisendroth of the University of Michigan described the poor judgment in this case as being symptomatic of broadcast efforts to be sensational and accurate at the same time.[25] NBC News president Michael Gartner hired two outside lawyers to conduct a full review of the facts and to provide legal advice to NBC.[26] Shortly after that, Gartner himself resigned from his position at NBC. Some critics viewed this fiasco as an example of an error attributable to a program that was still finding its way and attempting to attract attention to itself. Others regarded it as a failure to acknowledge ethical considerations in the field. Columnist Richard Cohen cited his former professor from Columbia University Graduate School of Journalism as one who always acknowledged intense competitive pressures in getting out an important story, but condemned the response of NBC in this case, as being based as much on business as on ethical concerns.[27] Short-term financial interests had seemed to take precedence over traditional journalistic norms at NBC.

Even in the development of CBS programs such as "48 Hours" and "Street Stories," critics are quick to point out that many stories still pander to ratings interests and that attempts at innovation have sometimes failed. One series, "West 57th," was soundly trounced for efforts at storytelling with an emphasis on visual appeal, playing down the narrative details of reports and focusing instead on the presentational techniques of other forms of commercial television including advertising, sports, and entertainment.[28] The approach assumed a visual literacy on the part of what it hoped would be a generation of younger viewers and, while this particular effort failed to attract a following, part of the success of some of the network's other offerings can be attributed to the distinct audience and approach of these programs.

SUNDAY MORNING

CBS "Sunday Morning" with Charles Kuralt attracts an upper-income viewership with a higher level of education and a leisurely, some insist "folksy," low-key appeal, carefully crafted with an orientation toward being an "electronic Sunday newspaper." Intentionally designed by former CBS News president Bill Leonard with the Sunday morning time slot in mind, the program was guided initially by executive producer Robert J. "Shad" Northshield, who went on to teach at Columbia University. He is thought of as the man behind the vision of "Sunday Morning," which has acquired the distinction of being regarded as literate television fare, a video work of art with emphasis on literature, classical music, the arts, and photography. These elements frequently combine to form a visual essay, reflecting its first producer's personal interests in areas such as wildlife photography and art history. This approach reduces broadcast rules of the road to a bare minimum.

Northshield started his work with CBS in 1953 and produced, among other things, "Seven Lively Arts." He left to become a columnist for the *Chicago Sun-Times*, then went to work for NBC as producer of "Today." This was followed by a stint as executive in charge of the news division and the "Huntley-Brinkley Report." He produced long-form documentaries in the early seventies, including a three-hour program on the civil rights struggle, "The American Revolution of '63," then handled network news coverage including election-night political chores and, ultimately, Watergate and the resignation of Richard Nixon.[29] His "Sunday Morning" assignment was a step back from hard news and its demands.

"Sunday Morning" frequently violates journalistic conventions at least indirectly, attempting to instruct viewers on how and what to think about a given subject, a tradition established in the video field over many years. For example, works of art on "Sunday Morning" are photographed in full frame first, then reduced to various parts, an attempt to duplicate the natural instincts of someone inspecting fine art while maintaining audio silence, or what traditional broadcasters would regard as the ultimate violation of production norms, "dead air." Beyond Kuralt's midprogram conversation with correspondents, the reporters are frequently hidden from view altogether, covering stories in the field but commenting only briefly, while their interview subjects are instructed to look directly at the camera rather than at an imaginary host, another violation of a convention set up for ease in editing and understanding.

"Sunday Morning" attempted to expand on the program's base of popularity under Linda Mason, to include hard news coverage consistent with a joint role she held that included responsibility for the weekend news on CBS. Innovations under her watch included international coverage of the Reagan-Gorbachev summit and travel to Japan and China. The program also employs its own television critics, which at one time included the former Pulitzer Prize–winning author of *The Newscasters*, Ron Powers. He has written extensively on the influence of the media and broadcast journalists whom, along with print journalists, he sees as not always performing "the vigorous, adversary, check on government intervening role" they traditionally played in America.[30] In spite of this indictment, CBS has continued to address important issues in a context that would attract viewers and advertisers.

GULF WAR COVERAGE

New competitive forces in the international news market and especially the introduction of CNN have hurt the competitive stance of CBS News, especially in the coverage of the war in the Persian Gulf. The traditional leader in military combat coverage, beginning with Edward R. Murrow, was embarrassed initially by its failure to get on the air early with a reporter from Bagdad, then was unable to offer a field report by Allen Pizzey once contact was made. CBS was able to redeem itself with early reports of Iraqi Scud attacks, the first network to do so, supplemented with coverage of the effects in Tel Aviv and descriptions of military footage of devastation from "smart" bombs that zeroed in on selected targets.

They also were first to report on the start of the ground war. Lesley Stahl offered early observations on the conflict along with Charles Kuralt, while Walter Cronkite was brought back to join anchor Dan Rather in the network news studios. This move was interpreted by some newspaper critics as a clear effort by CBS to bolster ratings and regain its status among broadcast news organizations. To that end, Rather was applauded for his interpretation of the events of the war from his perspective as the first American journalist to have interviewed Iraqi president Saddam Hussein prior to the start of the hostilities. Also, CBS's Bob McKeown was praised for being among the first to enter Kuwait City ahead of coalition troops.[31] CBS correspondent Bob Simon and his news team were captured by Iraqi soldiers and brutalized before being released. Protests that this treatment violated tenets of international law were not lost on network management, as were the monetary aspects of coverage. The fact that the network was willing to invest in war coverage with tremendously high financial stakes at a time when advertising was down was also viewed as a credit to CBS, as well as the other networks.

The other networks proved to be formidable competitors, with field reporters exhibiting courage in the face of military weaponry representing new technology. NBC's Arthur Kent gained recognition for his live reporting on the impact of Scud missiles, while ABC was credited for having first reported the start of the bombing of Iraq. CNN's Bernard Shaw, John Holliman, and Peter Arnett were distinguished by direct broadcasts from a hotel in Iraq at the start of the conflict through use of a satellite uplink which they monopolized to their benefit.[32] At one point, NBC anchor Tom Brokaw did the unthinkable and praised CNN's "enterprising" coverage in an interview with that network's Bernard Shaw. The fact that CNN was cutting into the lead of the established networks at that time makes the accomplishment all the more unusual.[33]

Although lean advertising revenue was due mainly to projections based on programming performance, anticipated in 1991 to be a $125 million dollar shortfall to the network, CBS was clearly committed to an all-out effort to regain status it lost from CNN in the early going.[34] On the other hand, as revenue was down, the extension of war coverage to late evening hour-long programming, close to documentary proportions, and the use of time stolen from affiliates may have had the opposite effect. The fact that advertising was at a low point at that time may have helped the network in their effort to provide war coverage, while they might have suffered considerably more if financial time had been more prosperous.

In narrowly defining the function of news and newsgathering with special emphasis on monitoring and reporting the activity of public officials and others affecting public life, some critics assume a role for journalists of always exploring new territory on the public landscape. As we have reviewed in this book, even some of the best CBS work has required a recommitment to old causes and time-honored traditions.[35] Those who have provided leadership at CBS have continually expressed a desire to maintain the standards set by Paley, White, Stanton, Murrow, and Klauber,[36] with an emphasis on telling important stories. The role models for CBS coverage of important stories, the managers, producers, writers, correspondents, and technical staff including photographers and editors, have created an impressive and ongoing body of work at CBS News with a commitment to the public interest and conventions of investigative reporting in the tradition of American muckraking. They are to be commended.

NOTES

1. Thomas H. Wyman, "The First Amendment and Professional Broadcast Journalism," Sloan Colloquium in Communications, Duke University, Durham, North Carolina, February 5, 1986.

2. Edward Bliss, Jr., "Eye Test," *Television Quarterly* 22(4) (1987): 9.

3. See, for example, Fred Rothenberg, "Documentaries Grow Scarce," *St. Louis Post-Dispatch*, September 3, 1984. Also, Dan Klugherz, "On Documentary . . . The End of Style," *Television Quarterly* 21(11) (1984): 17–20; and "The Vanishing Documentary," in Edwin Diamond, *The Media Show: The Changing Face of News* (Cambridge, MA: MIT Press, 1991), pp. 29–36; and Raymond L. Carroll, "Economic Influences on Commercial Network Television Documentary Scheduling," *Journal of Broadcasting* 23 (Fall 1979): 415.

4. Eric Sevareid, "What's Right with Sight-and-Sound Journalism," *Saturday Review*, October 2, 1976, pp. 18–21. Reprinted in George Rodman, *Mass Media Issues: Analysis and Debate* (Chicago: Science Research Associates, 1981), pp. 100–104.

5. Quoted in Barbara Matusow, "Intrigue at NBC," *Washington Journalism Review* (July-August 1983): 83.

6. Quoted in *Radio-Television News Directors Association Communicator* 26(10) (October 1983): 9.

7. "Same Harvest, Old Shame," "Frontline" PBS Television broadcast, April 17, 1990. Quoted in Aaron Mermelstien, "The Harvest of Shame Goes On," *St. Louis Sun,* April 17, 1990, p. 27.

8. "Prime Time Live," ABC Television broadcast, November 26, 1992.

9. George Beiswinger, "Media Museums," *Media History Digest* 8(2) (Fall-Winter 1988): 24; and "Vanderbilt University Is Repository for News Video Library," *Radio-Television News Directors Association Communicator* (October 1983): 38.

10. Quoted in Betty Houchin Winfield and Lois B. DeFleur, *The Edward R. Murrow Heritage: Challenge for the Future* (Ames, IA: Iowa State University Press, 1986), pp. 104–106.

11. Kay Lockridge, "Steadfast at '60 Minutes,' " *The Quill* (March 1976): 19; Arthur Unger, " '60 Minutes' Executive Producer Don Hewitt: 'The $60 Million Joe Sixpack,' " *Television Quarterly* 25(4) (1992): 23–36.

12. Judy Flander, "Hewitt's Humongous Hour," *Washington Journalism Review* (April 1991): 29.

13. Axel Madsen, *"60 Minutes": The Power and Politics of America's Most Popular TV News Show* (New York: Dodd, Mead and Company, 1984).

14. See David Shaw, "The Trouble with TV Muckraking," *TV Guide,* October 10, 1981, p. 10. See also Les Brown, "Taped-Over Shows Get CBS Disclaimer," *New York Times,* January 6, 1976; and Don Hewitt, "The Power of the Press," *Channels* (January/February 1984): 68–70.

15. "Clips of '60 Minutes' May Be Made Public in Suit against CBS," *Wall Street Journal,* March 18, 1983, p. 37; "Suit against CBS Settled," *Louisville Times,* April 25, 1980; and Monica Collins, " '60 Minutes' at Age 20: It Has Style, Substance and Success," *USA Today,* September 17, 1987.

16. Kay Lockridge, "Steadfast at '60 Minutes,' " *The Quill* (March 1976): 19; and also Don Hewitt, *Minute by Minute* (New York: Random House, 1985), pp. 104–107.

17. "60 Minutes," CBS News television broadcast, March 10, 1974. The segment is reviewed in Edwin Diamond, *The Tin Kazoo: Television, Politics and the News* (Cambridge, MA: MIT Press, 1975), p. 65.

18. Robert Chandler, vice president and director of public affairs, CBS News, letter to the author, April 20, 1978. See Michael D. Murray, "The Television Revolution: 1945–present," in *The Media in America,* William David Sloan, ed. (Scottsdale, AZ: Goruch Scarisbruck, 1993). Also, see John J. O'Connor, "How Fair Is the Fairness Doctrine?" *New York Times,* June 15, 1975, p. 27; and Jeffrey Klein, "Semi-Tough: The Politics behind '60 Minutes,' " *Mother Jones,* October 1979, pp. 26–31.

19. "Who Pays? You Do," "60 Minutes," CBS News television broadcast, November 25, 1979. See also Tom Dorsey, " '60 Minutes' Can Skirt the Spotlight As Well As Wield It," *Louisville Courier Journal,* June 9, 1981, p. C1; and " '60 Minutes' on Trial," *Interface* 2 (1981): 38.

20. The broadcast is published in *Sixty Minutes Verbatim* (New York: Arno Press/CBS News, 1980), pp. 149–153.

21. See Sandy Graham, "Illinois Power Pans '60 Minutes,' " *Wall Street Journal,* June 27, 1980, p. 1; "NBC Hires Lawyers to Probe Report that Sparked GM Suit" *St. Louis Post-Dispatch,* February 13, 1993, p. 8C.

22. "Rather Lather," *Newsweek,* September 2, 1974, p. 49.

23. "Dan Rather, Anchorman," *Newsweek,* February 25, 1980, pp. 71–72; "The New Face of TV News," *Time,* February 25, 1980, pp. 64–72; "The Houston Hurricane," *Time,*

February 25, 1980, pp. 72–75. Also, see Dan Rather and Mickey Hershowitz, *The Camera Never Blinks* (New York: William Morrow and Company, 1977); and Robert Goldberg and Gerald Jay Goldberg, *Anchors* (New Jersey: Carol Publishing, 1990).

24. See "CBS Buckles Down over Seat Belts," *Washington Journalism Review* (January/February 1993): 13.

25. "Good Morning America," ABC television broadcast, February 10, 1993.

26. Brian Donlon and James R. Healey, "NBC Looks at What Went Wrong; Staff Reprimands May Follow," *USA Today*, February 10, 1993, p. D3; "NBC Hires Lawyers to Probe Report That Sparked GM Suit," *St. Louis Post-Dispatch*, February 13, 1993, p. C8; William A. Henry III, "Where NBC Went Wrong," *Time*, February 22, 1993, p. 59; and Eric Mink, "Executive Quits amid NBC Flop," *St. Louis Post-Dispatch*, March 3, 1993, p. C1.

27. Richard Cohen, "NBC's Top Official Disgraced Journalism," *St. Louis Post-Dispatch*, February 16, 1993, p. B3.

28. See Les Brown, *Encyclopedia of Television* (New York: New York Times Books, 1977), pp. 308–309.

29. Production aspects of recent programs are described in Ron Powers, *The Beast, The Eunuch and the Glass Eyed Child: Television in the 80's* (New York: Harcourt Brace Jovanovich, 1990), pp. 165–174 and 320–326. Another recent criticism of the influence of production values was made by Morley Safer, Alfred I. DuPont Forum, Columbia University School of Journalism, January 30, 1992.

30. See Ron Powers, *The Newscasters* (New York: St. Martins Press, 1978), p. 236.

31. See Howard Rosenberg, "Dan and Saddam Show: CBS' Prime Time Coup," *Los Angeles Times*, August 31, 1990, p. F–1.

32. Howard Kurtz, "On Television, Gunfire Is Heard but Not Seen," *Washington Post*, January 17, 1991, p. A–28; and Richard Zoglin, "Assessing the War Damage: ABC Establishes Air Supremacy," *Time*, March 18, 1991, pp. 88–89.

33. Tom Shales, "War Footage and Network Skirmishes," *Washington Post*, January 19, 1991, p. C–1; and "CNN: Where Have All the Viewers Gone?" *Broadcasting*, July 1, 1991, pp. 45–47.

34. Wayne Walley, "Prestige of CBS Takes a Direct Hit from the Gulf War," *Advertising Age* 52 (July 1991): 3.

35. Hal Himmelstein, *Television Myth and the American Mind* (New York: Praeger, 1984), pp. 197–231.

36. "Dick Salant and the Purity of News," *Broadcasting*, September 19, 1977, p. 105.

AFTERWORD

From the outset, broadcast standards have been a variable commodity, always in flux, and the nature of documentary development has complicated decision-making even further. Many broadcast historians like to point out that broadcast journalism has always taken a back seat to entertainment, unlike the newspaper business, in which news came first. When the dramatization of "War of the Worlds" took place in the late 1930s, guidelines on proper behavior were yet to be developed for radio with respect to references to reality and even the appropriate use of radio jargon such as "bulletin" and "flash." It has been suggested that the strategies of offering compelling audio to mimic reality or, in some cases, placing a story within a story were merely devices to increase listenership.

Once some news standards were introduced and attempts at enforcement ensued, a number of questions remained concerning the use of commercial intrusion into the domain of news and information. This was complicated further by a press-radio "war" over resources and the nature of newsgathering services. Some newspaper publishers also involved in the broadcasting business tried to apply advertising standards to radio. This included efforts to rid radio news of "middle commercials" for items such as laxatives, which it was thought might denigrate important informational items such as reports on war casualties.

The fact that key news stories such as the kidnapping of the Lindbergh baby, which radio covered most completely, albeit under considerable criticism from the print media, frequently offered a chance to attract listeners also perhaps tainted expectations for sensational coverage. Radio's first major news voice, H. V. Kaltenborn, is best remembered for a live remote report from the field during the Spanish Civil War, a not-so-subtle prelude to "War of the Worlds." Many of the listeners taken in by that fictional broadcast cited the "permanent" talk of war as a rationale for their gullibility but also radio's emerging role as a conveyor of bad news on breaking stories. While the medium's most highly regarded news broadcaster, Edward R. Murrow, offered balanced, editorial opinion on the international scene with colleagues on the "World News Roundup," he also offered live dramatic, emotion-laden reports from air-raid shelters, bombing raids, and even a concentration camp during World War II.

Murrow's recruitment of a cadre of reporters such as Eric Sevareid, Howard K. Smith, and William Shirer, with both newspaper experience and academic credentials in various specialties, further enhanced CBS's status for newsgathering and reporting, but a subtle show-business element remained intact. Murrow's writing offered visual images of war-torn Europe, war atrocities, and carnage, with the stakes as high as one could conceive. That made it interesting and attractive for listeners who became loyal to CBS and stayed with the network and Murrow long after the war ended.

Later, with the advent of television, the Korean conflict offered another opportunity to present the challenge of war, but this time visually. The development of the film tradition also raised important questions for documentary producers and at various times entertainment values crossed the boundary into news in that area as well and sent mixed messages about the validity of this important means of communication. The use of actors in place of bona fide participants in an event, the choice of spokespersons and correspondents, the issue of integrating staged footage, selective editing, the role of music and narration in the presentation of a particular point of view—these issues evolved along with the earliest documentary efforts, to depict the real world on film and the arguments concerning these issues addressed in an artistic context.

Documentary film leader Robert Flaherty took great strides to commend a firm stand against the manipulation of content in an anthropological context, in the same way that journalists maintain the need for objectivity in their reporting. The problem, as we have seen in this book, is that the standards for behavior have been altered periodically with the intrusion of pervasive Hollywood entertainment values and the realization that the lines are not always so easily drawn in matters of public controversy. The issue of balance frequently intrudes into almost any discussion of fairness, and the early extended broadcast news reports offer examples of how difficult these judgments can sometimes be.

In dealing with juvenile crime and the murder of a youth as in the "Who Killed Michael Farmer?" radio documentary, the tendency is to identify with the victim and his family, although more contemporary efforts might also offer some sympathy for those who committed the act. The veracity of the "See It Now" report on Joseph McCarthy is still debated, as the fairness of almost all political reporting is constantly called into question. The issues of ulterior motives and the predisposition of reporters toward political issues and figures frequently come into play in the public dialogue on broadcasting.

Sponsorship has also been a recurring challenge for the more extended-length documentary efforts because they invariably ruffle feathers in the business community. Early treatment of the issue of cancer on a segment of "See It Now" entitled "Biography of a Cancer" left major tobacco growers annoyed, as did the much later, widely discussed and debated "CBS Reports" program "Harvest of Shame." Another documentary, "The Great American Funeral," caused morticians to wonder out loud whether this program was designed as a blatant effort to put them out of business. Inevitably a topic such as the treatment of the disadvantaged develops as a source of embarrassment to a sponsor as well, and the network news division often has had to justify biting the hand that feeds it. As a result, the short-form magazine story is currently being offered as an alternative, providing a chance for both sides to be heard. Although the newspaper press has often supported CBS efforts to report a critical story, they have shared the nation's concern when efforts have gone astray or awry.

By the same token, some commercial sponsors have benefited considerably in terms of prestige through an association with CBS News. The Xerox Corporation supported many information documentaries such as "The Making of the President" series, with programs completed in 1960, 1964, and 1968. Designed to provide information of an educational nature, many of the Xerox projects focused on space exploration and the environment, offering details on complicated questions leading up to policy questions for the government, but stopping short of taking a position.

CRITICAL CULTURE

Editorial voices have been heard in opposition to many of the CBS programs. While usually supportive, as with most of the early Murrow programs, the press has been critical, especially with respect to the extent of the broadcast commitment to the complicated issues they frequently address. While applauding efforts to let sources speak for themselves on many occasions, they have also often questioned the selection of sources. In examining a program dealing with the farm economy, for example, Jack Gould of the *New York Times* questioned CBS's failure to investigate the role of the middleman in the farm price equation. And, of course, underlying all of the criticism is the question of what political forces are at work to address the problem areas raised by the documentaries and network news shows. Critics such as John Crosby and Marya Mannes often went behind the scenes to find out why special stories are presented as they are, such as political convention coverage.

To its credit, CBS has frequently turned introspective and closely examined the field of journalism itself and the network's performance. It experimented with "CBS Views the Press," violating the norm of criticism being a one-way street with print counterparts and extending beyond the broadcast media to include scrutiny of American newspapers. Surprisingly, it has also periodically initiated series that offer viewers a chance to provide feedback, often questioning network policies and programs. The "CBS Reports" program "Anatomy of a News Story: TV Covers Itself" provided background on how detailed decisions were made and by whom in covering the 1972 Republican Convention in Miami.

"Inside CBS News" and "Letters to CBS" both qualify as efforts by network staffers to turn a critical eye on themselves; and, of course, the most popular and esteemed CBS News program, "60 Minutes," invites viewer reaction in the form of letters as part of the regular lineup of features. Having a resident social critic in the form of Andy Rooney also suggests an opportunity to look at the field of broadcasting on occasion and offer some insights into what is right or wrong with how broadcasters do their jobs, as in the recent Rodney King coverage, in which he questioned stations' decisions to show repeatedly a segment of the tape of the beating of King without offering broader perspective on the event. Much earlier, Rooney contributed to documentary television through an unorthodox look at the federal government that he wrote, produced, and hosted as part of "Mr. Rooney Goes to Washington," a caustic, sarcastic, and somewhat hilarious indictment of our national bureaucracy, broadcast January 26, 1975, shortly after Watergate.

Needless to say, there has been no shortage of feedback from government officials. In many instances, officeholders have been sought out for comment on complicated economic issues such as the challenges facing the family farmer or the distribution of food to homeless people. In some of those cases, major government spokespersons have cried foul about the way the story has been presented or the way they have been portrayed or edited. Government officials reacted unfavorably, for example, to the "Hunger in America" program and raised questions about misrepresentation of certain segments and overall content. In other instances, government sources ignored the production element and the content of the problem under study altogether, then exerted themselves or their opinion into the text of the debate over program arguments.

In the case of "Biography of a Bookie Joint" a number of critics were heard from the Boston area, the location of the documentary filming, with the FCC stepping in and offering an opinion on the fairness of the program. Program participants themselves have protested when they felt they had been misrepresented as in the case of "Sixteen in Webster Groves." In this instance, an entire community rose up in reaction to what it felt was an inaccurate and unfair characterization of its young people, a response management anticipated with a follow-up program, having correspondent Charles Kuralt return to the scene on the evening of the original broadcast to gauge reaction and let local residents let off some steam.

Three years later, CBS returned once again to that general area, on this occasion selecting the across-the-river location in "The Battle of East St. Louis," to examine racial tensions and explore efforts to improve relations through sensitivity training, focusing on attitudes toward white police officers in that predominantly black community. Once again, CBS returned to the scene six months later to gauge the effectiveness of what they had filmed. The success of that program in cooperation and consensus building was applauded although, by that time, the international scene was beginning to dominate press attention and the "CBS Reports" program "The Selling of the Pentagon" was at the forefront of attention.

Of course, reaction to the latter controversial program was reinforced by actions taken by both participants in the broadcast and government officials who viewed it as a direct assault on military public relations and the conduct of the war in Vietnam. This worked in concert with the conservative vision of CBS as the most liberal, some would claim left-leaning, element of broadcast news and led to a challenge on the floor of the House of Representatives, which Dr. Frank Stanton was forced to answer. Lobbying by the print media helped to win a positive outcome in that case and staved off a jail sentence for the CBS top executive, who refused to provide deep background on a major documentary effort.

A major lobbying campaign by the National Rifle Association resulted when the documentary "Guns of Autumn" suggested that hunters were being guaranteed a "kill" at a wildlife preserve of limited size and scope, rather than simply an opportunity to take part in a sporting event. "Echoes of the Guns of Autumn" was planned after CBS affiliate stations prescreened the original telecast, anticipating the need for a rejoinder of some magnitude. This follow-up telecast included a review of some protest letters received by the network and a discussion of stereotypes presented in the program. The manner in which the animals were presented also came into play in the response, with some newspaper critics taking CBS to task for the way the animals had been humanized to draw special sympathy from viewers. The hunters themselves responded with a letter-writing campaign and even a lawsuit, charging that they had been misrepresented and stereotyped as mindless and irresponsible in the documentary.

UNEXPLORED TERRITORY

On another occasion, a CBS program came under fire by the subjects of an investigation, who turned out to be well-known minority entertainers. These were successful artists, but they had been depicted, in their view, during "Black History: Lost, Stolen, or Strayed?" as contributing to a negative stereotype of the black race, through film portrayals making them appear as shiftless and lazy. Chief among those targeted by the film was Lincoln Perry, "Stepin Fetchit" in the movies, who immediately responded to the film by pointing out the positive inroads he had made by paving the way for other black performers. He offered specific examples of many movie innovations and "firsts" with which he was associated.

More recently, a similar response was anticipated with Bill Moyers's "The Vanishing Family" for "CBS Reports," which targeted minority youth and life in depressed urban conditions contributing to a high birth rate and low educational achievement. Although the program was rebroadcast and followed by a network discussion program, surprisingly little negative response was heard from the black community, with most newspaper critics, both black and white, lining up behind Moyers and his message that greater personal responsibility be taken while recognizing historic limitations imposed on black youngsters. Some critics credited the low-key, nonalarmist approach Moyers took to this topic with the success and credibility the project achieved, a striking contrast to other contemporary approaches.

While many of the more recent CBS efforts have been castigated for promotional emphasis, some clarification is needed as well, since objectives have changed with time. Documentary television historian A. William Bluem has advanced the view that all of television news is documentary in nature in so far as a comparison to the old-style, long-form, or as he put it, "Big D" documentary is concerned. The shorter-form magazine stories of "60 Minutes," "48 Hours," or "Street

Stories" could certainly be included in that comparison. This view was advanced further by Charles Hammond in his follow-up study in television documentary, over a decade ago.

In making this observation, both Bluem and Hammond also took time to examine those who worked in the long-form arena. Some emerged from the Hollywood tradition. Palmer Williams, who started with Murrow, labored initially on Frank Capra's "Why We Fight" military series. But others moved comfortably from print to broadcast journalism. Hammond cites Herbert Mitgang, for example, who returned to the *New York Times* after a stint as historian on the "CBS Reports" documentary "D-Day Plus Twenty Years." Joe Wershba also worked in the newspaper business before joining CBS.

Many of the long-form documentaries relied heavily on the printed word. The classic "Silent Spring of Rachel Carson" and a number of programs with a distinct political outlook began with major literary works. Before he embarked on a study of American teenagers, Arthur Barron attempted to draw parallels to written work, recounting rural poverty from *The Great American Novel*. Murrow made reference to *The Grapes of Wrath* as a prelude to "Harvest of Shame." CBS executive in public affairs Robert Chandler, who once functioned as a program producer, wrote a book based on the broadcast script from "The National Environmental Test," one of many "test" documentaries the network produced utilizing the resources of government departments and the National Park Service.

It has been argued that both "The Selling of the Pentagon" and "The Untold Enemy" began as research efforts for literary consumption first. J. William Fulbright studied the war effort, and the latter CBS efforts were the result of a major magazine investigation. The poignant "Any Place but Here," which looked at the placement of mental patients, evolved from a number of major works on the treatment of the mentally ill and efforts to place them outside of institutions. The thesis of "The Vanishing Family" was fashioned after an academic treatise entitled *The Visible Man*, with the issue and key arguments traced back even further to the study by Daniel Patrick Moynihan, *Family and Nation*. Many "60 Minutes" stories begin as newspaper articles, with the print reporters serving as consultants when CBS comes to town, a tradition adopted from "See It Now."

The problem we now encounter is that the imitative nature of the industry has created an environment in which the shorter studies prevail, a by-product of the success of "60 Minutes." While the prospect of buying work from independent producers is still a possible alternative, which could encourage more detailed and perhaps more daring content, history shows that these efforts are few and often flawed. The models of excellence for what amounts to the interpretation of events such as those we have examined, like Moyers's recent contributions, require careful study and understanding to demonstrate the need for their continuation, if broadcasting will continue to make a legitimate claim to journalism. Those programs help to create and continue a critical culture that contributes to the national dialogue on important issues of the day, in a forum that now dwarfs its traditional key resource, the newspaper industry.

Appendix A

TELEVISION'S DESPERATE MOMENT

Fred W. Friendly is Edward R. Murrow Professor Emeritus of Broadcast Journalism at Columbia University. He became well known initially as Edward R. Murrow's colleague and associate on key broadcasts, as part of "Hear It Now" on CBS Radio and "See It Now" and "CBS Reports" documentaries on television. Murrow and Friendly's denunciation of Senator Joseph R. McCarthy is one of the most controversial broadcasts in the history of electronic journalism. He resigned his post as president of CBS News in 1966 over a dispute in which the CBS management insisted on broadcasting a rerun of "I Love Lucy" instead of covering the Senate Foreign Relations Committee hearings on Vietnam. Friendly went on to serve as TV advisor to the Ford Foundation, host of a popular public television series based on Columbia University Media and Society Seminars, and author of three books: *Due to Circumstances Beyond Our Control, The Good Guys, the Bad Guys and the First Amendment*, and *Minnesota Rag*. Friendly retired from the Public Broadcasting Service (PBS), or what he termed "America's largest classroom," on December 15, 1991, at the age of seventy-six. He had spent fifty-five years in broadcast journalism, the last seventeen on public television.

The following conversation, focusing on the controversial McCarthy broadcasts, was taped during the winter of 1973 at the Ford Foundation, New York, and appeared in *Journalism History* 1(3) (Autumn 1974). It is published with permission.

A CONVERSATION WITH FRED W. FRIENDLY

MURRAY: How do you account for the influence of Joseph R. McCarthy in America in the early 1950s?

FRIENDLY: McCarthy captured the imagination of many people because obviously they wanted to believe a lot of it. They wanted to believe the Russians were poisoning American society and that there was a spy under every table.

MURRAY: Did the media contribute to this atmosphere?

FRIENDLY: The role of the media in this has never really been written. It was important that you cover McCarthy. Whether McCarthy was reported or just a sort of scoreboard, I don't know. But I do think a great part of the blame has to be laid at the feet of the media who exploited McCarthyism because it was a good story. They didn't like McCarthy but they kept building him up. And that was proper, if building him up was just the product of reporting him. But I don't think they did enough to show all the lies and all of the distortions— the way Watergate was reported. Today, if somebody says something that is palpably not true, the press reports it. It wasn't that way in the fifties and I think the "See It Now" broadcast on McCarthy was partly what set the example for future generations.

MURRAY: What was the background on the "Report on Senator Joseph R. McCarthy"? How did Murrow work with you? What kind of decision-making went into selecting filmed sequences on McCarthy?

FRIENDLY: We had photographed or recorded almost everything McCarthy had done for some length of time. Joe Wershba and Palmer Williams (both later with CBS's "60 Minutes") did most of that work. And we had enough film to last for more than three hours. I like the sequence with Reed Harris. Harris, who was the head of the Voice of America, had been accused by McCarthy of writing a Communist-inspired book years earlier. We could see that McCarthy was taking advantage of Reed Harris. We used it on the air once before. It was a marvelous sequence. I always knew we would use the one in which he attacked Adlai Stevenson because I knew there was an answer to all that. Much of what McCarthy said was extremely difficult to disprove. As you know, it's hard to refute a negative. But when he said, "Alger—I mean Adlai," I knew that Murrow was capable of systematically treating those allegations. As far as the selection of sequences, I made the first recommendations and then I had Murrow come over and look at a long cut. I made the first edit and he sort of approved it. Of course Joe Wershba and Palmer Williams contributed throughout.

MURRAY: One of the biggest criticisms of your McCarthy telecast, voiced by Gilbert Seldes of the *Saturday Review* and others, was that you and Murrow had a great deal of technical television expertise and that McCarthy was somewhat defenseless in view of his independently produced response. How would you respond to this accusation?

FRIENDLY: I think that they balance each other out. It is true that we knew how to do a better television program than he did, but he was a United States senator, he could have hearings any time of the day or night, he could subpoena people, he could attack people on the floor of the Senate with immunity. No one was balancing his fairness. Gilbert Seldes, who's a friend of mine, who I have a great deal of respect for, wasn't writing pieces saying Senator McCarthy shouldn't do this, or shouldn't do that. You have to balance these things against each other. And in the final analysis, what if we hadn't done the broadcast? And suppose McCarthy had triumphed, as he might well have, then where would Mr. Seldes and those who criticized the broadcast be? If we had it in our power to counteract the abuses, the one-sidedness of Joseph McCarthy and we hadn't used it, if Joseph McCarthy had taken over this government—the executive branch, as he very closely did. I'm not for one moment saying we stopped him or that we did it alone, but we helped. But if that had happened, where would Mr. Seldes and those who criticized us have been? I think we were balancing what we knew how to do well against what he did superbly well, which was to be a demagogue. And I'm sorry we had to do it that way. Murrow always said, "I hope we never have to do another broadcast like that." But it was the challenge of a lifetime, a desperate moment for the country, and not to have used it because of some series of rules that we would apply to ourselves and that Senator McCarthy would abuse to the ultimate would have made history judge us very harshly.

MURRAY: What were your general feelings toward McCarthy at the time of the broadcast?

FRIENDLY: I despised everything he stood for, although I never really met him. Because what he stood for was a big lie.

MURRAY: What about Murrow?

FRIENDLY: As far as I know he only met him once. Murrow went to a Gridiron Club dinner and as the dinner adjourned a face came out of nowhere and shook his hand and said: "Hi, Ed, shake, friendly enemies." And Murrow shook his hand not realizing that it was McCarthy. And he always said if he had only known who it was—he felt had. And he didn't want to shake hands with him or have anything to do with him. But that's the only time they met. We talked on the phone with McCarthy—we did a couple of broadcasts in which we had Senator Benton on one week and him the next. So I guess we did talk on the end of a telephone to him.

MURRAY: You've been criticized for some of the sequences which showed McCarthy in somewhat unflattering positions, the most extreme case being a shot of McCarthy belching during a speech in Washington. Can you say why you put it in?

FRIENDLY: The belching thing is a mockery. I mean anyone saying that's why we used it—we used that because in the quote "belching sequence" McCarthy was talking about General Ralph Zwicker. He was talking about Zwicker in Philadelphia with George Washington's mural in the background. That was one of the most important examples of McCarthy's excesses and character assassination that there was. I think the first edit of that was on paper where I took the notes of what he said and marked it up. The fact that he belched was strictly coincidental. I would no more put a piece or sequence in just because he belched—there wasn't time. We had twenty-five minutes in that whole broadcast. All you have to do is read the copy there to realize that that had to be in. Now, I certainly couldn't take those belches out; that would have been dishonest and I couldn't have done it. But that's ridiculous, and anyone who says that really doesn't know what they're talking about.

MURRAY: A lot of executives on the commercial networks and some academics would argue that television should avoid taking sides—that its function is always to be "neutral" and "objective." What is your feeling on this again today?

FRIENDLY: Well, I still believe that, except under very special circumstances, where the future of the republic is involved. There's a 1939 quote by Ed Klauber of CBS News which, in my opinion, describes what a documentary should and should not be. And I would say that that's true, but there are extenuating circumstances and these were extenuating circumstances. First, most of this broadcast was a pretty fair treatment of McCarthy as he would have seen himself. The last three minutes were a ringing analysis and editorial denunciation of Joseph McCarthy by Edward Murrow, who had every right to say that. And if we altered the rules we had set up for ourselves—all rules sometimes have to be broken. This was the only time we ever did it. I think we did it one other time in a program about poverty.

MURRAY: The "Harvest of Shame" broadcast?

FRIENDLY: Right. Two times for Murrow and myself in a career that spanned 20–25 years—we had no choice but to do it. To have remained silent would have been an abdication of our responsibility. We have to take the criticism for it and we have to take whatever credit goes along with it. I think history has decided that Murrow and those of us who worked with him did the right thing. Those who wish to criticize us can—we did it. I'd do it again.

MURRAY: In your book you said that at the start of the McCarthy program your hand was shaking so hard that when you tried to start your stop-watch, to time the broadcast, you missed the button completely on the first try because of extreme nervousness. Did you fear reprisals?

FRIENDLY: I certainly knew that nothing would be the same again. I knew that Murrow and CBS and I would be attacked and I knew that we were taking the whole future of broadcast journalism in our hands. Because if we did that program and CBS got shut down for it, which I never believed would happen, but there were those who believed that. I knew that this was the most important broadcast that I would ever have anything to do with and in a way it was one of the most important broadcasts ever done. As for the decision to make it, I mean there have been other programs on the air that were better and there were other programs that were precedents in historical context. But this was a broadcast that was only on the air because Murrow and his colleagues willed it to be on the air. But I knew that I would never have anything to do with anything this important in my life and I never did. And I was always "up" for a show and Murrow was always "up" for a show. When you watch any of those kinescopes of those broadcasts you'll see his knees shaking. He was good because he was nervous. He was not "cool" as someone in the younger generation might describe a public figure. But I knew that this was the journalistic effort of our lives. I knew it then and certainly nothing that's happened since suggests otherwise.

MURRAY: Is there anything about the broadcast that you would have done differently?

FRIENDLY: I think we should have done it earlier, and I think Murrow thought that too. It's awfully easy now that we know that history has judged McCarthy the way history has judged him to say we should have done the broadcast in 1953 or even 1952, but that's because we know how the struggle came out. I think Murrow felt that we had to be careful that we weren't too far ahead of public opinion. Normally, you should be way ahead of public opinion except we were in broadcasting—television, which was a brand new art—a brand new form of journalism, and it had not been established that it could do controversial subjects. As a matter of fact the broadcast established that, that is the most important part of that broadcast, not that it was key in the battle against McCarthyism, that was important, but the most important part was that it proved once and I hope for all that you could do controversial subjects and the company would still be there the next morning. There was a body of opinion that felt otherwise. So I guess we felt that if we were too soon, the risks to the company and to our program were just too high. In retrospect knowing that we could have taken that risk and the company endured, we now say—I say, that we should have done it a year earlier and I think Murrow felt that way, but who was to know that.

MURRAY: Somewhere you mentioned that various problems had arisen with the network management concerning publicity and finance of broadcasts like the one on McCarthy and an earlier civil liberties broadcast in defense of a young air force lieutenant, Milo Radulovich. Did the summer retrospective series of outstanding documentaries [1973] resurrect any apologies or belated congratulations from people in management?

FRIENDLY: The most interesting thing about that, for both the Radulovich and McCarthy broadcasts, was that Murrow and I asked the company to buy advertisements to alert people to the fact that these programs were on the air. When they refused to even talk with us about that, Murrow and I went out and bought the ads ourselves. Twenty years later, they repeat that broadcast and *they* buy a half-page ad for many thousands of dollars in the New York news. One of the things I mean to do before this year is out is to take the check (I still have the canceled checks for the ads) and the ads that we ran in 1953–54, plus the ad that they ran in 1973, and frame them side by side. If Murrow had lived he would have gotten more of a kick out of that, I can assure you. He had a great laugh and a marvelous sense of humor and he would have thrown his head back and said: "All you gotta do is live long enough and you see everything." In this case he didn't live long enough. But it's been twenty years. Imagine that. No ad when it was important and twenty years later when it was unimportant whether people looked at it or not (although I'm glad people did) there was a half-page ad—no questions asked.

MURRAY: In retrospect, what effect do you think the broadcast actually had on the political decline of Senator McCarthy?

FRIENDLY: I can't answer that. It's been so speculated on. I don't think it was the most important thing. I think the most important thing was the Army-McCarthy hearings and his encounter with Joe Welch, and that's what Murrow thought. I do think that what the broadcast did was stiffen a lot of other backs and that's what it will be remembered for.

MURRAY: When you first saw McCarthy's filmed reply to your broadcast, did you think it would be effective?

FRIENDLY: I knew it wouldn't be. First, it was a very sloppy job and he was very heavily made up. What he might have done was to attack the broadcast and do an analysis of the broadcast and what was wrong with it. But instead he just decided to defame Murrow for something he had done many years before that. But I knew it was a mockery. I think that broadcast did McCarthy far more harm than anything. That's what's so silly about what Gilbert Seldes said. Because nothing that we quote "edited" about McCarthy defamed him as much as what he put together himself.

MURRAY: You've said on record that you consider "Annie Lee Moss before the McCarthy Committee" [the "See It Now" documentation of the appearance of a black civil servant who lost her job because of unsubstantiated claims of subversion by the McCarthy committee] as the best documentary you've done.

FRIENDLY: The Annie Lee Moss program is, in my opinion, one of the best broadcasts ever done by anyone. If we had had the Annie Lee Moss footage earlier, I would like to think we never would have done the original broadcast on McCarthy. Because the Annie Lee Moss telecast showed a perfect example of McCarthy using all the power of the Senate of the United States and of his high office to destroy a woman. And to this day people say she was guilty— Roy Cohn, and more recently Bill Buckley said, "Well she was guilty you know." The important thing was not whether she was guilty or not but the important thing was the abuse heaped on this woman. I didn't know then nor did Murrow whether she was guilty—that was not the point of the broadcast. "The Case of Lieutenant Milo Radulovich" was very important too. I don't think we would have ever done the McCarthy broadcast if the Radulovich program and another early civil liberties broadcast hadn't taught us that we could get into controversial areas. The reason that whole series of broadcasts were important is it proved to broadcasters that you could do controversy and get away with it.

MURRAY: You've been accused of being an elitist.

FRIENDLY: That's the nicest thing ever said about me. I wish I were.

MURRAY: Is your position then that if each of the networks were fulfilling their responsibilities that the people would get a well-balanced view?

FRIENDLY: I think a well-balanced view is the product of a multitude of voices. What people tried to do at various times was to still voices. I wasn't worried about McCarthy getting short shrift. George Sokolsky, the *Chicago Tribune*, and lots of people in radio and television were extolling his virtues every day. He was on the air more than the president. We were the only voice on television—major voice—willing to take him on. I can't follow at all the argument that we were unfair to McCarthy. McCarthy was unfair to the country.

THE END OF AN ERA AT CBS

Bill Leonard joined CBS in 1945 as a radio reporter and on-air host, then moved to television with a weekly series about New York City, while also reporting for the "CBS Evening News." His early coverage of the underprivileged, the treatment of drug addicts, and the mentally ill earned him the Albert Lasker Award for Medical Journalism in 1956. He narrated the Emmy-winning documentary "Harlem: A Self-Portrait" in 1959 and was invited by Fred Friendly to become a "CBS Reports" staff correspondent.

Among other documentaries, Leonard also wrote, produced, and narrated "Trujillo: A Portrait of a Dictator" in 1960, for which he won the Ed Stout Award for Outstanding Foreign Reporting. He was put in charge of the CBS News election unit in 1962 and assumed the vice presidency of network news programming in 1964. In 1968 he initiated "60 Minutes" and a decade later, in 1979, was promoted to president of CBS News and started "CBS Sunday Morning." He also proposed an hour-long national nightly newscast at that time.

When Walter Cronkite decided to retire as CBS anchorman, Leonard negotiated a $22 million, ten-year contract for his successor, Dan Rather. The first executive in company history, other than CBS founder William S. Paley, to have the organization's retirement limit of age sixty-five pushed aside, Leonard eventually resigned his post as president of CBS News in 1982. He received the George Foster Peabody Award for Lifetime Achievement in Broadcasting and authored *In the Storm of the Eye: A Lifetime at CBS*, which details his experiences. He is currently director of the Alfred I. DuPont/Columbia University Awards recognizing excellence in broadcast journalism.

The following conversation, focusing on documentary television and network news operations, was taped in the winter of 1990, at Leonard's home in

Washington, D.C., and appeared in *American Journalism* 8(1) (Winter 1991). It is published with permission.

A CONVERSATION WITH BILL LEONARD

The CBS Tradition

MURRAY: You've always had a kind of bias toward news broadcasters with a newspaper background?

LEONARD: Yes, I have, and there is a reason for that. Newspaper people are trained fundamentally that the number one thing to do is get the facts and to get at the truth or as close to the truth as you can get. After that comes embellishment, sidebar, and color. But what you're trying to do is inform people so that they can make better decisions. Now, television introduces the visual, and the visual element can be so colorful that you can be swept along by that. The truth and facts can easily take a backseat if you're not careful. And if you let a movie director loose without any of that fundamental training—that what you're after is to get the facts—deeply ingrained, he or she can be after the "higher truth," if you will, as they see it; and not bothered by little things like facts—let's not let the facts get in the way. Perhaps, what may come out is a film but not a document. Well, sooner or later, you can become a pleader instead of a reporter, and that, I don't think, is the role that we believed in at CBS News. What I believed in is and I think Dick Salant and Edward R. Murrow and the people who went before me—the great producers, David Lowe, for instance, who did "Harvest of Shame," was able somehow to combine the ability to get at the facts and at the same time to make a moving motion picture, a moving document. Those are the great documentarians who could do one without sacrificing the other.

MURRAY: In studying the great CBS documentaries like "Harvest of Shame" and some in the "See It Now" series, one of the impressions you get is that in some ways with Murrow and those who followed him, a sort of star system evolved in the sense that the people mentioned, David Lowe and Fred Friendly, for example, did a lot of the work on those but received little credit. Do you think that was a positive development?

LEONARD: No, I don't think it was particularly good. But it was necessary, I think, speaking as someone who grew up as a correspondent, who was used to being on air. I had little background, and when I started producing documentaries, I was a little disappointed on one occasion when Fred Friendly said to me that he wanted Ed Murrow to narrate a documentary I did. I always thought that I was a pretty good narrator and a pretty good broadcaster. I swallowed my pride and Ed did it. But I realized his point years later when I had to make the same decision about other documentaries and other producers who wanted to narrate their own documentaries. That was when I felt that a documentary needed a Walter Cronkite or Charles Kuralt or somebody like that. What you're trying to do is convey the maximum amount of information in the most effective way, and that sometimes a well-known voice that people have confidence in and know can give a documentary an extra dimension. Now "60 Minutes" is built more or less on that principle, but it is impossible for the leading correspondents to do all the work on those stories. Although they sometimes do a lot of the work. They do maybe a week's work on something that takes six weeks. But they are involved. It's better to have their voice and their pictures and the combination. But is it something of a deceit? Yes, it is; because the impression is that it's just them, when in actuality, in spite of the fact that you show credits, it's more than one person.

MURRAY: You told me once before that even though major figures at CBS functioned as correspondents on key documentaries, they didn't play a major role in the documentaries. I guess that's true in most cases?

LEONARD: It is true in a lot of them. Other correspondents played a very major role. When I did a documentary at the start of my career, I did almost everything. I did that documentary on Trujillo that got some attention, and I was about the only one working on it. I wrote it, directed it, and narrated it. It was almost a one-man job. But later on, I don't think that happened as much. What usually happens is that a producer and perhaps an assistant or associate work for a long time and a correspondent works for a shorter time and is there a good deal, but not all of the hard work.

MURRAY: Was the Trujillo documentary the most demanding assignment you got?

LEONARD: That was the toughest one I ever did. It was very tough, because I definitely never thought I was going to get him. On the whole, we invested a great deal of my time and the crew's time in the Dominican Republic with the topic of the notorious dictator. Nobody had ever interviewed him. Basically, we approached it with the idea that if we showed up and spent a lot of time down there, showing faith that we were really serious about covering him, that maybe he'd show up and let us do him. It was a long-shot bet and it did pay off. We got the interview, and it just made the documentary.

MURRAY: When you were a reporter, did the CBS management ever get anxious about that kind of thing, sending somebody out in the field for an extended period of time and spending a lot of the company's money?

LEONARD: No. We were very insulated from that. They left Fred Friendly alone. I don't know whether we had such a thing as a budget. But he made the bet in this case and sent me down there. I never knew how much it was costing. And I know I invested the better part of a year and out of it, I finally got the interview.

MURRAY: I thought it was interesting, what you said about "60 Minutes," because a lot of those people such as Don Hewitt, Palmer Williams, and Joe Wershba, working behind the scenes, were actually at CBS in the "covered wagon age" of broadcast news and some of them are still at it at "60 Minutes." It's ironic that the public sees a litany of "stars" going through the system in front of the camera, but they don't really get to know the people behind the scenes who are really making things happen.

LEONARD: Well, "60 Minutes" without Don Hewitt wouldn't exist. "60 Minutes" with Don Hewitt is the fastball pitch. He keeps that engine running.

MURRAY: Do you remember the instance you gave about the broadcast that you did a lot of work on that Ed Murrow wound up narrating? Do you remember what that was about?

LEONARD: It was a documentary called "Is This Election Already Rigged?" It was about gerrymandering and it's a tough subject anyway. And I think Fred felt he needed all of the presence for a subject as dull as that, that Ed Murrow could give it.

MURRAY: Do you think Murrow's role in all of this and his influence in broadcast news is overblown? Do you think he's gotten more credit than he deserves?

LEONARD: No. Ed Murrow was a remarkable force, a remarkable person. Superficially, the most remarkable thing about Ed Murrow was his voice, which was unique. It had a resonance, but that was really, of course, minor. His absolutely pure-blue-flame integrity was important, and his courage, his absolute standards. He was a fine broadcaster, a good writer, not the greatest writer, just a very, very good one. But he had an absolute standard of integrity that shone through and he had all of the courage that a man can have.

MURRAY: Did it ever bother you that he wasn't a newspaperman? I guess after a while you got over it.

LEONARD: No, it didn't bother me. It didn't bother me because he would have been a fine newspaperman. There were some people that just rose above that. I wasn't a newspaperman for all that long; but I started out on a college newspaper right away and those were my standards. That is how I was trained. It's because I just didn't have anything else, that's all. But I understood that Ed Murrow and a lot of people who did well in this game and didn't sacrifice their standards had a little bit of show business bred into them somehow. Now Murrow, you recall, spent a lot of time in college as an actor. Walter Cronkite was a sportscaster. He even did re-creations. There's a little bit of actor in him. At Dartmouth, I was very much involved in college dramatics, and when I got out of college, I had to decide whether I would become an actor or go into the newspaper business.

MURRAY: I guess having that kind of exposure, plus the performance background people like yourself and Walter Cronkite had as kids, sportscasting and even re-creating events for radio, that must have helped later on with convention coverage and that kind of thing. Did you give Mr. Cronkite specific things to research for convention? How did it work?

LEONARD: No, I didn't do any such thing. He was the best. He was a guy who did his own homework. He did all of that himself and he did it in great detail. He would retire three, or four, or five days, making extensive notes about all of the races and all of the people who were going to be involved in the convention and on the floor. He knew a lot of them anyway. He knew the situation; but he would study, as if for an exam. And he would study harder than anyone I ever knew. He really would study for all of them. And he would compile a very, very complete notebook—a large notebook, which he would have with him in the booth. I never saw him refer to it but it was there. He would have almost memorized it. So those things that sounded as if they rolled off the top of his head were things he had studied thoroughly and had committed almost to memory; they were with him. And he just came prepared.

Convention Coverage: 1968

MURRAY: At the Democratic convention in Chicago in 1968, you had big problems. How did you handle them?

LEONARD: It was extremely difficult. We had two things happening at once. We had a city that was, not in flames; but rioting was going on outside the hall. We had a convention inside the hall. We had the police trying to keep us from covering the story outside. It was an extremely difficult thing to handle.

MURRAY: You were running not only CBS News coverage; but that was the start of the News Election Service and coordinating coverage for other news organizations. How did that get going?

LEONARD: The News Election Service started after the 1964 election, when we had mounted at CBS such a large private effort to both collect the votes and to use survey methods to determine very quickly who had won, that the Associated Press and UPI, in effect, gave up the ghost and came to us and said, "Listen. We better do this together, because it's too expensive to do it separately. And anyway, we can't compete with you guys anymore." That really got started after the primary election in California in 1964.

MURRAY: It's kind of unusual that print people were willing to concede that.

LEONARD: It was an extraordinary concession. They had just run out of the ability and the money to do as much as we could do. And so we all got together. We had to get Justice Department permission to have a consortium to collect the vote. And we all got together and formed the News Election Service.

MURRAY: During the 1968 Democratic convention, when Cronkite said, "It looks like we've got a bunch of thugs out here," how did you react to that? You were in charge; were you shocked that he would say that; or were you pretty much fed up yourself?

LEONARD: Well, I think we were all rather, well, not shocked by what he said. Walter was a human being, and the way the police were behaving in Chicago at that time—that's exactly what they were behaving like. I won't say the rioters weren't behaving like a bunch of thugs, too, but the police, particularly, were behaving very badly and very brutally at that time in Chicago. Later, of course, they called it a "police riot." So what Cronkite said was pretty much confirmed by the official investigation. And no, I had worse things to worry about at the time. It was a very tense situation. We didn't know what the police would do for us. It was a bad scene out there and, furthermore, we did not have the support of our affiliates at that time—of our own people or the country, who basically felt that anything the police did to suppress the rioters or demonstrators was good. They thought that what we were doing was siding with the left-wing demonstrators. So we had a problem on our hands with our own affiliates and with the public. But we had to do it the way we saw it.

MURRAY: Did Mr. Paley say anything to you about the 1968 convention coverage?

LEONARD: No, not a word. I never got any feedback from him on that.

Politics of Management

MURRAY: Mr. Paley passed away recently and there have been a lot of things written about him. In his biography, *Empire*, the author, Lewis Paper, quotes a source saying he was very persistent, and he quotes you as saying he could be ruthless, especially in personal matters, I'm paraphrasing, in getting rid of people, even if he cared for them. He viewed himself as an army general during wartime. Is that a necessary evil for a broadcast manager that they really have to be hard-nosed?

LEONARD: Everyone is different. Paley was extremely tough in that regard. He had his own way of doing things and nobody or almost nobody lasted with Paley.

MURRAY: In a couple of the books about CBS, you pick up the theme that he would periodically conclude about lieutenants that "This person is getting just a little big for their britches," you know, and that person would be gone in short order.

LEONARD: Whether he thought they were too big for their britches or whether they never quite lived up to what he hoped they would become, whatever the reason, one way or another, sooner or later, they fell by the wayside, whether they were president or not. Actually the higher you got, the more danger you were in. If you were a little below the salt, you could be there for years. People say to me, "Well, you lasted." And I think the reason that I lasted is that I only got to the top, if you will, at the end of my career, not at the middle of it. If I'd gotten too high up at CBS News when I was forty-five years old, I'd probably been out of there. It happened all the time.

MURRAY: But most of the guys were, more or less, professional managers. You'd done a lot of different things in broadcasting. You represented CBS here in the capital and all that over an extended period of time.

LEONARD: Yes, but it didn't much matter what you were or who you were. Correspondents he let go on forever, but once you got into the management game it was different. Once you became manager and you were in the flow or under his eye fairly directly, it was different. If you were a person who dealt with Paley on a daily basis, sooner or later, you made a mistake. And he was very unforgiving of mistakes. If you didn't stand up to him, you were in trouble, because you would probably lead him down the wrong path. If you knew what you were doing and he had a bad idea (which he frequently had) and you didn't oppose it, you'd lead him down a trail that would embarrass him and he would say to himself, "Why didn't he stop me from doing that?" So you were in trouble then. If you stood up to him, and sooner or later, you'd stand up to him and he'd say, "All right, if that's the way you want it," and now if you were wrong, then you were in serious trouble. He was a very difficult guy to work for; but he was intelligent. He was smart and asked perceptive questions. He also asked, sometimes, almost off-the-wall questions that were preposterous. You couldn't believe how bad they were. You couldn't believe that a man who was so involved and knew so much could ask a stupid question as he would sometimes ask. Then, the next minute, he would ask a question that was so perceptive that you couldn't believe you overlooked it. So he would keep you off guard. And because he was so powerful, those things scared you to death. But he was also very entertaining, very warm and sympathetic, very attractive, and just an interesting man.

MURRAY: One of the CBS books said that Paley gave the staff a different impression. It said the staff got the view that he was kind of a quiet person. But the way you describe him makes it sound like he could be really domineering.

LEONARD: Well, he wasn't. He was rather quiet. I recall a time when we were all having the argument over whether we would pay Dan Rather as much as his agent was asking and he hadn't said much. First, expressing terrible shock, then telling that little story about the people he acquired for the network in the early days at CBS, saying, "Well, I guess sometimes the most expensive things are the cheapest in the long run—and the cheapest things are the most expensive."

MURRAY: When you told Paley he could expect that the CBS News ratings would go down after Dan Rather took over, did he ever come back and say, "OK, I understand that we'll have a down period"? Did he follow up and ask, "When can we expect to come back?"

LEONARD: No. You told him that, but he really was very unhappy when the ratings went down, no kidding. He really didn't want to sit still for that at all.

MURRAY: But you covered yourself by saying, "This is likely to happen"?

LEONARD: Likely to happen? We knew it was going to happen. But he made it very uncomfortable and was very unhappy.

Changes at the Network

MURRAY: It sounded from your book that part of the deal of getting Dan Rather as anchorman was complicated by other offers he was getting. It looked like, "Well, if we lose him, we've lost one of our big hitters." At the same time, it didn't sound like the other competitor for the job, Roger Mudd, played it that way. He came across as being much more independent but if he had done the same thing and looked around for other offers, if he had gone to negotiate with another network, do you think he would have been better off?

LEONARD: I don't know. My first idea was the best. I would have liked to have had him as a dual-anchor with Dan Rather. But Mudd didn't feel Rather was in his class, and he didn't think they ought to do a dual-anchor. I probably should have spent more time trying to persuade him to do that.

MURRAY: Did you get a lot of feedback from the public on that decision? What about feedback in general to broadcasts over the years?

LEONARD: Of all the broadcasts we ever did, the one that I personally got the most mail on (because somebody in the press used my name) was "The Guns of Autumn." I got thirty-eight thousand letters on that.

MURRAY: Is that because the National Rifle Association organized it?

LEONARD: Yes. I was very proud of that broadcast, by the way. I thought it was terrific. It was my idea to do it, and I thought we did it extremely well. I didn't think you could lay a finger on that broadcast. I think that was one of the reasons it was so effective. It wasn't preachy. It just laid the facts out there.

MURRAY: Do you remember if any of those letters you received on that broadcast came from major figures, movers and shakers or government officials?

LEONARD: No. They were mostly form letters from people involved in hunting.

MURRAY: When that many letters hit you or when that volume comes in, if it says something critical, you have to take it seriously, right?

LEONARD: No. I knew not to take it seriously because I knew they represented a lot of people who believed very much that something that they liked was being threatened. It showed how effective the broadcast had been, so it didn't bother me.

MURRAY: On the issue of the decision-making at the network, in news, for example, how did the title of managing editor get established?

LEONARD: I didn't have anything to do with that. In the first place, it's a meaningless term. I didn't like the term particularly. On the plus side, it's a symbol that says the person who is presenting the news is deeply involved in the selection of the news. And that's a good thing. On the other side of the coin, it suggests that the correspondent is a news person there to collect the news and not to manage or organize the management of how it's done. But as a practical matter, Walter wanted and had earned the right to use that title. He was, indeed, very much involved in the production, the writing, selection, and editing of the news. Just the evening news, nothing else. He never got into another thing. I felt that it was something you earned and Walter had earned it. When the negotiations for Dan Rather came on, I didn't think that Rather had earned the title. I didn't want to give it to him, and it was one of the main sticking points of the negotiation. I had to give in on it; and I didn't want to.

MURRAY: You were involved in a lot of tough management calls like that. I read where Mr. Paley told you that he appointed Fred Friendly news chief at one point because he thought the place needed some shaking up. Do you think Paley regretted that later on since Friendly was such an active, independent person?

LEONARD: Yes. I think he regretted it. But he did a lot of things like that and later on regretted it. Sure, if he didn't regret it, he wouldn't have let him go.

MURRAY: Everyone in the news division was backing Friendly, right? In fact, in one of the CBS books it says that you were all willing to leave the company right along with him.

LEONARD: Sure, Fred Friendly was my boss. Remember, Fred Friendly had taken me when I was a local broadcaster and I had been for twenty years. I had a good job but didn't amount to much.

MURRAY: It seemed to me like you pretty much owned New York as a reporter and were doing well financially.

LEONARD: I was doing much better. I had a very good job, and it looked like I would do that for the rest of my life. But Fred Friendly thought that I should be doing more. I'd be at political conventions as a local reporter, and after each convention, and in 1952, CBS News would come to me and say that they wanted me to be a correspondent. But after every convention they would offer me less than half of what I was making in local television. And I couldn't go back to my wife and say I've just been made a CBS correspondent and I'm going to have my salary cut in half. So I continued to do what I was doing until Fred Friendly insisted and made it possible. When he became president of CBS News he said: "You've got to decide one way or the other what you're going to do." He said, "I want you to do this, that's all." So I owed my career to Fred Friendly. There wasn't any question about where my loyalties would be. He had been very good to me.

MURRAY: He also comes across as the man behind Edward R. Murrow.

LEONARD: No. He wasn't.

MURRAY: How come Murrow used to, not defer to him, but always, when things got tough, say, "Fred Friendly and I think. . . . " Again, today, you would never hear anything like that.

LEONARD: Now that was him being very careful to give Fred credit. And he was being very kind to give Fred credit. They did do things together.

MURRAY: I wonder why that never happens anymore? Nobody would know about behind-the-scenes contributors, even major ones? Again, isn't that part of a star system?

LEONARD: No. I think under the right circumstances, it would happen that way. It was Murrow's nature to be fair and he was. Fred was the engine behind a lot of the stuff they were doing. Ed was a little embarrassed, sometimes, as to how little he did, to tell you the truth. On "See It Now" he did do a lot more of the reporting than others. He was just giving credit where credit was due.

Challenges of Change

MURRAY: Why aren't we seeing any hard-hitting documentaries on CBS and elsewhere? Has journalism's ability or the commitment to it declined with the retirement of so many people over the last few years?

LEONARD: There were other people besides me who had the same standards that were very important at CBS News in the whole documentary area. Bob Chandler and Bud Benjamin. And they're gone. Bud retired and died. Bob Chandler left. Those were the main ones. When the three of us and our influence pulled out of there, I would think that that would make a considerable difference. I don't think there was anyone else who—if they knew, they didn't care; and if they cared, they didn't know.

MURRAY: Do you think it's likely that anybody would come along with the same kind of background and orientation to reestablish that tradition? You were a reporter and had that background.

LEONARD: I want to take that back. I think Howard Stringer carried on pretty much in that tradition, although without quite as strong a journalism background. But I think he was pretty much trained by us, but he moved on so quickly to other responsibilities that there wasn't time to put in other people under him who could really do the job.

MURRAY: When you launched "Sunday Morning," did you know how that would develop?

LEONARD: Yes, I did. "Sunday Morning" was launched right in the next room. The staff came down on a Sunday morning, sat down, and I told them how I wanted "Sunday Morning" to work. We talked about it for two hours, and it turned out exactly the way we planned it.

MURRAY: Did you know right away that Charles Kuralt would be the best one to do that?

LEONARD: Yes. If he'd do it.

MURRAY: Did you have any trouble getting him to?

LEONARD: Surprisingly, I think he liked the idea, but I wasn't sure.

MURRAY: Do you ever look back and think that maybe Kuralt would have been a good person to replace Walter Cronkite on the "CBS Evening News"?

LEONARD: Yes. I think if the negotiations with Rather had collapsed that's probably what we would have done, although who knows. I guess it would have been all right, but Kuralt didn't like the politics. He didn't like great events coverage. He didn't like being the anchorman. He couldn't have anchored the Gulf situation. He could have anchored evening news. But he couldn't have been your front man and your key man with the tough, ongoing assignments.

MURRAY: Just wasn't oriented that way?

LEONARD: Just didn't like it.

MURRAY: One of your dreams was to expand the national news to an hour. Do you think that will ever happen?

LEONARD: No.

MURRAY: It just isn't feasible?

LEONARD: No. The public just doesn't want it.

MURRAY: The CBS book by Peter Boyer discusses a 1981 meeting in Hawaii and says the network affiliates gave you a really hard time about an hour news expansion proposal?

LEONARD: They sure as hell did.

MURRAY: Do you see that as a really symbolic meeting, as far as killing off prospects for expansion are concerned?

LEONARD: That's right. Absolutely. If it was ever going to go, it was going to go then, and we thought we had it. But they just wouldn't do it.

MURRAY: What about public affairs programming? Any signs of life in that area?

LEONARD: As far as documentaries are concerned, it's been a long time since a documentary shook up the country. I could mention a half dozen that shook up the country over a period of twenty-five years, from the McCarthy broadcast right to "The Guns of Autumn." The country paid attention to those. How long has it been since a documentary really stopped people, made them think, and had an impact?

MURRAY: I thought the one Bill Moyers did on young parents—mostly inner city kids, a couple of years ago was well done but it didn't have the kind of public impact you're talking about. I really don't think it was promoted properly.

LEONARD: Well, that's part of what I'm talking about.

MURRAY: Do you think the fact that so many other kinds of things are available, programs like "60 Minutes" or "48 Hours," does that have an effect?

LEONARD: The trouble with "48 Hours" is that it lacks content. It has no content.

MURRAY: Is that because it's hard to turn out quality on a weekly basis?

LEONARD: No. It isn't that at all. It is hard to turn out on a weekly basis but it's mostly because nobody is saying, "What are we trying to do? What are we trying to get at?" There's no content. There's no journalism in "48 Hours." None at all! "48 Hours" skims but it doesn't ever go into any depth.

MURRAY: It's more like show biz?

LEONARD: It's voyeurism; it isn't journalism. It's O.K. It's pleasant, but it doesn't make you mad. It doesn't make you upset.

MURRAY: In a couple of these CBS books, the authors point to the funeral of Charles Collingwood as another symbolic event when the old guard got together and that marked the demise of the old CBS. That was presented as a symbolic ending of that era. Is that the way it was?

LEONARD: I think so. I mean, I think that's as good a time to say it ended as any. Look, things pass. Eras pass and companies don't last very long. Few companies last more than a hundred years. Good ones don't last fifty years. Extraordinary ones last a hundred years. Businesses change, conditions change, and this situation is not different. At CBS News, I think we had a dream that the news division would continue to get better. It isn't getting better. It's still pretty good and I'm still loyal to CBS, but that era is over.

Appendix C

BEHIND THE LINES

Ed Bliss began his association with CBS News in 1943. He was day editor at CBS Radio until 1955, when he was recruited to write and produce news for Edward R. Murrow. He held that position until 1961, when Murrow left to go to work for the United States Information Agency (USIA). Murrow died shortly after that, and Bliss was asked by Janet Murrow to edit the work of her late husband. The result was *In Search of Light: The Broadcasts of Edward R. Murrow*, published by Alfred A. Knopf, Inc., in 1967. Bliss worked briefly for Fred W. Friendly, then served as assistant to CBS News president Richard Salant until the network decided to initiate the first regular half-hour evening newscast. He became news editor of that program, with Walter Cronkite at the anchor helm, in September 1963.

Working with Cronkite, whom some regarded as the "most trusted man in America," presented many challenges and opportunities. Bliss was in the newsroom handling all of the major stories of that era, for example, including the assassination of John F. Kennedy. He left CBS News to start the broadcast journalism program at American University in Washington, D.C., having already coauthored the best-selling broadcast journalism textbook *Writing News for Broadcast* with another CBS veteran, John Patterson. He has written a wide variety of articles for both popular and trade publications, conducted workshops and seminars on writing and editing for the Radio-Television News Directors Association (RTNDA), and serves as judge for the annual competition of the Walter Cronkite Scholarship for the National Academy of Television Arts and Sciences–Midwest Chapter.

He is now retired and resides in Alexandria, Virginia, with his wife, Lois. From his unique perspective as CBS News veteran turned academic, Bliss recently published the first comprehensive history of broadcast journalism,

Now the News, for the Columbia University Press. In this telephone interview, he discusses his work in broadcasting, experiences with both Edward R. Murrow and Walter Cronkite, and observations on the field, as a prelude to receiving the Paul White Award, October 2, 1993, from the RTNDA, meeting in Miami Beach.

A CONVERSATION WITH EDWARD BLISS, JR.

MURRAY: What was your background and what prepared you to work in journalism?

BLISS: I was born in China. My parents were missionaries there. My father was a doctor, and my mother was an English teacher. And I came back to this country when I was nine. I was going to be a doctor like my father, but I found that I was not very good in those subjects. And I had been editor of the paper at my prep school, the Northfield–Mount Herman School in Massachusetts, and I just loved it, so much so that I found myself skipping movies shown at the school (even though I was a movie buff) and even skipping meals to work on projects for the paper.

MURRAY: How did you land your first job?

BLISS: When I got through with school at Yale in 1935 with a B.A. degree, I was a pre-med major but had no intention of going into medicine. So I started out during the depths of the Depression. I applied at the *New York Times*, naturally, to be a copy boy, but nothing came of it. So I went to the *Herald Tribune*, then worked my way up the coast to the Hartford papers, around Boston, and ended up, after thirty-two papers, at a place that I had never been in, at a paper I had never heard of. I didn't even know how to pronounce the name of the town. It was Bucyrus, Ohio, the county seat for Crawford County, and that was the very best thing that could have happened to me.

MURRAY: What kind of paper was it? Did anybody in particular help guide your early career at that newspaper?

BLISS: It was a very clean little paper edited by a man, Rowland R. Peters, who had been a reporter for the *Chicago Tribune*. So he was a veteran, and Bucyrus was his home town. It was very good training. He was getting on in years and, like so many people, had had all he wanted of the rat race. And not only that, of course, he was now editor of the paper and thoroughly enjoyed it. He was a very civil, decent man, and he wrote all of his own editorials. He didn't use any canned editorials that came in the mail. It was a daily newspaper and since it was the county seat I was covering not only fires and the police beat but also had to cover the courthouse and learn what went on at probate court and in the courtroom. It was just wonderful background for a year. I worked my way up to seventeen dollars a week and asked him how much further I could go there. He said: "Probably not any further unless I die. As for pay, I can't assure you anything beyond twenty-five dollars a week."

MURRAY: How did you make the decision that you needed to go to New York?

BLISS: I was ambitious. The Broadway Limited used to go through town there and I would watch it coming in and the gates would go down on North Sandusky Street and I would say to myself, "Someday, I'm going to follow you to New York City." Well, I didn't go to New York City then, I went down to Columbus, Ohio, and got a job in 1936 on the Scripps-Howard paper there. It was the best paper in town. We were all sure of that. The other paper, the *Dispatch*, had more circulation but we thought our paper did a better job. And I was very fortunate there because it was also a very well-run paper. I stayed there until 1943. I had gotten married in 1940 to a lovely young woman from North Carolina, a teacher of the blind at the state blind school, and bought a home in 1942. Then in 1943 I was working on a book, a biography of my father, and a publisher in New York, W. W. Norton, was interested. I sent them some sample chapters, and one of the editors asked if they would pay the way, would I come to New York? I went to New York and they took me to lunch to talk about it and I was thrilled to death. Here I was, going to "Baghdad on the Hudson" at last. This was February 1943.

MURRAY: How did you make the CBS connection?

BLISS: Two friends of mine who had been cub reporters with me had gone to CBS News. While I was in New York, I dropped up there to have lunch with one of them, Lee Otis, and he said there was a vacancy here because Dallas Townsend had enlisted in the army and he was a writer on the "Overnight." So there is an opening. He said, why don't you apply for it? I did not have any idea of what I was applying for, but, as you know, they did the usual thing—they gave me hours and hours of AP and UP copy and had me write a script with an hour to look over it and an hour to write it and I passed the test. This was around Wednesday, and they wanted me to report to work on Monday.

MURRAY: I'll bet your wife liked that?

BLISS: I started on the "Overnight," going in to work at midnight and working until 9:00 A.M. I went from writer to "Overnight" editor, then to night editor and finally early in 1955, I got hours, 9 to 5, that would give me more time with our two children and my wife—in other words, banker's hours, finally. But I no sooner got that when Edward R. Murrow asked me if I would go on his staff in place of his writer/editor, Jesse Zousmer. Zousmer along with Johnny Aaron were also producing "Person to Person." They had also been working on his nightly radio show, writing the first half of his Monday-through-Friday radio broadcast, which was a hard news summary, and Murrow would take care of what came to be called "commentary." Of course, they did not allow that word to be used on the air at that time. It was news analysis, and Murrow would write it himself or else schedule a correspondent from overseas who was a specialist, the kind of thing you hear today on "MacNeil-Lehrer."

MURRAY: When did you start with Mr. Murrow and what was that like?

BLISS: In October of 1955 I went with Ed and it was, of course, a tremendous experience and, I always felt, a great honor. I worked with him doing that for five years as writer, editor, and producer. When I say producer, that consisted mostly of cutting magnetic tape after it came in, and I should say supervising because a tape engineer did the cutting. Then that last year, 1960, before he went to the USIA, I produced a weekly half-hour program for Ed called "Background."

MURRAY: How did you wind up working with Fred Friendly?

BLISS: When Murrow went to USIA, I was bequeathed to Fred's gentle care. And that was a great experience for a year. I was sort of an associate producer, double-checker, or whatever you want to call it, doing anything and everything with Fred, except going on the air.

MURRAY: How did you feel about your work with Fred Friendly and then Richard Salant, during that period? How did Salant work with you? And how did you move up in the organization?

BLISS: By the end of that time, I could see that Fred was not going to make me an actual producer of a program. I really don't remember how it happened, but I remember telling him that I was going to have to do something else. I ended up as assistant to Dick Salant, who was president of CBS News at that time, and that was just terrific working with Dick. You could not have worked with a better man. If you sent him a memo with a question, for example, you would never have to wait and wonder what his answer would be. He wouldn't dictate a memorandum. He would just scribble on the bottom of your note and initial it: "Let's, R. S. S.," or "Hell No, R. S. S." You knew exactly where he stood every minute. He had a great sense of humor, a high sense of dedication, and as much integrity as you could imagine a man having. His death shook me, and I was so sorry.

MURRAY: Mr. Salant would sometimes like to point out that he was trained as a lawyer, not a broadcaster with an extensive journalism background. You mentioned that recently in a piece for the *RTNDA Communicator*.

BLISS: That's right. He would say, "I do what you tell me to do," which was nonsense. But he would ask advice. He was a lawyer, and of course as a lawyer at CBS he had dealt at times with journalistic problems. But he was editor of the law review at Harvard, and I think there was a lot of journalism in his bones. He was also editor of his prep school paper back at Exeter at the same time that I was editor of my paper. He graduated from Harvard in 1935, and I graduated from Yale the same year, and he sometimes kidded me about that—saying it was very unlikely that we were going to get along.

MURRAY: Was he upset that a Harvard man would have to ask a Yale man how to get the job done?

BLISS: No, *he* knew how to get the job done. I carried out assignments and would sometimes sit around in my office with very little to do and then all of a sudden he would say: "By noon Thursday I would like to have a rundown on how many minutes we have devoted to racial demonstrations and violence in the North as compared to the South, over the past six months." It seemed like an impossible task to complete in forty-eight hours. I would have to call Lois at home and say, "Don't expect to see me for the next few days." And I would get a room across the street and just work my tail off. I would turn in all kinds of things. It was stimulating, but then I would go three or four days with very little to do. I would sit in my office and write letters and wait for the next assignment.

MURRAY: What was your most demanding job?

BLISS: In 1962 I was assigned to produce a half-hour documentary for Frank Stanton about the so-called "Rayburn Rule." Sam Rayburn made sure that cameras and microphones were not to be allowed at public hearings in the House of Representatives. The stand that Stanton, Salant—really everyone at CBS, plus almost everybody else in broadcasting—took was that our tools, including cameras and microphones, should be allowed if it was a public hearing.

MURRAY: What was Dr. Stanton's role in that?

BLISS: They wanted me to do it as a documentary giving both sides, but at the end Stanton was to come on and deliver a five-minute editorial giving the CBS position. When it was all done Dick reviewed it first and approved it. And then we had Stanton come down to the screening room and look it over, and, much to my relief, he approved it. He said just two words, which I value. He said: "Good job." And I felt so relieved because this was my first television production effort ever and it was for the top man at the network, so you can imagine how I felt. And then Paley killed it because it was for all of our stations, and the stations were getting a little restless, especially affiliates in the southern states. Some of them had been deserting CBS for other networks because of the more aggressive way CBS was covering the civil rights movement.

MURRAY: Did you ever get any feedback on why Paley killed it?

BLISS: I asked Stanton about it later and he said Paley just thought it was inappropriate for CBS to be imposing an editorial on stations. Anyway, they did show it to some interest groups on the Hill, and from what I hear it got on one station in Texas.

MURRAY: They tested it in Rayburn's backyard, and it didn't fly?

BLISS: That's right, I never thought then of the irony of that. But it was a great time, and I'm sure it helped me when CBS decided to start the regular half-hour evening news program in September 1963. Cronkite asked me if I would be his news editor.

MURRAY: You've been asked many times about comparisons between Murrow and Cronkite—I noticed your reference to that comparison most recently in a textbook, *The Broadcast Century*, by Robert Hilliard and Michael Keith. It sounds like in the final analysis, Mr. Cronkite was more at home in the studio?

BLISS: That's right. Murrow did not even feel comfortable before a microphone. He would perspire profusely and give his whole being to the reading of the script. It's interesting that only once did he ever refer to his discomfort before a microphone and that was the last broadcast he made before he went on his sabbatical. He referred to "this frightening microphone."

MURRAY: When you first heard that he was going to make the transition from radio to television did you think he would do well?

BLISS: I never had any doubt. Murrow would not attempt something he could not do well. Someone said that once, and I agreed fully. He never learned to swim, for example, which was unusual for a country boy. I have seen Polecat Creek, I made a pilgrimage to his boyhood home in North Carolina, and you would not want to swim in it—it is small and fit only for polecats. He did not dance because he was so busy and into everything from dramatics to becoming head of the ROTC company and campus politics there at Washington State University. By this time he felt he would be behind everybody in dancing. So if he couldn't do it well, he would not do it. But yes, I think everyone felt that he could pull it off and make that move to television.

MURRAY: Did you ever go into the field with Murrow or Cronkite for special political programs or primary coverage? Bill Leonard told me he was always impressed with Cronkite's level of preparation and that, in fact, he [Cronkite] put together books on subjects for the evening news or documentaries.

BLISS: I can remember going with Cronkite for primary coverage to California, Oregon, and Indiana. But, absolutely, he prepared those books and I think he did that pretty much on his own, although he may have gotten some help from the CBS reference library. You know Robert Trout did the same kind of thing, he had the same kind of books. It was his wife, Kit, who did the research and did updates for his personal reference books. Cronkite did that in preparation for the political conventions and space shots. I remember coming back into the newsroom one night after going to the theater, and it was close to midnight. There was one lone light on in what we used to call the "Cronkite Area." Everything was in shadow and silent except teletypes moving copy. No other soul in the place. There was this one light on in Cronkite's office, and he was in there studying these great charts showing where the space orbits would go. He was there studying. He was determined to understand what these astronauts were talking about.

MURRAY: The Kennedy assassination—you relayed the information to Cronkite on JFK's death. What kind of day was that for you? How did you handle it? I'll bet you have gotten a lot of inquiries on that?

BLISS: Well, I have been asked about that by a lot of people—every student and every interviewer always asks about it. Of course, it's a day one will never forget. It's strange, we were so busy it's all a big blur in my mind. You know we all turned into reporters around the desk that day. I do remember talking to Billy Graham and asking him for a comment. But mostly, during that time, I screened the copy before it got to Cronkite, so it would not be redundant. So all of the copy went through me and then I would hand it to Walter. That's how I happened to hand him the final confirmation that President Kennedy was dead. You don't forget that, of course. I was really rather glad to be busy because there was the monitor and if you watched too much—especially the funeral and that final procession up to Arlington Cemetery—I would have cried.

MURRAY: You always worked pretty much behind the scenes. Were you ever tempted to go from writer to on-air performer, like Andy Rooney?

BLISS: There was a time I thought I could make an on-air contribution to a program called "News of America" which Paul White started up and aired an hour after the "World News Round-Up." John Hersey's story of Hiroshima had appeared in the *New Yorker*, and I was struck by it, especially since the entire issue had been turned over to that book. If you turned the pages you saw ads for Chanel, silk stockings, gowns and that sort of thing, but the story was about flesh dropping from limbs and the devastation of the bombing of Hiroshima and I wrote a piece about it and recorded it. It was about a minute and a half. I went over to Broadway and did it. Ted Church by this time had succeeded Paul White and he listened to it and said, "Hey, that's pretty good, we'll put you on the air." I said, "I knew when I cut it that if it wasn't all right, I could do it over. I might go on the air and sputter around and make a mess of it." He said, "Well, that's true," and that was the end of it. I told my students never to take that approach. But I think it turned out all right. I think I am what I am supposed to be, an editor. I am quite sure I am a better editor than I would be a reporter on the air.

MURRAY: In the Gary Gates history of CBS, *Air Time*, he said that after you made the switch to academia and the broadcast journalism program at American University, some feared your students might get the impression that if they were fortunate enough to make it to the network, they might think their future bosses would be as generous and kind as you. What strategies did you use to impress them with the idea that it is a really tough business?

BLISS: My approach was to try to impress students with responsibility, first of all, and writing, clear writing, for good communication. It worked beautifully at American University because, until I got there, the students had been going on the air on a closed-circuit station. I was able to wrangle from WAMU-FM, the university station, the right of students to do three newscasts a day and be heard all throughout the Washington area, plus a half-hour magazine program on Sunday. Of course, that took a lot of the students' time and it helped me teaching journalism. Once in a while a student would come in all starry eyed, attracted to the glamour of television and all of that, and then I would tell them how many hours a week they would have to work on the newsdesk. Most would go out the door, and I would never see them again. Of course, other people, like Bob Edwards of National Public Radio, Deborah Potter of CNN, and ABC's chief Congressional correspondent now, Jackie Judd, felt it was wonderful to work all of those hours. And, as you know, it's a self-screening process. I was very fortunate to get those hours on the station because that solved my problem right there, about who would be my students and the approach I could take.

MURRAY: In a lot of the things you have written, including a recent article for *Television Quarterly* and your new history of broadcast news, *Now the News*,

BLISS: The news on radio and television is their major competitor and you cannot help but feel, if you are in the employ of a newspaper, that they've got the glamour jobs, with the highest pay. Connie Chung coming on the air, with Dan as coanchor, was front-page news all across the country. Can you imagine a reporter from the *New York Times* going over to the *Los Angeles Times* and being front-page news? There is just no comparison of three and four million dollars a year in salary. And the newspaper people work just as hard, and they don't get three or four million dollars a year.

MURRAY: What about weekly magazines?

BLISS: Newsmagazine critics point the finger at television and say how obsessed it is with sex and violence, and I think they *are* too obsessed with it. Just last week, the covers of *Time* and *Newsweek*. One has a cover story saying "Sex for Sale" in letters almost two inches tall. The other has letters almost as tall with the words "Lesbians" on the outside. This is the pot talking to the kettle. We *all* need to clean up our act.

MURRAY: What about the Spiro Agnew period? How did you feel about his charges and the attack on the press during that era—print and broadcast news? Were you still at CBS then?

BLISS: I was teaching at the time and felt that some of it was warranted. When you fire a shotgun blast like that, some of the pellets will hit home. But some of the things he said were just crazy. Here were all of these broadcasters who were being described as New York–Washington axis types. They were from all over the United States. You couldn't possibly have a bigger spread on the backgrounds of these various people. And then, of course, the charge that they only talked to each other; almost *never* would they talk to each other.

MURRAY: In the clinics you have conducted over the years for the RTNDA to improve writing quality, what kinds of broadcasts or examples do you use from Murrow's work to help direct employees in the newsrooms of today?

BLISS: When you speak about writing and Edward R. Murrow, I think about what he did during the war or his summation at the end of the McCarthy broadcast, or his Buchenwald broadcast with the description of the two men, they must have been over sixty years old, crawling toward the latrine. "I saw it, but I will not describe it," he said. His flight over Berlin, when he went out with the RAF and told what he saw on the ground, what he referred to as an "orchestrated hell." This was good writing.

MURRAY: What's the problem? Why aren't we turning out better writers? I guess you can't help but critique what you hear today?

BLISS: Everybody says they want good writers but they can't find them. News directors don't have the time to train them. Stations that are making money in big markets should hire editors the way networks do, but they don't. They have the producer or anchor look over the copy, and that's it. But you need good editors to help some of those sentences. Here's one I heard on a channel here in Washington last night: "He brings it off nice—he does it perfect." Schools—grade schools and high schools—should do a better job.

MURRAY: You are receiving the RTNDA's highest honor in the fall, the Paul White Award, and of course, Walter Cronkite, Dan Rather, and all the CBS executives will be there for the presentation, along with the nation's broadcast news directors, both radio and television. What will you tell them about the status of broadcast news? Any observations or suggestions on what is going on right now, or what they might do to improve it?

BLISS: My great fear is that I will appear to be preaching. That is my great fear, and I don't want to do that. And my age is against me too. I obviously appear as an old man, and these will be young men and women in the audience. I have to be very careful not to sound like the "old guy" talking about the "old days"—how we did it *right* then. There are a lot of things being done right today. But there are far too many things being done wrong today.

MURRAY: When did things start to change?

BLISS: It goes back to something that happened maybe fifteen or sixteen years ago, when the bottom line became more important than the responsibility of the station to inform. It always was a business, but back then you did a good job because of the prestige it gave you as a station or network. You competed for quality. Take the sweeps period today, for example. There was a sweeps period last month. If you look at the programming that was broadcast—the latest news from Hollywood or the latest in swimsuits, not because swimsuits are important or interesting. Swimsuits give you an opportunity to show a lot of skin. That is demeaning to journalism. It's this problem that broadcast news became such a great profit center. It used to be something that a station did because of fear that their license might not be renewed, and because they wanted to show how good they were as journalists, or to demonstrate they were a lot better than that station down the street. But now the emphasis is not on quality; it's on how much revenue you can return. That's a damn shame.

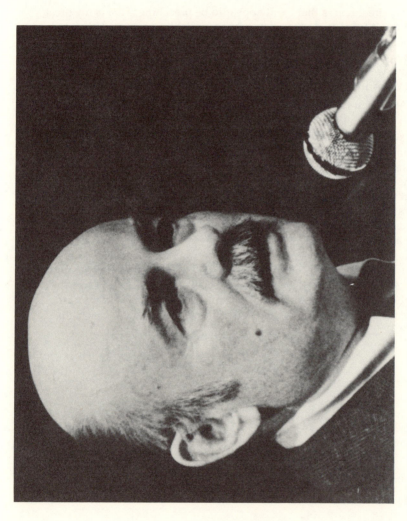

Edward Bliss, Jr., was a writer and program producer for Edward R. Murrow, then editor of "The CBS Evening News with Walter Cronkite." In between, he worked for CBS News presidents Fred W. Friendly and Richard Salant. Later, he founded the broadcast journalism program at American University and authored the first comprehensive history of broadcast news. Courtesy of Edward Bliss, Jr.

"AND THAT'S THE WAY IT IS" (AND WAS) IN PUBLIC AFFAIRS TELEVISION

Walter Cronkite achieved a unique status in American journalism history. The premier network anchorman at CBS, he was regarded as the "most trusted" news source in an era dominated by television coverage of major events. He is associated with most of the major stories of his day: the Kennedy assassination and funeral, the Vietnam War, the moon landing, and Watergate. Cronkite was one of the first American journalists accredited to cover World War II. He worked briefly for Harrison Salisbury in London in 1942 and reported eyewitness accounts of the North African campaign, the invasion at Normandy, and the Battle of the Bulge. He helped to establish international news bureaus for United Press, covered the Nuremberg trials as chief correspondent, then became Moscow bureau chief. With the outbreak of the Korean War, he joined CBS News, hosting such series as "Eyewitness to History" and "The Twentieth Century."

He became anchorman of the CBS Evening News in 1962 and introduced the first half-hour national newscast the following year. His coverage of key stories earned him a popular following among viewers and tenure as "managing editor" of the nightly news. His 1965 visit to Southeast Asia was followed by a personal assessment of military policy after the Tet Offensive in 1968, in which he spoke out against prospects for success. He is associated with a number of contemporary stories including coverage of Richard Nixon's travel to China and Moscow, the Watergate follow-up, and a special Bicentennial celebration. On occasion, Cronkite has publicly condemned the broadcast practices of focusing attention on feature news and hiring broadcast reporters without significant experience in journalism, and he has also called for the expansion of the network evening newscasts. He retired as CBS anchorman in

1981 but contributes occasionally to network special projects including political convention coverage. He also retains a place on the CBS Board of Directors.

The following telephone interview was taped during the winter of 1993, and focuses on Cronkite's contributions to documentary television.

A CONVERSATION WITH WALTER CRONKITE

MURRAY: You have had contact with all of the major national and international political figures of our day. Who do you think has done the most with respect to the way they handle themselves on television and in the way they prepare for broadcast coverage or meetings with the press, including television interviews?

CRONKITE: As far as political candidates are concerned, it's been a generational thing. They seem to get better and better with each generation, at least in terms of sheer presentation and dedication to doing a professional job.

MURRAY: You had a great deal of contact with John F. Kennedy. In fact, in the first half-hour national television newscast you included an interview with him on the subject of Vietnam. Do you feel he came across on television as well as everybody says, as the first full-fledged candidate of the video age?

CRONKITE: I remember that particular Kennedy interview very well. The interesting thing about it is that when I got up to Hyannis, where we planned to do the broadcast the day before. I arrived on a Sunday night, and Bob Pierpoint met me at the hotel. And it turned out that we were sort of in disarray over the fact that the Associated Press came out with a story that the president was going to make a statement on Vietnam as part of our news program. This implied that questions had been discussed in advance and arranged with the president's press aide, Pierre Salinger, as part of the preparation for the interview. Pierre Salinger denied that, of course, and he was upset, and I was very upset myself—especially with the AP guy, because that was not ever our approach by any means, and certainly not at that particular time. We were planning to focus on economics. We did not give out any questions in advance and I had no such agreement with them. We would certainly not allow any review of questions in advance of the interview and neither would the president have suggested them. We did not submit questions and we never did that, except on one occasion with Franco, and we did not use it because it turned out not to be any good anyway.

MURRAY: What about Lyndon Johnson and the press? Could he have saved himself on the Vietnam issue if he had come on television and leveled with the American people and taken a more honest approach at the outset of his term about our military and foreign policy?

CRONKITE: Well, it would have been effective had he come out with an honest approach, but I am not sure he had the information for an honest appraisal. Johnson was like a lot of people at that time with respect to understanding the nature and extent of the war. I think the realization of conditions and the activity of the South Vietnamese military really came, for most people, with the Tet Offensive.

MURRAY: After you came back from Vietnam the second time, after Tet, and reported what you saw—I'm sure you recall the well-known quote about President Johnson saying to an aide, that if he lost you on that issue he may have lost the entire American people. What did you think of that? Did you hear about that statement right away?

CRONKITE: No. I learned about that much later. I was not surprised that he would have made that statement because in addition to myself, a lot of people were thinking that way by then. The Viet Cong operations and conduct of the war were then seen fully by the American people. I think the broadcast probably had some small effect, but it was fairly evident by that point that the war policy was not working. Some people have picked up on that statement and played it up beyond its real influence.

MURRAY: After that time, the so-called liberal press came under fire by the Nixon administration. Today, it seems people are much more willing to admit to an identification to liberal causes and embrace liberal ideals. In fact, I have heard it said that you now support liberal causes. Should journalists admit to that—if that is how they feel? Have you changed your position on this?

CRONKITE: No, I have not changed. I think a working journalist, doing daily news broadcasting or any kind of newsgathering, has to be as objective as they can be. I think journalists have to subscribe to that ethic, so they should be concerned about liberalism or anything else creeping in.

MURRAY: Edward R. Murrow is identified as someone who stood up both for and against certain causes as he did with the McCarthy broadcasts. Did you ever get to work with him very much?

CRONKITE: Ed tried to hire me in Europe and I was doing other things. We did work on some projects, but not really extensively.

MURRAY: The process of developing a documentary. How does that start out?

CRONKITE: Somebody in the shop gets an idea and has the enthusiasm and interest for a subject, and it goes on from there.

MURRAY: The long-form documentaries? We don't see too many of those any more. What's your thinking on it? Why is that—the networks don't want the hassle or the public just does not care for them?

CRONKITE: I don't know whether it's the chicken or the egg. But we're going to test the theory again on the Discovery Channel later this year. In fact, I have a contract to do some of that kind of programming again for the "Encyclopedia" program each year, for the next three years. We're going to see how that works out.

MURRAY: Does it ever bother you when you see conditions or policies you investigated years ago, like apartheid in South Africa, continue unabated?

CRONKITE: Yes, because I think sometimes they often change for the worse.

MURRAY: Do you ever go back and study those old broadcasts at the Museum of Television and Radio?

CRONKITE: It's right down the street and I have visited on occasion. But do I go back and review my work after it's done? Not really.

MURRAY: I saw Ed Bradley on "Later with Bob Costas." He said, like so many of the other younger people who got into broadcasting in the last generation, that you inspired him with coverage of important stories like coverage of the Kennedy assassination, the space program—and your enthusiasm for the big story. He even mentioned one documentary in detail, "D-Day, Plus 20 Years." In fact, he related an anecdote that he observed as a kid, and then later heard more about when he reached CBS—that in one segment of that documentary General Eisenhower was driving—at least part of the time, and you were behind the wheel for the rest. And there was some speculation, that maybe Eisenhower wasn't the best driver in the world, maybe the by-product of being chauffeured as a general and later in office as commander-in-chief. Is that the way that was?

CRONKITE: No, actually we were in a jeep and he was describing this fabulous scene at Normandy Beach on D-Day. I drove down the beach at the start of the program while he described what had taken place. Of course, the idea was that he was showing *me* what happened. Then Fred Friendly said, "You know, there is something wrong with your driving him, Walter, *he* should be driving instead of you." So he asked the general, "Do you drive?" And he said, "Sure." He said, "Then we should have you driving." He seemed willing, so he got behind the wheel and he didn't seem to mind. Fred got him to drive and describe that scene to me. His wife, Mamie Eisenhower, who was standing with my wife near the filming, asked Betsy if whether what she thought she was seeing was correct—that they had just exchanged drivers, and that Dwight was going to be doing the driving. Betsy said that "It looks that way," and Mamie turned back toward her and added: "My dear, your husband has never been in greater danger. Dwight hasn't driven in twenty-five years." Actually, he did need some assistance getting it into gear, but we made it.

MURRAY: Bill Leonard told me that you are distinguished most from your peers by the extensive homework you did on various documentaries and special projects, especially in planning for political conventions. How and where did you do that research?

CRONKITE: Most of it was done right here in my office. You have to remember that I had all of the resources of CBS News behind me and they were very extensive. I could demand any material needed.

MURRAY: It seems as if you studied and planned for some of these broadcasts for great lengths of time and then, ironically, a lot of the major stories developed on the spur of the moment, such as the historic Sadat and Begin meeting, although your role in that is misunderstood, right? You just asked the right questions?

CRONKITE: That's correct. Yes. I had no intention of bringing up a meeting between the two in the Middle East. But there had been some speculation that such a thing might be happening for us because of what Sadat had said in his Parliament in front of some Canadian parliamentarians, when he had addressed himself to a meeting and said, "I will go to Jerusalem." And that started the story of whether there would be such a meeting, where they both would be attending. It became an issue. When the Canadians got to Tel Aviv and Jerusalem, someone among them suggested that Sadat would be willing to meet, and Begin said, "Let him come." And that story got it started because it was suggested that it had been mentioned to Begin. He said, "He can come anytime."

More rumors started over that weekend on the issue of their getting together and I was able to get Sadat on a satellite call and I said, "When do you think there will be such a meeting?" And actually, by the time it developed as a story over the weekend in Europe and that night, I had heard Sadat say many times as a figure of speech that he wanted peace, and that in fact, in his lifetime, there would be peace. And getting the satellite interview Monday morning, I asked him about what he had said, and he gave his conditions for peace—that the Israelis would have to withdraw from the Golan Heights and withdraw from the Sinai, and return to Jerusalem. Those were his conditions for peace, but he said upon further questioning then that he was willing to meet with Begin to discuss peace anytime, without condition. Begin accepted and history was made.

SELECTED BIBLIOGRAPHY

UNPUBLISHED MATERIAL

Bilski, Theodore J. "A Descriptive Study: Edward R. Murrow's Contribution to Electronic Journalism." Ph.D. diss., Case Western Reserve University, 1971.

Bliss, Edward, Jr. Personal correspondence, June 11, 1975.

——. Personal correspondence, May 4, 1988.

——. Personal correspondence, November 2, 1988.

Cahill-Spencer, Patricia. "Red Shadows: Joe McCarthy and Television." M.A. thesis, University of Kansas, 1971.

Caliteaux, Karen. "The Political Blacklist in the Broadcast Industry: The Decade of the 1950's." Ph.D. diss., Ohio State University, 1973.

Chandler, Robert. Personal correspondence, April 20, 1978.

Cooke, Alistair. Personal correspondence, September 14, 1989.

Cronkite, Walter. "The Journalist at Thermopylae." Address at Johns Hopkins University, Baltimore, MD, February 9, 1967.

Deaver, Jean F. "A Study of Senator Joseph R. McCarthy and 'McCarthyism' As Influences upon the News Media and the Evolution of Reportorial Method." Ph.D. diss., University of Texas, Austin, 1969.

Dowling, Frederick R. "The Style of Five Radio Commentators." Ph.D. diss., University of Wisconsin, Madison, 1955.

Friendly, Fred W. Personal correspondence, June 8, 1989.

——. Personal correspondence, May 30, 1990.

——. Personal correspondence, May 31, 1992.

——. Remarks before the Radio-Television News Directors Association. Salt Lake City, UT, August 29, 1986.

Leonard, Bill. Personal correspondence, June 7, 1990.

——. Telephone interview, September 5, 1990.

——. Personal correspondence, May 14, 1992.

Murray, Michael D. " 'See It Now' vs. McCarthyism: Dimensions of Documentary Persuasion." Ph.D. diss., University of Missouri, Columbia, 1974.
Murrow, Janet. Personal conversation, April 24, 1992.
Schlesinger, Arthur, Jr. Personal correspondence, August 3, 1992.
Small, William. Personal correspondence, June 23, 1992.
Stanton, Frank. Personal conversation, February 7, 1992.
———. Personal correspondence, February 25, 1992.
———. Remarks before the Institute for Education by Radio-Television, Ohio State University, Columbus, OH, May 6, 1959.
Wershba, Joseph. Personal conversation, November 9, 1973.
Williams, Palmer. Personal conversation, November 9, 1973.
Woolley, Russell. "The Radio Speaking of Edward R. Murrow." Ph.D. diss., Northwestern University, 1955.
Yeager, Murray R. "An Analysis of Edward R. Murrow's 'See It Now' Television Program." Ph.D. diss., University of Iowa, 1956.

BOOKS

Arlen, Michael. *Living Room War.* New York: Viking Press, 1969.
Barnouw, Erik. *The Image Empire: A History of Broadcasting in the United States*, vol. 3, from 1953. New York: Oxford University Press, 1970.
———. *The Golden Web: A History of Broadcasting in the United States*, vol. 2, 1933 to 1953. New York: Oxford University Press, 1968.
———. *A Tower in Babel: A History of Broadcasting in the United States*, vol. 1, to 1933. New York: Oxford University Press, 1966.
———. *Tube of Plenty: The Evolution of American Television.* New York: Oxford University Press, 1975.
Barrett, Marvin, ed. *Moments of Truth?* New York: Thomas Y. Crowell, 1975.
Baughman, James L. *The Republic of Mass Culture.* Baltimore: Johns Hopkins University Press, 1992.
Bayley, Edwin R. *Joe McCarthy and the Press.* New York: Pantheon, 1981.
Benjamin, Burton. *Fair Play: CBS, General Westmoreland, and How a Television Documentary Went Wrong.* New York: Harper and Row, 1988.
Bergreen, Lawrence. *Look Now, Pay Later: The Rise of Network Broadcasting.* Garden City, NY: Doubleday and Company, 1980.
Bliss, Edward, Jr., ed. *In Search of Light: The Broadcasts of Edward R. Murrow, 1938–1961.* New York: Alfred A. Knopf, 1967.
Bliss, Edward, Jr. *Now the News: The Story of Broadcast Journalism.* New York: Columbia University Press, 1991.
Bluem, A. William. *Documentary in American Television.* New York: Hastings House, 1965.
Bluem, A. William, and Roger Manvell, eds. *Television: The Creative Experience.* New York: Hastings House, 1967.
Boddy, William. *Fifties Television: The Industry and Its Critics.* Urbana, IL: University of Illinois Press, 1990.
Bogart, Leo. *The Age of Television.* New York: Frederick Ungar, 1972.
Boyer, Peter J. *Who Killed CBS? The Undoing of America's Number One News Network.* New York: Random House, 1988.

Brewin, Bob, and Sydney Shaw. *Vietnam on Trial: Westmoreland vs. CBS.* New York: Atheneum, 1987.

Brown, Les. *Encyclopedia of Television.* New York: New York Times Books, 1977.

——. *Television: The Business behind the Box.* New York: Harcourt Brace Jovanovich, 1971.

Buckley, William F., and L. Brent Bozell. *McCarthy and His Enemies.* Chicago: Henry Regnery, 1954.

Campbell, Richard. *"60 Minutes" and the News: A Mythology for Middle America.* Urbana, IL: University of Illinois Press, 1991.

Carey, James W. *Communication as Culture: Essays on Media and Society.* Boston: Unwin Hyman, 1989.

Carey, James W., ed. *Media, Myths, and Narratives: Television and the Press.* Newbury Park, CA: Sage, 1988.

Chester, Edward W. *Radio, Television, and American Politics.* New York: Sheed and Ward, 1969.

Cohn, Roy. *McCarthy.* New York: New American Library, 1968.

Cook, Fred J. *The Nightmare Decade: The Life and Times of Senator Joe McCarthy.* New York: Random House, 1971.

Cronkite, Walter. *Theodore H. White Lecture, Harvard University.* Cambridge, MA: Joan Shorenstein Barone Center on the Press, Politics and Public Policy, Kennedy School of Government, 1990.

Culbert, David H. *News for Everyman: Radio and Foreign Affairs in Thirties America.* Westport, CT: Greenwood, 1976.

Czitrom, Daniel J. *Media and the American Mind: From Morse to McLuhan.* Chapel Hill: University of North Carolina Press, 1982.

Dayan, Daniel, and Elihu Katz. *Media Events: The Live Broadcasting of History.* Cambridge, MA: Harvard University Press, 1992.

Diamond, Edwin. *Good News, Bad News.* Cambridge, MA: M.I.T. Press, 1978.

——. *The Media Show: The Changing Face of the News.* Cambridge, MA: M.I.T. Press, 1991.

——. *The Tin Kazoo.* Cambridge, MA: M.I.T. Press, 1975.

Douglas, Susan J. *Inventing American Broadcasting, 1899–1922.* Baltimore: Johns Hopkins University Press, 1987.

Emery, Edwin, and Michael Emery. *The Press and America: An Interpretative History of the Mass Media.* Englewood Cliffs, NJ: Prentice-Hall, 1954.

Emery, Michael C., and Ted Curtis Smythe, eds. *Readings in Mass Communication: Concepts and Issues in the Mass Media.* Dubuque, IA: William C. Brown, 1974.

Epstein, Edward Jay. *News from Nowhere: Television and the News.* New York: Random House, 1967.

Fang, Irving. *Those Radio Commentators!* Ames, IA: Iowa State University Press, 1977.

Faulk, John Henry. *Fear on Trial.* New York: Simon and Schuster, 1964.

Feuerlicht, Roberta S. *Joe McCarthy and McCarthyism: The Hate That Haunts America.* New York: McGraw-Hill, 1972.

Foote, Joe S. *Television Access and Political Power: The Networks, the Presidency, and the "Loyal Opposition."* New York: Praeger Publishers, 1990.

Friendly, Fred W. *Due to Circumstances Beyond Our Control.* New York: Random House, 1967.

Fulbright, J. William. *The Pentagon Propaganda Machine.* New York: Liveright, 1970.

Gans, Herbert J. *Deciding What's News: A Study of the CBS Evening News, NBC Nightly News, Newsweek and Time*. New York: Vintage Books, 1980.

Gates, Gary Paul. *Air Time: The Inside Story of CBS News*. New York: Harper and Row, 1978.

Gitlin, Todd. *The Whole World Is Watching*. Berkeley, CA: University of California Press, 1980.

Goldberg, Robert, and Gerald Jay Goldberg. *Anchors: Brokaw, Jennings, Rather*. New York: Birch Lane Press, 1990.

Haiman, Franklin S. *Freedom of Speech: Issues and Cases*. New York: Random House, 1967.

Halberstam, David. *The Powers That Be*. New York: Alfred A. Knopf, 1979.

Hallin, Daniel C. *The "Uncensored War": The Media and Vietnam*. Berkeley, CA: University of California Press, 1986.

Hammond, Charles Montgomery. *The Image Decade: Television Documentary, 1965–1975*. New York: Hastings House, 1981.

Head, Sydney. *Broadcasting in America: A Survey of Television and Radio*. Boston: Houghton Mifflin, 1976.

Hewitt, Don. *Minute by Minute*. New York: Random House, 1985.

Hilliard, Robert L. *Writing for Television and Radio*. Belmont, CA: Wadsworth, 1984.

Himmelstein, Hal. *Television Myth and the American Mind*. New York: Praeger Publishers, 1984.

Hughes, Emmet John. *Ordeal of Power*. New York: Atheneum, 1963.

Jacobs, Lewis, ed. *The Documentary Tradition*. New York: W. W. Norton, 1971.

Joyce, Edward. *Prime Times, Bad Times: A Personal Drama of Television News*. New York: Doubleday, 1988.

Kahn, Frank, ed. *Documents of American Broadcasting*. New York: Appleton Century Crofts, 1973.

Keeley, Joseph. *The Left-Leaning Antenna: Political Bias in Television*. New Rochelle, NY: Arlington Books, 1971.

Kendrick, Alexander. *Prime Time: The Life of Edward R. Murrow*. Boston: Little, Brown and Company, 1969.

Koch, Howard. *The Panic Broadcast*. Boston: Little, Brown, 1970.

Lang, Kurt, and Gladys Engel Lang. *Politics and Television*. Chicago: Quadrangle Books, 1970.

Leonard, Bill. *In the Storm of the Eye: A Lifetime at CBS*. New York: G. P. Putnam, 1987.

Leonard, Thomas C. *The Power of the Press: The Birth of American Political Reporting*. New York: Oxford University Press, 1986.

Leroy, David, and Christopher H. Sterling, eds. *Mass News: Practices, Controversies and Alternatives*. Englewood Cliffs, NJ: Prentice-Hall, 1973.

Levin, G. Roy. *Documentary Explorations*. Garden City, NY: Doubleday, 1971.

Lichty, Lawrence W., and Malachi G. Topping. *American Broadcasting: A Sourcebook on the History of Radio and Television*. New York: Hastings House, 1975.

MacDonald, J. Fred. *Blacks and White TV*. Chicago: Nelson-Hall, 1992.

——— . *One Nation under Television: The Rise and Decline of Network Television*. New York: Pantheon Books, 1990.

MacNeil, Robert. *The People Machine: The Influence of Television on American Politics*. New York: Harper and Row, 1968.

Madsen, Axel. *60 Minutes: The Power & Politics of America's Most Popular TV News Show*. New York: Dodd, Mead, 1984.

Marzolf, Marion Tuttle. *Civilizing Voices: American Press Criticism, 1880–1950*. New York: Longman, 1991.

Matusow, Barbara. *The Evening Stars: The Making of the Network News Anchor*. Boston: Houghton Mifflin, 1983.

Mayer, Martin. *About Television*. New York: Harper and Row, 1972.

McCabe, Peter. *Bad News at Black Rock: The Sell-Out of CBS News*. New York: Arbor House, 1987.

McKerns, Joseph, ed. *Biographical Dictionary of American Journalism*. New York: Greenwood Press, 1989.

Metz, Robert. *CBS: Reflections in a Bloodshot Eye*. New York: Signet, 1975.

Mickelson, Sig. *The Electric Mirror: Politics in an Age of Television*. New York: Dodd, Mead and Company, 1972.

──── . *From Whistle Stop to Sound Bite*. New York: Praeger Publishers, 1989.

Moynihan, Daniel Patrick. *Family and Nation: The Godkin Lectures, Harvard University*. New York: Harcourt Brace Jovanovich, 1986.

Murray, Robert K. *Red Scare: A Study in National Hysteria*. Minneapolis: University of Minnesota, 1955.

Murrow, Edward R. *This Is London*. New York: Simon and Schuster, 1941.

Murrow, Edward R., and Fred W. Friendly, eds. *See It Now*. New York: Simon and Schuster, 1955.

Nimmo, Dan. *The Political Persuaders*. Englewood Cliffs, NJ: Prentice-Hall, 1970.

Nimmo, Dan, and James E. Combs. *Mediated Political Realities*. 2d ed. New York: Longman, 1990.

O'Connor, John E., ed. *American History, American Television: Interpreting the Video Past*. New York: Frederick Ungar, 1983.

Paley, William S. *As It Happened: A Memoir*. Garden City, NY: Doubleday and Co., 1979.

Paper, Lewis J. *Empire: William S. Paley and the Making of CBS*. New York: St. Martins Press, 1987.

Persico, Joe. *Murrow: An American Original*. Englewood Cliffs, NJ: Prentice-Hall, 1988.

Powers, Ron. *The Beast, the Eunuch and the Glass Eyed Child*. New York: Harcourt Brace Jovanovich, 1990.

──── . *The Newscasters*. New York: St. Martins Press, 1978.

Quinn, Sally. *We're Going to Make You a Star*. New York: Simon and Schuster, 1975.

Rapping, Elayne. *The Looking Glass World of Nonfiction TV*. Boston: South End Press, 1987.

Rather, Dan, with Mickey Herskowitz. *The Camera Never Blinks: Adventures of a TV Journalist*. New York: William Morrow, 1977.

Read, William H. *America's Mass Media Merchants*. Baltimore: Johns Hopkins University Press, 1976.

Reasoner, Harry. *Before the Colors Fade*. New York: Alfred A. Knopf, 1981.

Rorty, James, and Monche Deter. *McCarthy and the Communists*. Boston: Beacon Press, 1954.

Rosenthal, Alan. *The New Documentary in Action*. Berkeley, CA: University of California Press, 1971.

──── . *Writing, Directing and Producing Documentary Films*. Carbondale, IL: Southern Illinois University Press, 1990.

Rosenthal, Alan, ed. *New Challenges for Documentary*. Berkeley, CA: University of California Press, 1988.

Rovere, Richard. *Senator Joe McCarthy*. New York: Harcourt, Brace, 1959.

Rubin, Bernard. *Political Television*. Belmont, CA: Wadsworth, 1967.

Schiller, Dan. *Objectivity and the News: The Public and the Rise of Commercial Journalism*. Philadelphia: University of Pennsylvania Press, 1981.

Schoenbrun, David. *On and Off the Air: An Informal History of CBS News*. New York: E. P. Dutton, 1989.

Schorr, Daniel. *Clearing the Air*. Boston: Houghton Mifflin, 1977.

Schudson, Michael. *Discovering the News: A Social History of American Newspapers*. New York: Basic Books, 1978.

Seldes, Gilbert. *The Public Arts*. New York: Simon and Schuster, 1956.

Sevareid, Eric. *Not So Wild a Dream*. New York: Atheneum, 1976.

Slater, Robert. *This . . . Is CBS: A Chronicle of 60 Years*. Englewood Cliffs, NJ: Prentice-Hall, 1988.

Sloan, William David, James Stovall, and James Startt, eds. *The Media in America: A History*. Scottsdale, AZ: Gorsuch Scarisbruck, 1993.

Small, William. *To Kill a Messenger: TV News and the Real World*. New York: Hastings House, 1970.

Smith, R. Franklin. *Edward R. Murrow: The War Years*. Kalamazoo, MI: New Issues Press, 1978.

Smythe, Mabel M., ed. *The Black American Reference Book*. Englewood Cliffs, NJ: Prentice-Hall, 1976.

Sperber, A. M. *Murrow: His Life and Times*. New York: Freundlich, 1986.

Start, Clarissa. *Webster Groves*. Webster Groves, MO: City of Webster Groves, 1975.

Sterling, Christopher, and Kitross, John. *Stay Tuned: A Concise History of American Broadcasting*. Belmont, CA: Wadsworth, 1978.

Swallow, Norman. *Factual Television*. New York: Hastings House, 1966.

Thomas, Lately. *When Even Angels Wept: The Senator McCarthy Affair*. New York: William Morrow, 1973.

Tuchman, Gaye. *Making News: A Study of the Construction of Reality*. New York: Free Press, 1978.

Udelson, Joseph H. *The Great Television Race: A History of the American Television Industry, 1925–1941*. University of Alabama Press, 1982.

Wallace, Mike, and Gary Paul Gates. *Close Encounters*. New York: William Morrow, 1984.

Watkins, Arthur V. *Enough Rope: The Inside Story of the Censure of Senator Joe McCarthy*. Englewood Cliffs, NJ: Prentice-Hall, 1969.

Watson, Mary Ann. *The Expanding Vista: American Television in the Kennedy Years*. New York: Oxford University Press, 1990.

Westin, Av. *Newswatch: How TV Decides the News*. New York: Simon and Schuster, 1982.

White, Paul. *News on the Air*. New York: Harcourt, 1947.

White, Theodore H. *The Making of the President 1968*. New York: Pocket Books, 1970.

Winfield, Betty Houchin, and Lois B. DeFleur. *The Edward R. Murrow Heritage: Challenge for the Future*. Ames, IA: Iowa State University Press, 1986.

Wyckoff, Gene. *The Image Candidates: American Politics in the Age of Television*. New York: Macmillan, 1986.

Yellin, David G. *Special: Fred Freed and the Television Documentary*. New York: Macmillan, 1972.

SELECTED ARTICLES

"Accused Reservist Is Ruled Bad Risk." *New York Times*, October 14, 1953, 17.

"ACLU Aimed at Jenner." *Indianapolis Times*, November 30, 1953, 10.

"ACLU Has Rights Too." *Indianapolis Star*, November 20, 1953, 29.

"ACLU Prefers Few Reds to Intimidation." *Indianapolis Star*, November 21, 1953, 1.

Adams, Val. "CBS Appeals Action by Union." *New York Times*, February 7, 1958, 45.

"Air Force Will Fight Ouster." *New York Times*, September 24, 1953, 23.

Alter, Jonathan. "Bill Moyers Examines the Black Family." *Newsweek*, January 27, 1986, 58–60.

——. "The Struggle for the Soul of CBS." *Newsweek*, September 15, 1986, 53–54.

"An Organization Is No Better Than the Men Who Lead It." *Indiana Catholic Record*, November 27, 1953, 1.

"The Aroma of Decency." *New York Herald Tribune*, March 19, 1954, 19.

Auletta, Ken. "Look What They've Done to the News." *TV Guide*, November 9, 1991, 4–7.

"The Baited Trap." *Time*, March 29, 1954, 77.

Balutis, Alan P. "Congress, the President and the Press." *Journalism Quarterly* 53 (1976): 509–515.

——. "The President and the Press: The Expanding Presidential Image." *Presidential Studies Quarterly* 7 (1977): 244–251.

Baughman, James L. "The Strange Birth of 'CBS Reports' Revisited." *Historical Journal of Film, Radio and Television* (2) (1982): 28–38.

Becker, Samuel L. "Presidential Power: The Influence of Broadcasting." *Quarterly Journal of Speech* 47 (1961): 14–17.

Beiswinger, George. "Media Museums." *Media History Digest* (Fall-Winter 1988): 24.

Bergreen, Lawrence. "The Moyers Style." *American Film*, February 1980, 53.

"Bill Moyers: In a Medium of Sound-Bite Journalism, He Serves up Porterhouse." *American Film*, June 1990, 17–20.

Bliss, Ed. "What Makes Don Hewitt Tick?" *RTNDA Communicator* (September 1987): 32.

Boyer, Peter J. "CBS Asks Advice on Cronkite Show on Apartheid." *New York Times*, November 5, 1987, p. 25.

——. " '60 Minutes' Star Is Critical of CBS." *New York Times*, August 6, 1986, 19.

Broder, David. "Drumbeat for the Family." *Washington Post*, January 26, 1986, B7.

Brown, Les. "Taped Over Shows Get CBS Disclaimer." *New York Times*, January 6, 1976, C1.

Carmody, John. " 'The Guns of Autumn': A Recoil, A Response." *Washington Post*, September 27, 1975, C1.

Carroll, Raymond L. "Economic Influences on Commercial Network Television Documentary Scheduling." *Journal of Broadcasting* 23 (Fall 1979): 415.

Carter, Bill. "Whatever Happened to Documentaries?" *Washington Journalism Review* (June 1983): 43–46.

"The Case of Lieutenant Radulovich." *Variety*, October 28, 1953, 25.

"CBS Buckles Down over Seat Belts." *Washington Journalism Review* (January/February 1993): 13.

"CBS Declines to Air Jefferson Day Speech." *Broadcasting*, April 7, 1947, 26.

"CBS Gives Employees Bad News." *St. Louis Post-Dispatch*, April 9, 1991, 7B.

Chandler, Robert. "Putting the CBS News Budget into Perspective." *Broadcasting*, April 13, 1987, 32.

"Civil Liberties Union Is Refused War Memorial for Meeting." *Indianapolis Star*, November 17, 1953, 1.

"Civil Liberties Unit to Meet in Church." *Indianapolis Star*, November 19, 1953, 26.

"Civil Liberties, Unlimited." *Indianapolis Times*, November 19, 1953, 22.

"Clips of '60 Minutes' May Be Made Public in Suit against CBS." *Wall Street Journal,* March 1983, 37.

Cohen, Richard. "And for Government Aid." *Washington Post,* January 26, 1986, B7.

――――. "NBC's Top Official Disgraced Journalism." *St. Louis Post-Dispatch.* February 16, 1993, B3.

Collins, Monica. " '60 Minutes' at Age 20: It Has Style, Substance and Success." *USA Today,* September 17, 1987, C3.

"Communications Board Investigating Broadcast That Caused Hysteria." *St. Louis Post-Dispatch,* October 31, 1938, 1.

Corrigan, Patricia. "Class of '67: Image Still Rankles." *St. Louis Post-Dispatch,* July 6, 1992, 3D.

――――. "Webster Groves: Are Teens Still Clad in Diapers?" *St. Louis Globe-Democrat,* March 4, 1986, B1.

Corry, John. "Weighing the Facts in Westmoreland vs. CBS." *New York Times,* September 4, 1983, B19.

Crater, Rufus. "Perspective on the News: What the Shooting Was All About." *Broadcasting,* July 19, 1971, 20–22.

Cronkite, Walter. "Keynote Address." Conference of College Broadcasters at Brown University. *College Broadcaster* (February 1989): 26.

"Dialed Hysteria." *Newsweek,* November 7, 1938, 13.

"Dick Salant and the Purity of News." *Broadcasting,* September 19, 1977, 105.

Dorsey, Tom. " '60 Minutes' Can Skirt the Spotlight As Well As Wield It." *Louisville Courier Journal,* June 9, 1981, C1.

"Edward R. Murrow Airs Dispute on 'See It Now.' " *Hoosier Legionnaire,* December 1953, 4.

"Edward R. Murrow of CBS: 'Diplomat, Poet, Preacher.' " *Newsweek,* March 9, 1953, 40.

"Edward R. Murrow, of the 'See' around Us." *Daily Variety,* January 6, 1954, 196.

"Eisenhower Quoted to Security Panel." *New York Times,* September 30, 1953, 25.

"Executive Committee Unanimously Backs Amos." *Hoosier Legionnaire,* December 1953, 4.

"Eyes of Conscience." *Newsweek,* December 7, 1953, 65–66.

"Face Off on the First Amendment." *Broadcasting,* April 26, 1971, 36.

"F.C.C.: History of a Flop." *Business Week,* February 4, 1939, 15.

"F.C.C. Shakeup." *Newsweek,* October 25, 1937, 32–34.

Flander, Judy. "Hewitt's Humongous Hour." *Washington Journalism Review* (April 1991): 29.

"4 Youths Held in Fatal Gang Fight; Police Patrol Scene." *New York Times,* August 1, 1957, D17.

Friedman, Steve. "Neighborhood Folklore." *St. Louis Magazine,* September 1986, 49.

Friendly, Fred W. "The Unselling of the 'Selling of the Pentagon.' " *Harpers,* June 1971.

Friendly, Jonathan. "CBS Producer Defends Program on Vietnam." *New York Times,* July 17, 1982, 44.

Gent, George. "The Black Soldier." *New York Times,* July 10, 1968, L79.

――――. "Show on Negroes Arouses Viewers." *New York Times,* July 4, 1968, L41.

――――. "TV: Common Struggle?" *New York Times,* July 17, 1968, L87.

Gilliam, Dorothy. "The Crumbling Black Family." *Washington Post,* January 30, 1986, C3.

Godfrey, Donald G. "CBS World News Roundup: Setting the Stage for the Next Half Century." *American Journalism* 3 (3) (Summer 1990): 164–172.

Gould, Jack. "Body, Soul and CBS." *New York Times*, July 31, 1968, 83.

———. "Radio-TV: Street Gangs." *New York Times*, April 22, 1958.

———. "TV: Hagerty's Role Discussed." *New York Times*, February 28, 1958, 45.

———. "TV: Human Document." *New York Times*, February 3, 1958, 46.

———. "Video Journalism: Treatment of Radulovich History by 'See It Now' Is Fine Reporting." *New York Times*, October 25, 1953, 13.

Graham, Sandy. "Illinois Power Pans '60 Minutes.' " *Wall Street Journal*, June 27, 1980, 1.

"Guilt by Kinship." *New York Times*, October 21, 1953, 13.

Hart, Jeffrey. "Moyers Said It Well in Series on Blacks." *St. Louis Post-Dispatch*, February 5, 1986, 3B.

Henry, William A., III. "Autopsy on CBS 'Expose.' " *Time*, July 26, 1982, 40.

———. "Don Hewitt: Man of the Hour." *Washington Journalism Review* (May 1986): 26.

Hernon, Peter. "Class of '66 Remembers." *St. Louis Post-Dispatch*, July 7, 1986, 1A.

"Hue and Cry: TV's Hope for a Brighter Tomorrow." *Daily Variety*, January 6, 1954, 86.

"Hunger Pains." *Newsweek*, June 10, 1968, 100.

"Ike's Praise Cited by Barred Group." *Indianapolis Times*, November 18, 1953, 3.

Irvine, Reed. "The Selling of 'The Selling of the Pentagon.' " *National Review*, August 10, 1971, 23.

Jordan, Jim. "Legion Brands Civil Liberties Unit 'Vicious Racket.' " *Indianapolis Times*, November 22, 1953, 4.

Katz, Jon. "Brooding, Pious and Popular: Bill Moyers Is the Media's Pastor of Public Affairs." *St. Louis Post-Dispatch*, March 25, 1992, 78.

Klein, Jeffrey. "Semi-Tough: The Politics behind '60 Minutes.' " *Mother Jones*, October 1979, 26–31.

Knap, Ted. "Murrow to Televise Civil Rights Dispute." *Indianapolis Times*, November 20, 1953, 1.

Kurtz, Howard. "On Television, Gunfire Is Heard but Not Seen." *Washington Post*, January 17, 1991, A28.

Levins, Harry. "Film Still Drives 'Em Crazy after All These Years." *St. Louis Post-Dispatch*, March 6, 1989, 2D.

"Liberties Group Hails War Memorial Ban." *Indianapolis Times*, November 17, 1953, 1.

"Lieutenant's Kin Guarded after Threats." *Detroit News*, September 28, 1953, 1.

Lockridge, Kay. "Steadfast at '60 Minutes.' " *The Quill*, March, 1976, 19.

Mannes, Marya. "The People vs. McCarthy." *Reporter* 10 (April 27, 1954): 26.

Martin, Ernest F., Jr. "The 'Hunger in America' Controversy." *Journal of Broadcasting* 16 (1972): 185–194.

"McCarthy in Broadcast Calls Critics Untruthful." *New York Herald Tribune*, March 12, 1954, 1.

"McCarthy Says Red Decodes Secrets, but Army Denies It." *New York Times*, February 24, 1954, 1.

Mermelstein, Aaron. "The Harvest of Shame Goes On." *St. Louis Sun*, April 17, 1990, 27.

Merron, Jeff. "Murrow on TV: 'See It Now,' 'Person to Person,' and the Making of a 'Masscult Personality.' " *Journalism Monographs* 106 (July 1988).

Mink, Eric. "Warning to Blacks and Whites." *St. Louis Post-Dispatch*, January 24, 1986, 9F.

Moley, Ray. "Radio Dangers." *Newsweek*, November 14, 1938, 48.

Moore, Mike. "Cronkite Basted; Society Lambasted." *The Quill* (December 1985): 37.

"Mrs. Moss Confused but Feels No Anger." *Washington Post*, March 14, 1954, 1.

Murray, Michael D. "The End of an Era at CBS: A Conversation with Bill Leonard." *American Journalism* 8 (Winter 1991): 48–61. See Appendix B.

——. "Persuasive Dimensions of 'See It Now's' 'Report on Senator Joseph R. McCarthy.' " *Communication Quarterly* (Fall 1975): 13–20.

——. "Television's Desperate Moment: A Conversation with Fred Friendly." *Journalism History* 1 (1974): 68–71. See Appendix A.

——. "To Hire a Hall: 'An Argument in Indianapolis.' " *Communication Studies* 10 (2) (Spring 1975): 12–20.

"Murrow: The Man, the Myth and the McCarthy Fighter." *Look*, August 24, 1954, 27.

"Murrow Wins the Nation's Applause." *Broadcasting*, 46, March 15, 1954, 7.

"The Night Martians Came to New Jersey." *People Weekly*, October 31, 1988, 45.

Novak, Michael. "The Content of Their Character." *National Review*, February 28, 1986, 47.

O'Connor, John J. " 'The Guns of Autumn' Hunting the Hunters." *New York Times*, September 14, 1975, D25.

——. "How Fair Is the Fairness Doctrine?" *New York Times*, June 15, 1975, D27.

"Officer Maps Appeal to Ike on Air Force Ouster." *Detroit News*, October 14, 1953, 1.

"Once Upon a Time, Madam, There Just Were No Communists." *Indianapolis Times*, November 14, 1953, 1.

"One Last Word." *New York Herald Tribune*, March 15, 1954, 17.

"Orson Welles on Problems of Making Drama More Intimate." *New York Times*, August 14, 1938, 1.

Philips, Wayne. "Truman Disputes Eisenhower on '48." *New York Times*, February 3, 1958, 1.

"Praise Pours in on Murrow Show." *New York Times*, March 11, 1954, 19.

"Proposes Congress Curb Radio 'Abuses.' " *St. Louis Globe-Democrat*, October 31, 1938, 1.

"Radio Broadcast Causes Panic: Widespread Hysteria over War Drama." *St. Louis Globe-Democrat*, October 31, 1938, 1.

"Radio Does U.S. a Favor." *Variety*, November 2, 1938, 1.

"Radio Listeners Alarmed by Fictional Broadcast of Attack by Men from Mars." *St. Louis Post-Dispatch*, October 31, 1938, 1.

"Radio Listeners in Panic, Taking War Drama as Fact." *New York Times*, October 31, 1938, 7.

Rice, Patricia. "CBS Reports: Dan Rather Visits Voters in Webster Groves." *St. Louis Post-Dispatch*, September 19, 1992, 3A.

Rogers, Jimmie N., and Theodore Clevenger, Jr. " 'The Selling of the Pentagon'; Was CBS the Fulbright Propaganda Machine?" *Quarterly Journal of Speech* (1971): 266–273.

Rosenberg, Howard. "Dan and Saddam Show: CBS' Prime Time Coup." *Los Angeles Times*, August 31, 1990, F1.

Rothenberg, Fred. "Documentaries Grow Scarce." *St. Louis Post-Dispatch*, September 3, 1984, 10C.

Rusher, William. "Power of the Press: Listening to Liberals." *St. Louis Post-Dispatch*, February 12, 1986, 3B.

Rutkus, Denis S. "Presidential Television." *Journal of Communication* 26 (1976): 73–78.

"Salute to a Brave Man." *New York Herald Tribune*, March 12, 1954, 19.

"Schulte Hits at Use of Center by Civil Liberties Union." *Indianapolis Times*, November 24, 1953, 1.

Seldes, Gilbert. "Murrow, McCarthy and the Empty Formula." *Saturday Review*, April 24, 1954, 27.
"Senator Attacks: Hits Back at Stevenson, Murrow and Flanders in Radio Broadcast." *New York Times*, March 12, 1954, 1.
Shales, Tom. "The Black Family: A Tale of Pain." *Washington Post*, January 25, 1986, C1.
——— . "War Footage and Network Skirmishes." *Washington Post*, January 19, 1991, C1.
Shaw, David. "The Trouble with TV Muckraking." *TV Guide*, October 10, 1981, 10.
Shayon, Robert Lewis. "What's Wrong with Documentaries." *Saturday Review*, January 23, 1965, 55.
Sherill, Robert. "The Happy Ending (Maybe) of 'The Selling of the Pentagon.' " *New York Times Magazine*, May 16, 1971.
" '60 Minutes' on Trial" *Interface* 2 (1981): 38.
Smith, F. Leslie. " 'The Selling of the Pentagon' and the First Amendment." *Journalism History* 14 (1975): 2–5.
Smith, Sally Bedell. "Paley Sees a 'Tragedy' in a Hostile Shift at CBS." *New York Times*, May 1, 1985, D1.
Stanton, Frank. "The Critical Necessity for an Informed Public." *Journal of Broadcasting* 3 (1958): 193–204.
"Stepin Fetchit Calls His Film Image Progressive." *New York Times*, July 24, 1968, L83.
"Student Gets Ferguson Aid in Air Force Ouster." *Detroit News*, September 24, 1953, 1.
Swaydos, Harvey. "Fred Friendly and the Friendly Vision." *New York Times Sunday Magazine*, April 23, 1967, 31–32.
Taylor, Clark. "Network Anchors Mull Credibility of TV News." *Los Angeles Times*, November 28, 1984, 6.
"They're Standing in Line behind CBS." *Broadcasting*, April 19, 1972, 19–20.
Thompson, Dorothy. "On the Record." *New York Tribune*, November 2, 1938, C3.
"Too Realistic Radio Play Starts Wave of Hysteria over City." *St. Louis Post-Dispatch*, October 31, 1938, 1.
Tuchman, Gaye. "Objectivity as Strategic Ritual: An Examination of Newsmen's Notions of Objectivity." *American Journal of Sociology* 77 (1972): 660–680.
"TV and McCarthy: Network's Decision and Murrow Show Represent Advance for Medium." *New York Times*, March 14, 1954, X13.
"2 Judges 'Spank' Parents of Boys." *New York Times*, April 22, 1958, 35.
Ungar, Arthur. " '60 Minutes' Executive Producer Don Hewitt: 'The $60 Million Joe Sixpack.' " *Television Quarterly* 25 (4) (1992): 23–26.
——— . "300 Minutes with Mike Wallace at Sixty-Seven." *Television Quarterly* 22 (1) (1986): 7–25.
"University of Michigan Student Fights Expulsion from Air Force." *Detroit News*, September 23, 1953, 1.
"Unmasking the Pentagon." *Newsweek*, March 8, 1971, 25.
"Veterans Rally to Legion Stand on ACLU." *Hoosier Legionnaire*, December 1953, 4.
" 'War of the Worlds' Fetches $143,000." *St. Louis Post-Dispatch*, December 16, 1988, 24E.
Watson, Mary Ann. "The Golden Age of American Television Documentary." *Television Quarterly* 23 (Summer 1988): 57–75.
"When Television Came of Age." *St. Louis Post-Dispatch*, March 21, 1954, 2E.
Whiteside, Thomas. "The One-Ton Pencil." *The New Yorker*, February 17, 1962, 42.
"Wires and Calls to Murrow Strongly Anti-McCarthy." *New York Herald Tribune*, March 11, 1954, 3.

Young, Perry Deane. "From Saigon to Salvador: Revisionism Reconsidered." *The Quill* (May 1983): 7.
Zoglin, Richard. "Assessing the War Damage: ABC Establishes Air Supremacy," *Time*, March 18, 1991, 88–89.

INDEX

About the Author

Michael D. Murray worked for CBS News while still an undergraduate student at St. Louis University. He is chairman of the Department of Communication at the University of Missouri-St. Louis. He recently received the Goldsmith Research Award from Harvard University and was the Weld Senior Fellow at Stanford University.